About This Book

The words and excitement surround us. On demand. Convergence. Access. Point of need. Re-usability.

They sound good, but what do those words mean? How do they change the shape of education in organizations? What is available for individuals? Here we describe, in vivid detail and through scores of examples, the shift from knowledge in the classroom to knowledge everywhere. We tour job aids and performance support at work, at home, and in transit in between.

The movement is driven by impatient executives, managers, and employees. They will not wait for a class to be scheduled. They want what they want when they want it, and in a form that is targeted, compact, updated, and integrated with a client's question, daily workflow, or a bulky system.

In this book, we've tamed performance support into Planners and Sidekicks. Planners are in our lives *just before or after* the challenge. They help us decide whether Avian Flu should alter trip plans or to reflect on how we could have improved the presentation offered at the sales meeting. Sidekicks are at our side *during* the task. For example, the quick food cook reads the job aid as she creates the new food product. The quarterback glances at his wrist in the huddle. The writer pecks away and smiles at how Wikipedia sports a red line under it in this sentence.

Performance support is what instructors, supervisors, employees, and people do. Yes, us too. No longer satisfied to mount a great event, rule a classroom, or command curriculum enshrined in three-ring binders, training people are growing into workforce learning professionals, performance consultants, and blended and e-learning specialists with responsibility for solution systems and strategic accomplishments. Our work extends beyond classrooms and to delivering influence, information, policies, cheerleading, and guidance where and when needed. That's right—via job aids and performance support.

Do you wonder about the possibilities? Do you question your readiness or your people's readiness for independent effort via performance support? Do you want to see what others have done and to examine the elements that contribute to success? Do you want to know about software that might lend a hand? Are you eager to look into the future? We welcome you to read all about it here.

About Pfeiffer

Pfeiffer serves the professional development and hands-on resource needs of training and human resource practitioners and gives them products to do their jobs better. We deliver proven ideas and solutions from experts in HR development and HR management, and we offer effective and customizable tools to improve workplace performance. From novice to seasoned professional, Pfeiffer is the source you can trust to make yourself and your organization more successful.

Essential Knowledge   Pfeiffer produces insightful, practical, and comprehensive materials on topics that matter the most to training and HR professionals. Our Essential Knowledge resources translate the expertise of seasoned professionals into practical, how-to guidance on critical workplace issues and problems. These resources are supported by case studies, worksheets, and job aids and are frequently supplemented with CD-ROMs, websites, and other means of making the content easier to read, understand, and use.

Essential Tools   Pfeiffer's Essential Tools resources save time and expense by offering proven, ready-to-use materials—including exercises, activities, games, instruments, and assessments—for use during a training or team-learning event. These resources are frequently offered in looseleaf or CD-ROM format to facilitate copying and customization of the material.

Pfeiffer also recognizes the remarkable power of new technologies in expanding the reach and effectiveness of training. While e-hype has often created whizbang solutions in search of a problem, we are dedicated to bringing convenience and enhancements to proven training solutions. All our e-tools comply with rigorous functionality standards. The most appropriate technology wrapped around essential content yields the perfect solution for today's on-the-go trainers and human resource professionals.

Pfeiffer
www.pfeiffer.com

Essential resources for training and HR professionals

MORE PRAISE FOR *JOB AIDS AND PERFORMANCE SUPPORT*

"Rossett and Schafer provide a straightforward, jargon-free outline to help us appreciate important new concepts. Their examples are simply expressed, but stimulate challenging thoughts for practitioners. The authors are optimistic about the potential of technology for transforming the practice of learning at work. However, they are realistic about the challenge that lies ahead. Above all, they are capable of demystifying the complex."

> —Martyn Sloman, adviser: learning, training and development, Chartered Institute of Personnel and Development, United Kingdom

"In Chapter 1, Rossett and Schafer promise us 'a job aid on job aids and performance support.' They deliver on their promise . . . magnificently! This book provides a road map to the creation and use of job aids to support performance in almost every conceivable situation."

> —Marguerite Foxon, manager, Global Leadership and Evaluation, Motorola

"At Applied Global University, our focus is to provide learning that supports corporate direction, responds quickly to customer needs, and provides maximum value. Performance support tools that are immediate, targeted, and robust are a critical component of this strategy. Rossett and Schafer provide the roadmap and 'how to' guide we need to achieve those goals!"

> —Diana Hayden, managing director, Applied Global University

"If you share my belief that sustainable competitive advantage is fueled by the effective acquisition and application of knowledge, this book should be in your library. Along these lines, Rossett and Schafer present fresh ideas and practical tools in a 21st century context-from technological trends to evolving social norms. This is a refreshing look at the business of learning."

> —Cameron Hedrick, senior vice president, Talent and Organizational Capability, Citigroup, North America Operations and Technology

"Vivid real-world examples and excellent visuals bring to life what you can accomplish with innovative job aids and performance support. I came away with the wheels turning and can't wait to try some new ideas with my clients. Job Aids and Performance Support is very readable, and I expect my copy to be dog-eared in no time."

> —Julie E. Hymes, learning solution architect, Resolute Learning

"This is the perfect book for meeting today's performance challenges in an emerging global economy. As organizations cut their training budgets and realize the relevance of job support to achieve business goals, there is growing acceptance of performance support as an innovative alternative to classroom-based training. When performance improvement is vitally needed, this book, packed with useful explanations, descriptions, and examples, does a great job of demystifying the transition from traditional training solutions!"

> —Margaret Martinez, CEO, The Training Place, Inc.

"In a faster and 'flatter' world of work, performance support is essential! Placing knowledge, support, and granular learning in the workplace and at the fingertips of employees is crucial. Allison Rossett and Lisa Schafer have created a highly valuable guide!"

> —Elliott Masie, founder, The Masie Center's Learning CONSORTIUM

"If performance support is 'job aids on steroids' according to Rossett and Schafer, consider this book your protein shake."
　　　　　—Cindy Molina, director of training, USE Credit Union

"The classroom of the future will look nothing like it does today. Due to the advances outlined in this book, information will be more accessible then ever before. Rossett and Schafer do a brilliant job of bringing performance support and job aids into their rightful place in the hierarchy of learning. This book will not only change the way you look at these valuable tools, it will also change the way you look at learning in general."
　　　　　—Bob Mosher, director, Learning and Strategy Evangelism, Microsoft Learning

"Chapter 3 is a great refresher on how performance support tools can and should be used. This book is a valuable resource for training practitioners in helping shift the focus from purely training, to that of performance and business results."
　　　　　—Coley O'Brien, director of training, Sears Company: Sears Holdings Corporation

"This book is a very practical guide showing how to build job aids to supplement or replace training, and to support job performance. It takes you step-by-step through the assessment of the needs for a performance support, how to start such a process and strategies for implementation."
　　　　　—Carmen Panzar, learning and development director, Citigroup-Audit and Risk Review

"The authors put to rest many wayward beliefs about performance support, offering us significant and contemporary proof about these valuable tools-what works, how, when, where, and why. And as always, Rossett and Schafer provide abundant real-world examples, tips, and resources for getting started and implementing practical strategies. What a terrific book for improving and accelerating human performance!"
　　　　　—Frank Rogalewicz, consultant, Leadership and Organizational Effectiveness,
　　　　　Lockheed Martin, Integrated Systems and Solutions

"With wisdom, perspective, research, and tons of real-world examples, Allison Rossett and Lisa Schafer illuminate the power that performance support systems bring to the brave new world of cognitive overload, task attention disorder, and the wireless frontier. Although venerable tools like the 'to-do' list have, since antiquity, helped lift human cognition above its inherent limitations, the authors illustrate a plethora of new possibilities. Using wave after wave of example, the book urges us nimbly and insistently toward a more effective balance of training and support."
　　　　　—Will Thalheimer, president and principal researcher, Work-Learning Research

"A timely and much-needed update on the state of the performance support field. Building on the acclaimed A Handbook of Job Aids, Rossett and Schafer provide a highly informative blend of theoretical concepts, practical applications, and strategic implications. A must read for both performance improvement practitioners and executive decision-makers who are charged with delivering organizational results."
　　　　　-Christian Völkl, management consultant, E&E information consultants AG, Berlin, Germany

"Knowledge is everywhere. Paradoxically, most training and education professionals do not yet know how to create programs that make knowledge everywhere. Rossett and Schafer's book provides much-needed concepts, tools, and examples to shape a high-performance workplace where knowledge is truly available everywhere."
　　　　　—Feng-Kwei Wang, executive director, ITRI College, Industrial Technology Research
　　　　　Institute (ITRI), Taiwan

Pfeiffer™

Job Aids and Performance Support

Moving from Knowledge in the Classroom to Knowledge Everywhere

Allison Rossett & Lisa Schafer

Wiley Publishing, Inc.

Published by Pfeiffer

A Wiley Imprint

989 Market Street, San Francisco, CA 94103-1741   www.pfeiffer.com

Pfeiffer books and products are available through most bookstores. To contact Pfeiffer directly call our Customer Care Department within the U.S. at 800-274-4434, outside the U.S. at 317-572-3986, or fax 317-572-4002.

Pfeiffer also publishes its books in a variety of electronic formats. Some content that appears in print may not be available in electronic books.

Acquiring Editor: Matt Davis
Director of Development: Kathleen Dolan Davies
Developmental Editor: Susan Rachmeler
Editor: Rebecca Taff
Senior Production Editor: Dawn Kilgore
Manufacturing Supervisor: Becky Carreño

ISBN 10: 0-7879-7621-0

ISBN 13: 978-0-7879-7621-7

Library of Congress Cataloging-in-Publication Data
Rossett, Allison.
  Job aids and performance support : moving from knowledge in the classroom to knowledge everywhere / Allison Rossett & Lisa Schafer.
    p. cm.
  Includes index.
  ISBN-13: 978-0-7879-7621-7 (cloth)
  ISBN-10: 0-7879-7621-0 (cloth)
  1. Employees—Training of. 2. Teaching—Aids and devices. I. Schafer, Lisa, 1965- II. Title.
  HF5549.5.T7R648 2006
  658.3'124—dc22
                              2006023712

Printed in the United States of America

Printing 10   9   8   7   6   5   4   3   2

To the one who has supported the book writing many times, Sue, and to the newbies, Julie and Gregory

Contents

List of Figures, Tables, and Exhibits

Foreword

In 1970, the very first time I sat at an IBM 3280 green screen character-based computer terminal, I knew. I knew that, even though the capabilities were limited, the potential was incredible. Quickly, however, the Law of Diminishing Astonishment surfaced. My awe turned to frustration. *How come I can't. . .? Why doesn't it. . .? Why do I have to remember all of these commands?*

We moved from forms data entry to basic word processing programs: command driven (remember shift/control/alt/p), line editors without word wrap, embedded format commands that were obscured so you couldn't see what the document would *really* look like when printed. Users (what we were called then) truly wanted to *know in advance of doing* when DOS-based PCs arrived. The a> or c> prompt responded only with Abort, Retry, or Fail when you didn't get the command right—or the right command—before hitting "enter." And then it required you to reboot.

Performance support back then was:

- Documentation that you couldn't find or understand because the underlying assumptions about what you knew were invalid.

- *Hey, Ed!* Asking someone nearby who knew maybe two things more: no help desks.

Usually the effort to learn the software was greater than the time available at the moment of need, so you settled and actually changed your goals, while knowing that somehow, some way, there existed a way to insert a page break. I recall, embarrassingly, that one time I actually unplugged the printer to stop the page print. I had looked up Stop Printing, Page Break, End of Page, and other synonyms in the manual. To no avail. Later, after spending so much time with the vendor support person that I had to send flowers out of gratitude, I learned it was indexed under Embedded Format Commands! Oh yeah. . . . That was obvious. Whose point of view did the indexer take? Certainly not the practical, goal-oriented, get-it-done, non-technician's view. Certainly, that manual showed no concern about *my* view.

Today we have increasingly intelligent performance support that often presents itself as good software design. As Allison Rossett and Lisa Schafer illustrate with rich examples in this much-needed book, performance support has reached new heights. These new support environments are ubiquitous and delivered in so many ways. It's hard to characterize them because they are big and small, stand-alone and embedded in devices, and applied to many performance goals, work processes, and tasks.

Today's performance support is a *conceptual framework* that allows designers and developers to:

- Optimize power and simplicity when supporting task or processes

- Balance structure and freedom when appropriate: forcing required actions without performer discretion or allowing flexibility based on user competence or confidence and the consequences of failed actions

- Integrate knowledge or content in many ways, including natural language on displays, rule processing at the software level, dialogs that suggest options or considerations, and feedback that is rational and clear and filtered and relevant

- Represent content in its most powerful form using demonstrations, illustrations, rich graphical representations that are superior to those possible in an analog world, data manipulation, and alternative views of the content to accommodate performer preferences or styles, and so on

- Use wireless and alternative delivery devices for *availability at the moment of need,* rather than delivery way in advance or long after. (iPods and cell phones might be among the most significant devices for support in the future!)

To me the measure of how far we have come from the days of data forms and field help is demonstrated by the many web-based applications we use daily to perform incredibly complex tasks that once relied on experts with system knowledge to perform:

- Making and changing reservations on a reservation system used to take airlines up to five years to teach staff. Now anyone can do it in seconds!

- Asset allocation of financial investments is done by many and without significant financial expertise.

- We configure our own equipment and systems based on personalized needs.

We don't always think of these environments as support because they have arrived so quickly and easily, but they are. We wonder how we fared without them.

THE IMPORTANCE OF THIS BOOK

Job aids must match the needs of the task and the performer. Nothing but electronic aids can do that sufficiently. In bringing the concept of performance support into straightforward frameworks and providing terminology and concepts to guide analysis and design, Allison and Lisa do us a huge service. They define the variables to be considered, categorize them, and then inform us with practical and affordable examples. That should provide readers with the confidence to move forward. I commend them on their foresightedness and capable thought.

This book is important to me right now in 2006 because I have retired after over twenty-five years of advocating performance support throughout its evolution. I wrote a rallying call in my 1992 book, *Electronic Performance Support Systems: How and Why to Remake the Workplace Through the Strategic Application of Technology,* after years of working in the computer-based training arena. I spoke to thousands of people all over the world about the new alternatives and tried to generate excitement and conceptual frameworks. Mostly I tried to change the point of view of training professionals stuck in a paradigm that grew increasingly less relevant in a changing, complex, and increasingly electronic and global world. I grew frustrated as I looked back at how long that paradigm shift was taking because of my urgency about the needs of performers and my insights into what was possible. But as a good friend said to me once, *Everything takes longer than it takes.* The technical, logistical, process, knowledge, political, and economic factors have to be aligned. And that takes time and critical mass.

Rossett and Schafer's book is important to me because it represents the fact that this concept has arrived . . . and is being implemented daily by normal people and applied to normal tasks. A Midwestern car wash uses it. A grandmother plans for her newborn grandchild's college education with it. It's not restricted to development by MIT engineers to support nuclear power plant shutdown (among the first applications). Performance support is becoming ubiquitous. It is practical. It is affordable. It is doable. And I am grateful for any part I have played in adding to the progress.

I am also grateful to Allison Rossett for her years of personal friendship and professional commitment to her work and to the advancement of thought. She is a gift to all who know her. Her collaboration with Lisa Schafer yielded a strong result—this book. We all benefit from it.

Gloria Gery
Tolland, Massachusetts
June 2006

Preface

Long ago humans squinted at cave walls for guidance on hunting and cooking. Now we turn to mobile phones, personal information managers, desktop computers, and even laser beams for advice on just about everything. From retirement planning to auto repair, closing a sale, choosing the right password, speeding up a hard disk drive, getting the best price, dressing for success, dieting, dating, and thriving within organizational culture, we are not alone anymore.

That is what this book is about. It is about the shift from knowledge in the classroom to knowledge everywhere. Our focus is performance support.

Performance support is happening where we work and live. Under a tree and at a park bench, in a submarine, at a parent-teacher meeting, in a cubicle, or on the manufacturing floor, people reach beyond themselves for help in doing what needs to be done. It comes to us as extensive computer systems and as notes scribbled on the backs of envelopes. I create one every day, as I add, edit, and erase items on my to-do list. Right now, on a scratch pad next to my left hand, is a longish list. What's there? Some names and numbers representing calls I should have returned yesterday. A nudge to get to the gym today, with a parenthetical reminder that I skipped yesterday. There's also a reminder to keep working on my taxes and another pushing me to send a note thanking the people who contributed to a Saturday class. And then there is this Preface. That's the item on my list with two bright red lines under it.

The best way to appreciate performance support is to look at examples showing how performance support solves problems and elevates practice.

I can remember twiddling my thumbs while waiting to do laundry in my dorm at college. When I wanted to do the wash, the washers and dryers were almost always busy, causing frustration, late nights, and early mornings. When I did get to it, the room, with scattered piles of laundry, wet and dry, disgusted me. This was the result of aggressive launderers who chucked wash on the table if you weren't there to claim it. Enter e-Suds. e-Suds is civilizing the process by introducing information and technology. USA Technologies installed Internet-based laundry systems on several university campuses. The system tracks the use of washers and dryers and then alerts students by email, cell, or PDA to the status of their laundry and the washers and dryers in close proximity. Imagine the benefits of knowing the "wash cycle is complete" on your load, or that a washer and dryer are available in Chavez Dormitory, floor 3, north end.

My baby boomer life cries out for performance support. *The Wall Street Journal* (Greene, September 26, 2005, R1) described what Intel found when researching digital entertainment preferences. To their surprise, boomers did not want another way to watch TV. Most of all, they wanted help with their aged parents, especially support in dealing with dementia. This led the company to create a system to cope with not recognizing faces and voices, and not remembering what was talked about during the last conversation. Their system, "caller ID on steroids," responds when the phone rings, with a photo, name, and topics covered during the last interaction, so that the senior can engage with more certainty and comfort.

And boomers need help themselves, too. My neck gets stiff more often now. The stiffness reduces my eagerness and ability to crane and twist to see what's around me. This leads me to be, I'm afraid, just a little less thorough when driving in my car. Amazingly, my friend's new car compensates. It warns him when he's about to bump something such as another car, person, shrub, or fire hydrant. That's great customized support in context and at the moment of need. While my GPS is a fine sidekick on the road, I now hunger for this feature.

Those are problems solved by performance support. But what about elevating performance at work? As a doctor approaches a hospital bed, radio frequency identification (RFID) can notify her personal digital assistant about this patient's condition, history, medication, and recent test results. Of interest in this example, the physician could be alerted to a new publication relevant to this patient's disease state. Standing beside the bed, the doctor is able to scan the text and determine what these findings might mean for this patient.

As you can see from these examples, performance support is immediate, present, targeted, and useful. In many ways, it is everything typical classroom instruction is not.

Training departments provide classes. Most are measured by how many they offer and how much they are appreciated.

Customers, citizens, and employees have different needs. They seek help answering questions, meeting expectations, contributing to strategic goals, responding to the unforeseen, dealing with torrents of information, and acting even smarter than they are. This book is about delivering that help in the form of information, guidance, and even advice, to those who need it, when and where they need it, through job aids and performance support.

It is beginning to happen. Annual studies by ASTD and *Training* magazine confirm the slow, steady trend away from classroom delivery and toward more technological approaches. Information, lessons, instructors, and events, not to mention music and entertainment, will be ubiquitous. They will go where they are needed and welcomed.

This shift to knowledge everywhere makes incredibly good sense. It suggests a revolution in workplace learning and support. But revolution is too strong a word for where we are today. Intimations, hints, glimmers, beginnings. Those words describe it better.

That is where Lisa Schafer and I come in. In this book we define possibilities. We honor the roots of performance support. We introduce two kinds of support, *planners* and *sidekicks*. We share scores of examples and introduce people doing great things in car washes, the Library of Congress, the executive suite, cubicles, and repair centers. We describe how the shift to distributed knowledge changes what everyone does, including professionals in our field. We point to promising vendors and software. We remind about the power of blending performance support and instructor-led programs. And we close with cautions. Performance support is best in the hands of savvy, motivated users.

We admit it. We are fans of job aids and performance support. In this book we use ideas, stories, examples, commentary, authorities, and resources to encourage changes in business as usual. As you'll see, Lisa Schafer and I advocate a systematic shift from knowledge limited in time, place, and influence to knowledge everywhere, just about all the time. We hope to win you over and help you help the people you care about.

Allison Rossett
San Diego, California
June 12, 2006

Introduction

This book tells the story of change and opportunity.

The first edition of this handbook was a tale of job aids and training and development. While there were hints at what computer technology would mean, the first edition dwelled on offices and factories, laminated cards, checklists, documentation, manuals, and workplace posters.

Of course the job aid has changed, right along with everything and everyone else. Enter computers. Enter software. Consider advances in the science of learning. Ponder the possibilities created by mobile devices like cell phones, iPods, and personal digital assistants. Then place all that in the context of heightened expectations about performance and results.

Leaps in technology are matched, perhaps even exceeded, by enlarged roles and hopes for the people dubbed trainers. No longer satisfied to mount a great event, rule a classroom, or command curriculum enshrined in three-ring binders, trainers are growing into workforce learning professionals, performance consultants, and blended and e-learning specialists with responsibility for solution systems and strategic accomplishments. Their work extends beyond moments in time and place to influence, information, and even lessons that go where the challenges of work and life are. They must provide support when and where required, by people or by systems that deliver the smarts to those with needs. That's right— via job aids and performance support. Welcome to the era of convergence!

WHAT IS PERFORMANCE SUPPORT?

A helper in life and work, performance support is a repository for information, processes, and perspectives that inform and guide planning and action.

Let's look at each component in this definition.

"A helper in life and work." That's the spirit of the concept. Performance support represents converged information and work, residing next to the individual, in close proximity to the challenge in order to offer help when help is needed.

Performance support gets its identity, in part, by being distinct from the individual, yet very, very close. On shelves above employees' desks, in pockets, on dashboard displays, on walls next to equipment and chemicals, in drawers beneath computer keyboards, on cell phones, underneath and inside phones, via headphones, and even on matchbook covers, performance support enriches life and work.

An engineer is better able to execute a product launch because the organization has captured approaches and examples from the past and made them readily available on a PC. A driver avoids an odd-shaped shrub because his new car signals that it is there. A new retiree ponders the costs associated with an around-the-world cruise. With that question in mind, she receives customized financial guidance from her mutual fund company's website reflecting her holdings, her life expectancy, her risk tolerance, and her other goals.

The engineer, driver, and retiree are receiving the help they crave in a new way. In the old days, they would have turned to driver's ed, or the product launch manual, or retirement planning class. What they are getting now is targeted, tailored, and immediate.

"Repository for information, processes, and perspectives." Performance support must store and make accessible critical information, processes, wisdom, and perspectives.

Am I ready for retirement? How much money will I need, given my circumstances and preferences? What is in hand? What is likely growth in the future? What must be done to close a gap, if there is one?

How do we launch products in this company? What lessons about product launch have we learned in the past? Information, rules, approaches, and viewpoints must be assembled in order to begin to answer these questions.

Right now and in this place, are there threats near my car? What threats? Where are they?

"Informs and guides." Sometimes a situation is so unforgiving that a specific response must be informed by performance support, either via technology or a print aid. When displays in a nuclear-power plant alert to a problem, for example, the operator's response must be precise. No gray area here. No ambiguity. No opportunity for individual foibles. The same is true for the preflight precautions taken by the crew of a commercial airliner. Even though they have done it many times, a print job aid, the most basic form of performance support, tells the pilot and co-pilot what to do. The consequences of an error are too significant to allow pilots to do their thing or to have a bad day or moment.

As guides, performance support expands perspectives and approaches to a job, task, or opportunity. Motorola provides an elegant example. Eager to encourage more participation by students in classes, Motorola adorned tent cards with a space for names on one side and guidance on the other. Ask questions. Apply what you are learning to your work. Acknowledge others' contributions. Ask another question. And so on and so forth. So simple, so useful.

Apple Computer was eager to help new people orient to work swiftly and comfortably. They used technology to collect opinions from more veteran employees on topics as diverse as managing priorities and locating a good Thai restaurant. They made it all available online.

Those resources were designed to guide decisions and to enhance confidence. Let's move into the quick-food world. It is active and pressured back there, where the food is produced. The new burger chef at a quick-food restaurant feels better about those first hours on the job because food production and safety procedures are posted in plain view.

Performance support can also deliver attitude adjustment. In *The New Yorker,* a writer described encountering an "instructive note about how not to have a breakdown" when the copy machine breaks down. Item 4 on the list taped to the machine reads: "Please try not to take it personally when the machine has its problems . . . it's just a machine. In other words, please don't bang, beat, bruise, or otherwise abuse it. It won't help." No rules or instructions here; enjoy gentle and comforting advice on how to handle the inevitable aggravations associated with using this copy machine.

Guidance can extend to nagging. B.J. Fogg (2003) introduced the concept of "captology." Captology is a made-up word which stands for *computer-as-persuasive-technology.* A favorite example is quitnet.org. On that website, people who want to quit smoking commit to the effort and receive support for the challenges to come. When the smoker signs up, she is asked how much she smokes and for how long. Guidance is tailored to individual responses; subsequent guidance targets key needs, such as selecting the right date to commence the effort to quit. You wouldn't want to commence two weeks before your daughter's giant wedding. Information is pushed to members based on what research indicates they need to give up cigarettes. Imagine that, after a beastly day at work, you find yourself dying for a smoke. Go to the website, and you are offered an opportunity to join a group. They encourage you to stay the course and stay away from cigarettes.

"Planning and action." Early definitions of job aids (Harless, 1986) highlighted procedures, action, and information. Rossett and Gautier-Downes (1991) expanded the definition to incorporate more cognitive perspectives that include approaches to a problem and ways of reflecting and analyzing. While performance support is of obvious value in identifying and fixing a spelling error in a word processed document or purging the house of the smell of fish, benefits extend to topics like planning retirement and evaluating strategies to mitigate security concerns. Consider burger assembly. Burger assembly is an example of *sidekick* performance support. It is there as the tasty components are put together. Getting ready for retirement requires *planner* performance support. The program helps reflect on all that is involved in readying for a successful retirement.

WHAT IS *NOT* PERFORMANCE SUPPORT?

Not everything is performance support. For example, tools and instruction are not.

Tools, like flashlights and office chairs, are often confused with job aids because they too support people in their work. However, there is an important distinction between tools and performance support. The care tag on a new blouse, a preflight checklist, and a computerized telephone directory are different from that office chair and flashlight because they are repositories for information. The support of work is necessary but not sufficient to make something a job aid or performance support. To qualify, the object must house valued information, processes, or perspectives that target a need or task.

Pencils, tractors, hard hats, and file cabinets are tools. User documentation, safety signs, fidelity.com, and quitnet are performance support. Although all support the ability to perform effectively or safely, only the latter four store information in order to guide and elevate thought and action.

Instruction is not performance support. It is planned experience that enables an individual to acquire skills and knowledge to advance the capability to perform. Instruction builds human capacity. Surgeons, landscapers, managers, performance consultants, and instructional designers all invest in instruction to build their capacity, what they know by heart, what they will be able to do with fluency.

When successful, instruction, in a time-consuming process involving presentation, practice, and feedback over time, results in a change in the mental state of the individual. Later, organizations continuously draw on this enhanced mental state by asking employees to manage, to create, to solve problems, to engineer, to deal with the unforeseen, and to anticipate.

A system that combines instruction and support is compelling. Consider an airline pilot. They are well trained, of course, but also reliant on performance support for emergencies, certainty, compliance, and habits. Support is there at the moment of need in the form of print documentation and a cockpit that is chock full of information and guidance. A landscaper might turn to a reference manual to determine the watering needs of an unfamiliar plant. And a doctor might refer to a PDA to check for drug interactions when considering medication for a particular patient. The pilot, landscaper, and doctor invested years and effort in smartening up; their performance will be even niftier when bolstered by performance support for unfamiliar, critical, or non-recurrent challenges, details, or updates.

WHAT IS TO LOVE ABOUT JOB AIDS?

Why were job aids popular? Why do they remain so today? Three answers—convergence, simplicity, and relevance.

Identified with the work, job aids go where the action is, in straightforward fashion. If you want to know how to change the message on your answering machine, a job aid sits beside you to help with the task. Need a quick comparison of your product to the other guy's? Once again, a salesperson and potential customer appreciate the opportunity to look together at an authoritative table that makes comparisons. Eager to remember all the things you are required to buy at the grocery store, not just those that pop into your mind while wandering the aisles? Yet again, job aids provide what is needed to get the task done at the moment and in the place of need. With little cost, fuss, and bother, they converge with the challenge of recording, buying, picking, fixing, deciding, or selling.

Rossett and Mohr (2004) described what one inventive U.S. Coast Guard officer did to help his crew monitor engineering equipment on the Coast Guard cutter Red Birch. Lieutenant Junior Grade Jonathan Heller wanted to reduce the number of personnel required when the ship was at the pier.

Heller did not have the luxury of running a one-week training course on checking gauges and recording data for the entire crew. Instead, his crew recommended helping the non-engineering types by drawing red marks on the gauges to make it easier to discern when a reading was outside normal range. Theirs was the most simple of job aids, a red mark on the gauges signifying "trouble."

As you can see, job aids come in all shapes and sizes. Imagine a fading Post-it™ Note marked "Water Me!!!" taped to an office fern; another is a laminated card in an emergency room so it withstands errant sprays of blood and guts; another is a checklist that helps prepare for a meeting; and another is a detailed manual that explains new software.

Job aids earn affection because they help people handle tasks that matter to them in a not-very-costly fashion, from mixing a Cosmopolitan, to installing Bluetooth on a personal digital assistant, to making sure that everything is packed for an international trip. A well-worn recipe book is a classic collection of job aids. It's relevant because you or somebody you care about wants to feast on those casseroles, sauces, and desserts.

Technology presents even tastier possibilities today. We call them performance support. Job aids are a familiar form of performance support.

Technology, of course, adds much to a shopping list scrawled on a piece of paper. Through software, a shopping list can be compared with dietary, price, or caloric restrictions, leading to advice about the quality of your intended purchases, given your goals or needs. Advantages include the ability for users to quickly access large quantities of information, support for simultaneous multiple users, global update and distribution, and personalized guidance.

Consider the package you sent from Boise to Brussels. Online tracking tells you where your package is, while supporting the simultaneous searches of thousands of others who are equally concerned about the whereabouts of their parcels. From print job aids to adaptive technology-based systems, performance support delivers the goods by going where they are needed, when they are needed, with tireless speed and adaptability.

WHAT IS TO LOVE ABOUT PERFORMANCE SUPPORT?

As you can see, there is a lot to love. Today, the growing popularity of performance support is derived from the same three factors that earned affection for job aids decades ago, convergence, simplicity, and relevance, plus a worthy addition, personalization.

Convergence

Imagine this situation. You are expected at a meeting at a building across town. You have no clue how to get there. Your colleague swiftly whispers directions while also participating in a conference call. You listen, nod, and head out of the building. Not surprisingly, half-way across town, you can't remember whether you turn right or left after the library. Convergence is what you need. Convergence, in the form of notes that captured your colleague's directions for referral while driving across town, or even better, and far more converged with the effort, a GPS (global positioning system). With the GPS, a sultry voice offers immediate prompts to get you to your destination, including, of course, which way to turn after the library.

Proximity is at the heart of convergence. The information and guidance is where you and the challenge are. At the desktop, in the car, in the cockpit, or on the run, when and where they are needed, performance supports remind about how many calories have been consumed today as you consider adding a bear claw sweet to your coffee order. When on a rainy, dark, and unknown road, they are a familiar voice offering directions about what to do next. At the automatic teller machine (ATM), they are words on the screen, in the language you selected, about how to extract cash.

Simple as Pie

No fuss, just focus. Effective performance support helps individuals decide what to purchase, when to sell, and how to fix. While effective instruction is comprehensive and prepares individuals to handle the unforeseen, performance support is targeted to the task at hand. IBM's Tony O'Driscoll, in a personal communication, said it eloquently: "Parsimony is the key. It is not about serving up everything that might be relevant to what you are trying to do today. It is about content and resources that solve the immediate now and the immediate how for the task that you are trying to get accomplished."

Want to fix a hole in jeans or a wall? Want to respond appropriately when someone calls you by the wrong name? Want to prevent your pet from getting carsick? Ehow.com provides guidance from soup to nuts. Take the topic of vinyl records. No history, no chemistry. Nothing deep, and nothing extra about vinyl records. Ehow provides procedures for storing and cleaning your vinyl treasures. While the ehow site is vast in scope, search technology allows you to seek and find just what you need.

Relevance

Dieters, burger chefs, doctors, and ship boarding officers want to accomplish their goals. That's why they look to performance support.

U.S. Coast Guard officer Dan Hardin, a commercial fishing vessel safety coordinator, decided to use performance support to improve inspections on fishing vessels. Prior to the use of the performance support tool, boarding officers were required to attend a one-week course on the intricacies of enforcing hundreds of pages of federal regulations for fishing vessel safety. The complex laws applied to many boats and situations, and sometimes resulted in inconsistent or inaccurate choices by boarding officers. Hardin's PDA-based support tool eliminated much memorization. His solution presents a series of questions about the vessel: length, number of personnel on board, type of vessel, type of engine, and so forth. Based on answers to questions, the PDA generates a customized checklist of safety requirements for firefighting, lifesaving, and bridge equipment appropriate to each vessel. Instead of laboring to determine whether the law requires this particular ship to carry one of three different types of life rafts, an inflatable buoyant apparatus, life float, or nothing at all, boarding officers, with PDAs in hand, now spend their energy on, for example, inspecting life rafts to ensure that they're properly set up to release should the ship sink.

Personalization

Some performance support acts as if it knows you. It adjusts information and guidance based on what you need and want. It brings help to your situation and context.

Technology makes it happen. For example, not only does a personal digital assistant (PDA) record what was eaten today, it also offers up suggestions for a dinner that addresses caloric allocation, allergies, and food preferences. The same is true for the doctor who approaches a bedside in the hospital. Through RFID (radio frequency identification) links to the patient's medical chart and history, the physician is much smarter about history, needs, and allergies and can receive alerts if a dangerous drug interaction is prescribed or relevant research has been published.

Another example is an online tool that asks questions and then provides advice, based on your answers. At San Diego State University (SDSU), and in many other places, an individual who is contemplating enrollment in our online graduate program is queried about issues from the capacity to send email attachments to the ability to follow through on commitments and work in teams. After responses are received, the system comments on this respondent's readiness to pursue a degree independently and online.

ARE WE FORGETTING TRAINING AND DEVELOPMENT?

Certainly not.

We're interested in making the most of resources, training, and other methods, in service to performance and accomplishments.

Donald Clark (2003) put it this way:

> We must look beyond the boundaries of traditional training, and beyond the boundaries of the course. Certainly this will take us into performance support and knowledge management, but we must go further, bleeding e-learning into corporate communications, workplace learning, marketing, recruitment, customer learning, searches on the web and the real world. This expansive view of learning delivery offers lots of scope for exciting new approaches to blended learning.
>
> . . . The learning organisation is built not on the premise of more training. In fact, in the case of formal training, less rather than more may be required. . . .

It makes sense to look at all this, as Douglas and Schaffer (2002), Rossett (2001, 2002), and Levy (2005) did, in light of the movement from an instruction-centric world to one that is more focused on results.

Of course, most workforce learning professionals are devoted to improving performance and work. If performance support contributes, as it can and does, that is great. If training is essential, because employees must know it by heart or require skills to take advantage of resources or not knowing threatens professional standing, so be it. The point is not to cast off training and development, or even to advocate for it, but to use it judiciously, appropriately, often in concert with performance support.

The goals are what matters. They are plentiful, from planning an effective meeting, writing a good brief, qualifying a client, spelling correctly, to making a good decision about what to eat or where to go for more information about salt, calories, or cholesterol. Which strategies and what guidance system will bring about these desired results? What instruction is necessary to enhance individuals' abilities to seek and find what they need? Let's look at two examples of the combination of performance support and instruction.

Consider potatoes. The following scenario illustrates the close connection between instruction and performance support, in this case, the familiar job aid:

Speedy Burger has invested in new equipment for cutting, stacking, and storing French fries in fast-food outlets across the country. At a regional meeting, store managers are introduced to a twenty-two-minute videotape and two laminated checklists designed to assist them in helping their employees to learn to use the new equipment. Each manager is asked to instruct his or her employees according to the following procedure:

1. Set up the new machine. Place a dozen potatoes beside the machine.

2. Show the videotape.

3. Reiterate the safety issues highlighted in the videotape.

4. Elicit employee questions or concerns regarding safety or the procedure for making French fries.

5. Demonstrate loading by following the procedure outlined on the first laminated card.

6. Ask employees to work with partners and to load potatoes into the machine, following the procedure on the first laminated card.

7. Make certain that each of the partners has the opportunity to load the potatoes, using the procedure on the first laminated card.

8. Provide feedback to the employees and ask pairs who encountered problems to try the procedure again.

9. Demonstrate activating the machine, again reiterate safety concerns, and then ask an employee to try it.

10. Use the procedure outlined on the second laminated card to demonstrate how to take cut potatoes out of the machine, drawing attention once again to safety.

11. Ask half of the group to follow the procedure on the first card to load and activate the machine and the other half to remove cut potatoes by following the procedure on the second card.

12. Provide feedback and then ask the individuals to exchange cards and roles.

13. Elicit questions.

14. Remind employees about the popularity of French fries and their importance to the business, the benefits to be derived from use of the new machine, and the importance of safety features. Show them where the two laminated cards are posted.

15. After employees have returned to work, introduce the third laminated card to assistant store managers. This card lists daily and weekly maintenance tasks and illustrates necessary steps. Demonstrate maintenance tasks by following the procedures listed on the card and then ask each assistant manager to do the same. Provide feedback on each person's performance and reiterate the importance of maintenance to safety, productivity, and cleanliness. Remind the assistant store managers of the importance of coaching employees.

16. Provide managers with copies of the two laminated cards so that they will have them for their reference, for the training, and for employees to refer to later.

The following scenario is based on a program with electronic performance support, coaching, and many kinds of interventions, including education. It is a real U.S. Coast Guard leadership development initiative, circa 2005. Thanks to Erica Mohr for the example and to Commander Bill Kelly for leadership on the project:

The Coast Guard is eager to help its members get smarter about leadership and management. In the past, simple leadership lesson plans were provided on a website to download and articulate to the crew. This new system delivers unit-specific feedback about local leadership strengths and weaknesses and provides a variety of interventions (much more than just training) to improve leadership performance.

1. Employees complete a thirty-six-question online assessment, answering questions about the leadership at their local unit. Figure 1.1 illustrates the system.

Figure 1.1 The Coast Guard's Online Leadership Assessment

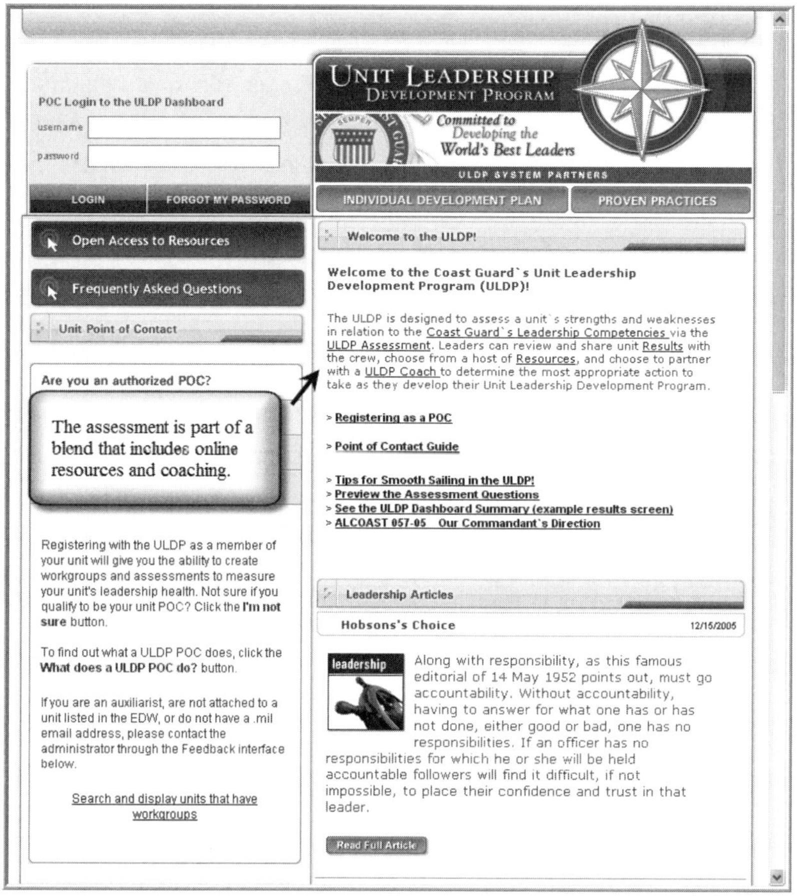

Source: U.S. Coast Guard. Used by permission.

2. Results are provided to each unit commander in an easy-to-read stoplight format. Results are broken down into nineteen leadership competencies, and for each competency a red, yellow, or green score is calculated. Red, not surprisingly, signifies a critical gap. Figure 1.2 illustrates the advice that one leader received.

3. Results are then linked to a library of resources, ranging from standard lesson plans to videos with discussion questions, to suggestions for policy changes and implementation of best practices. Each resource is categorized into the nineteen leadership competencies. Units can choose an appropriate intervention specific to their leadership weaknesses, as revealed by the tool.

4. But the support doesn't end there. Units are provided a leadership coach who is certified and available to provide advice ranging from simple questions about how to navigate the website to conducting interviews and focus groups to help the executive select an appropriate intervention.

Figure 1.2 Leadership Assessment Results Presented in a Stoplight Format

Source: U.S. Coast Guard. Used by permission.

ABOUT THE HANDBOOK
Goals for the Handbook

This handbook has six goals:

1. To serve as a "job aid on job aids and performance support";

2. To define performance support so that it advances the convergence of learning, information, and work;

3. To encourage the use of performance support by individuals and organizations;

4. To encourage the development and implementation of *great* performance support;

5. To advance the shift from training to performance, to boost transfer, to reduce the need for transfer, and to enhance the practice of professionals in learning, training and performance; and

6. To enhance performance, accomplishment, and results, for individuals and organizations, in work and in life.

Audience

This book was written for people who are responsible for improving the way that people do their work. Many are called trainers; others are known as technical writers, instructional designers, performance consultants, e-learning specialists, human resources managers, personnel managers, course developers, education specialists, workforce learning professionals, and documentation managers. What they have in common is that they are charged with helping people in their organizations to be competent in responding to requests, changes, innovations, products, customers, and problems.

Initially, we wrote for full-time human performance professionals. However, friends and colleagues from other arenas (city government, psychological services, and small businesses) looked at the chapters and pointed to applications to their own situations. For example, a psychologist saw ways to use job aids in simplifying and standardizing the training she does for psychology assistants. An attorney thought of ways to use performance support in preparing witnesses to testify in court. The coordinator of several dozen part-time sales people described ways to use job aids in keeping her workers up-to-date on new products and services—without taking them away from selling in order to attend training.

Thus the vision of the audience for the handbook was broadened to include both full-time professionals and those who count education, training, and information as only portions of their jobs. The writing, organization, and examples are suited to the serious student of the topic, the experienced workforce learning professional, and the person who sees possibilities to do one thing better.

The handbook is meant to make the reader's life easier and to stimulate thought, reading, and new directions for action. We are unabashedly committed to more performance support in life and work because we believe in the concept. Parents, divers, pilots, teens, engineers, supervisors, retirees, and mechanics can advance progress on their goals through performance support.

This book is about performance support and serves as performance support itself. Later, when the need arises, we invite you back to read, examine examples, and visit recommended online resources. Not everybody will create job aids and performance support. In some cases, the book will reveal ideas about what you might seek out elsewhere, from vendors, perhaps. Go get it, for yourself and for your clients.

Format

There are ten chapters in the book.

Chapter 1	Here we set the table for the book. We define job aids and performance support, link them to each other and to instruction, and define what they are and what they are not. In brief, we put these forms in the context of new ways of thinking about workforce learning and support. We also define the purpose for the handbook, its audience, and its chapters.
Chapter 2	When would you use performance support? When might you look in a different direction?
Chapter 3	Where does performance support come from? What about job aids? What are the roots of these embedded approaches? Why are we interested in performance support now? How does it fit the new ways that organizations and individuals are attempting to achieve goals?

Chapter 4	This chapter presents the two kinds of performance support, Planners and Sidekicks. We update the types that were presented in the *Handbook of Job Aids* and expand to take advantage of the options created by technology.
Chapter 5	Here we look at performance support in action for one of the two kinds of performance support, *Planners*. We present five Planners, seeking lessons from use in real organizations to solve important problems.
Chapter 6	Here we look at performance support in action for one of the two kinds of performance support, *Sidekicks*. We present four Sidekicks, focusing on integration of the support with the work.
Chapter 7	This is for the person who is now eager to go forward. How do you move forward to create useful performance support in your organization?
Chapter 8	What is the essence of effective performance support? We'll focus on eight attributes and turn to one company, IBM, to see how it supports sellers and leaders through on-demand resources.
Chapter 9	In Chapter 9, we present implementation strategies. We highlight blending, and discuss strategies ranging from sponsorship to multidisciplinary teams, measurement, communications, and change management.
Chapter 10	This chapter closes the book by looking into the future. How will newer technologies create new means to support performance and accomplishment? If there is less training, then what approaches and strategies will increase? Are there any costs to this shift to performance support?

REVIEW OF CHAPTER 1

Definition of Performance Support

A helper in life and work, performance support is a repository for information, processes, and perspectives that informs and guides thought and action.

Benefits of Job Aids and Performance Support

- *Converged.* Job aids and performance support are one with the work. They converge with the task, such as notes that captured directions to the meeting, or even more insinuated into the effort, a GPS system, whose sultry voice offers immediate prompts to get you where you want to go.

- *They go where the work is, rather than taking you away from the work to go to training.* Job aids and performance support are there, at the desktop, in the car, or on the run, when and where they are needed. In the midst of the question, concern, or problem, they remind about how many calories were consumed today. When on a dark and unknown road, they are a familiar voice with directions about what to do next.

- *Simplicity.* No frills, no fuss, just focus. Effective performance support helps individuals decide what to purchase, when to sell, and how to fix. While effective education is comprehensive and prepares individuals to handle what might come their way, performance support is targeted to keeping your cat from getting car sick or getting the smell of fish out of the house.

- *Personalized.* Some performance support understands you and adjusts information and guidance accordingly. What can you afford to buy? Is this an appropriate candidate for this job? How can you avoid avian flu, given your travel schedule? Performance support tailors information and guidance to your circumstances.

Instruction, Tools, and Performance Support—What's the Difference?

- Although *performance support* and *tools* support performance, only performance support stores information to be used by people to decide what to do. Documentation, checklists, and computer software are examples of performance support. A stapler and a portable vacuum cleaner are examples of tools; no information there.

- *Instruction, training, or education* provide preparation to perform, just in case somebody needs to know or do something. Performance support is more targeted, immediate, and specific. People turn to performance support to deal with something in particular.

- *Instruction changes the insides of people, what they know by heart.* Performance support is outside, an asset to which people refer when in need. Management development is an example of instruction because it is devoted to building the internal capacity of the individual. Performance support might be used by a manager to remind him how to approach a performance appraisal.

PREVIEW OF CHAPTER 2

Chapter 2 asks hard questions about when and when not to use performance support.

RESOURCES

Clark, D. (2003). *Blended learning* (white paper). Retrieved August 20, 2005, from www.epic.co.uk/content/resources/white_papers/blended.htm

Clark, R.C. (1986). Part I: Task-general instructional methods. *Performance and Instruction, 25*(3), 17–21.

Douglas, I., & Schaffer, S. (2002). Object-oriented performance improvement. *Performance Improvement Quarterly, 15*(3), 81–93.

Fogg, B.J. (2003). *Persuasive technology: Using computers to change what we think and do.* New York: Morgan Kaufmann.

Harless, J. H. (1986). Guiding performance with job aids. In *Introduction to Performance Technology,* pp. 106–124. Silver Springs, MD: International Society for Performance Improvement.

Levy, J. (2005, March). A parallel universe. *Chief Learning Officer,* www.clomedia.com, p. 13.

Rossett, A. (2001, June). E-trainer evolution. *Learning Circuits.* www.learningcircuits.org/2001/jun2001/rossett.html

Rossett, A. (2002, March). Overcoming insomnia in the big tent of e-learning. *Performance Express,* www.performancexpress.org/0203/

Rossett, A., & Gautier-Downes, J.D. (1991). *A handbook of job aids.* San Francisco: Pfeiffer.

Rossett, A., & Mohr, E. (2004, February). Performance support tools: Where learning work and results converge. *Training and Development, 58*(2), 35–39.

Sugrue, B., & Kim, K.H. (2004). *State of the industry.* Alexandria, VA: ASTD.

The When and Where of Performance Support

The hardware store employee must assemble bicycles for display. A firefighter must be able to couple a hose in no time at all. A customer service representative has trouble remembering what to say in different and pressured situations. Teachers don't see the need for the new attendance tracking software; they like the old one. Would performance support be appropriate in these cases? For which aspects of these challenges would it be apt? This chapter explores when and when not to use performance support.

WHEN TO USE PERFORMANCE SUPPORT

If people could remember everything, then performance support would not be necessary. Job aids, documentation, audio prompts, software—performance support all—are used largely because of limitations on memory and unwillingness to invest in developing memories.

Memory can be categorized in two ways: long-term memory (LTM) and short-term memory (STM). Long-term memory represents information that is stored, encoded, and retained in the brain as associations and networks. Memories are stored in LTM, whether they are recollections about chopping down Christmas trees with Grandpa, the political history of Malta versus Yalta, the definition of "pusillanimous," or a favorite brand of extra virgin olive oil.

The movement of information from STM into LTM, into meaningful networks, is called *learning*. It costs time and money to learn. The cost is in the nature of the experiences required to move random and fleeting data points into organized and meaningful memories. Consider what is involved in learning multiplication tables, in moving a bunch of numbers from STM into LTM. Consider driving an auto, explaining the three branches of the U.S. government, and motivating an employee. Lots of learning is involved in these goals. Think about all that effort, presentation, practice, feedback, and repetition over time.

Short-term memory (also referred to as working memory) is limited, usually to five to seven pieces of information. A good illustration of the limits on STM is the process of transferring a credit-card number from a bill to the check that will pay the bill. Some people capture four numbers at a time; others can capture five, six, seven, or as many as eight numbers. People differ in the number of times they have to go back to the credit card before they can reproduce the number. And people get annoyed when they have to record or transfer even longer numbers. The problem comes from the limits of memory and the memory decay that occurs when people rely on STM.

Because STM has limited capacity and because moving data into LTM expends resources, for repetitive practice over time and settings, professionals concerned with effective performance confront a challenge. Should they spend the time and resources needed to do what it takes to enable people to know their jobs by heart? Given the changing nature of work, is it possible to memorize significant portions of a volatile job? What about making investments in employee learning and then seeing that colleague employee skip to a competitor? These are the circumstances that encourage individuals and organizations to rely on performance support.

Edwin Hutchins' 1995 work on cognitive distribution is important. He complained about how cognitive science tends to limit the unit of analysis to the individual. Instead, he urged attention to social and cultural contexts, where artifacts around the individual boost cognitive activity. Remember quitnet, the website devoted to smoking cessation? Cognitive activity associated with smoking is affected by information, guidance, community, and measurement, on the site and in interaction with the smoker.

What about those tasks that are tedious or burdensome? Ruth Clark (1986) offered the following recommendation:

> Designers should encourage learners to use working memory to process information, not to store it. For example, as learners first practice a new procedure, give them access to clear, written, summary steps for reference so all working memory can be directed toward executing the procedure. The use of job aids, in the form of a written procedure table in this instance, can be especially powerful for this purpose. With enough repetition of the task, it will become automatic and bypass working memory. Then the job aid will become unnecessary. (p. 19)

People should look to performance support in the following situations:

1. *When the performance is infrequent.* Performance support is indicated when an individual cannot be expected to remember something done rarely. Whether people rely on aids to provide the details of an acquaintance's address or to compare product specifications or to carry out the procedure for changing the message on an answering machine, performance support boosts infrequent performance. Even Albert Einstein relied on performance support. A famous story tells of Einstein admitting to not knowing his own phone number because he didn't see any reason to know it, since he called it rarely and could look it up, when necessary.

2. *When the situation is complex, involves many steps, or has many attributes.* Work grows more complex and regulated. Performance support makes good sense for individuals who confront lengthy, difficult, and information-intensive challenges, such as those presented by Sarbanes Oxley and HIPAA. How does an employee secure data in a computer system so that certain employees may access those data but others may not? How do office managers know whether their operations are in or out of compliance with HIPAA? How do employees activate new features of the numerical-control lathe? What factors must a manager keep in mind when putting an employee on notice? When terminating an employee? Which product is compatible with earlier products and versions, and in what ways? Training makes less sense here than omnipresent access to performance support, which can boost performance and track effort.

3. *When the consequence of error is intolerable.* The following are examples of such situations:

- A salesperson promises compatibility between an existing computer system and a large new system. Alas, the client purchases the new system and finds it incompatible.

- An accountant initializes a computer disk and in the process deletes several clients' financial histories, including tax records.

- A doctor prescribes a medication to which a patient suffers a grave reaction. Why? The physician forgot either what drug this patient was already taking or the interaction between the new and the old.

- A new employee is responsible for classifying and matching blood types but is not sure exactly how to do it.

- An engineer is calculating tolerances for a bridge.

- A middle schooler is taking an important test.

Yes, a test. When we wrote *The Handbook of Job Aids,* the debate about the use of calculators in schools and during testing was joined. Many were against. They reminded us that educated people knew their figures by heart. A growing number were in favor. They pointed to the omnipresence of calculators, that the educated person takes advantage of accessible resources, and that how the calculator was used was more important than the actual computations. In this book we can report that the battle is just about over. In 1994, the Scholastic Aptitude Test (SAT) opened the doors to calculators in their tests.

4. *When performance depends on a large body of information.* Getting work done in the "Information Age" depends on ready access to large amounts of information on people, places, things, and policies. Print and automated performance support is essential when there are voluminous answers to questions about who, what, when, where, and how. Training catalogs provide a good example. Not even the most motivated employee can be expected to know the entire list. Technology steps in here, allowing employees and supervisors to search the database for the right offering, right time, and right place.

5. *When performance is dependent on knowledge, procedures, or approaches that change frequently.* In the past, an employee could feel relatively comfortable after training for and settling into a position. That is no longer true. The

shelf life of knowledge, procedures, and approaches is short. The contemporary salesperson, for example, must stay abreast of changing products, features, markets, and compatibilities. The same is true, of course, for doctors, accountants, and customer service providers. Answers that are right early on Monday could be wrong on Tuesday. In fact, they might be wrong by noon on Monday.

6. *When performance can be improved through employee self-assessment and correction with standards in mind.* A case has been made by Aronson (1999) for the power of self-persuasion to influence performance improvement. Clarity about what constitutes excellence and clear communication surrounding it helps people help themselves. For example, a highway-maintenance employee can become more safety conscious under snow conditions immediately after reading a document that reminds and coaches on the unique aspects of that situation. Similarly, a manager can conduct a more sensitive performance appraisal when a performance support tool suggests corrective actions tailored to the employee under review. A trainer is likely to return to the classroom with heightened skills if, during the lunch break, he or she has pondered the morning's teaching efforts in light of a checklist or rubric (see http://edweb.sdsu.edu/webquest/rubrics/weblessons.htm) that highlights ways to improve.

7. *When there is high turnover and the task is perceived to be simple.* Organizations are less willing to invest in training when employees might be short-timers or the work challenge is judged to be minimal. For example, a woman publishes a small, commercial directory of goods and services. Her salesforce is active for only a few months each year, turns over frequently, and handles a very simple product line with a rate card that is set for the year. She relies on support because she wants her salespeople in the field, not at training sessions. Performance support makes sense in emergency medicine too. If you had to call for urgent medical attention for a loved one, whom would you like to answer the phone? A physician, of course. Alas, it is not going to be a physician who answers the phone. The responder is likely to be someone who has been trained to use a performance support tool. The online tool prompts questions and, based on responses from callers, suggests both the next question and appropriate comment. The tool allows the person on the phone to act smarter than she is—and to get the job done.

8. *When there is little time or few resources to devote to training.* This is a "real-world" book. Because it is that, we acknowledge that organizations often turn to print and inexpensive computerized performance support when they are unable or unwilling to invest in education and training. Job aids, in particular, are popular in situations with scarce resources. Organizations are likely to favor an investment in reusable assets that remain with the organization over developing people, especially if the people are likely to depart or the task is judged to be uncomplicated. That works well in those circumstances. Marc Rosenberg's sidebar makes a strong case for the value to be derived from performance support.

TOM GILBERT WAS RIGHT

Marc J. Rosenberg

Of all justifications for performance support, "economic worth" may be the most important. And to make a sound economic worth argument, look no further than Tom Gilbert.

Gilbert, the father of Human Performance Technology (or Human Performance Improvement) demonstrated that the value gained from any behavior change, i.e., the performance, must be based on the cost of the effort versus the benefits received, expressed as follows:

$$\text{Worthy Performance} = \frac{\text{Value of the Accomplishment}}{\text{Cost of the Behavior}}$$

Thus, the worth of any performance intervention increases as its value increases and its costs decrease. But if costs are too high, or the value is too low, the performance we get may not be worth the effort. Let's apply this to training versus performance support decision making.

Because training focuses on the tough job of improving or modifying human behavior, it is usually an expensive solution. When used in critical situations (for example, nuclear safety, medical practice, or military effectiveness), where certainty of competence is essential, training is highly appropriate. The costs are high, but so is the value (like personal security or the value of human life).

But in many situations, such as when training is called upon to compensate for poor documentation, bad processes, or deficient resources and tools, training's focus is often on temporary workarounds and coping strategies. In these cases, the limited value of the accomplishment cannot justify the high investment in the training solution alone, putting the overall worth of the intervention into question. Performance support offers a better way to meet this challenge.

Because performance support and performance-centered design are more closely aligned with work practices, we have opportunities to improve workplace performance directly. Instead of using training to explain a murky document, we fix the document. Instead of relying on courses to elaborate on complex or difficult processes, we rethink the processes and put information all around them. Instead of teaching people to get by with inadequate resources and tools, we enrich those resources and tools. With performance support, we attack the performance problem at its root, mitigating the need for so much costly training.

Of course, training can be and often is a part of a comprehensive solution. But when we think about value versus cost in determining how to improve performance, training is increasingly not the total answer. We must expand our toolkit to include performance support interventions that lower our overall investment while more directly and more permanently improving performance.

This is our challenge when we "blend" interventions to solve performance problems. We must recognize that relying solely on blending *instructional* solutions is not always the best way to meet the economic worth test for long-term, sustainable, and valued performance improvement. Including performance support in the mix lowers overall investment, reduces time to competence, and makes the solution more durable over time, all of which lowers the denominator of the formula (cost), thereby increasing the overall worth of the intervention. By integrating performance support, sometimes even considering performance support as a first resort and training as a secondary solution, we will meet Gilbert's challenge of generating worthy performance.

Marc J. Rosenberg, CPT, Ph.D., (www.marcrosenberg.com), is a management consultant, educator, and expert in the world of training, organizational learning, e-learning, knowledge management, and performance improvement. Marc is author of the best-selling *e-Learning: Strategies for Delivering Knowledge in*

(Continued)

WHEN IS PERFORMANCE SUPPORT INAPPROPRIATE?

Here are the circumstances in which a workforce learning professional might want to avoid performance support.

When Aided Performance Would Damage Credibility

An ineffective manager is a good example. Should the unit leader counsel a troubled employee while referring to a checklist? Should that same manager work on goals with a team with eyes focused on a poster that reminds him how to boost morale?

Or suppose a person has the following symptoms: slight fever, headache, stuffy nose, and sore throat. During a visit to a family physician, the doctor listens to those symptoms; thinks about them for a few seconds; and then fires up her computer to search in a database. Now suppose the person has different symptoms: slight fever; headache; stuffy nose; sore throat; spots in front of the eyes; and a rash on the chest, palms, and the soles of the feet. Another doc listens to those symptoms; thinks about them for a few seconds; and then turns to a database on his computer.

Which doctor inspires confidence? Most would reject the first doctor. She should know what to do about the symptoms of the common cold. It is the second physician who inspires confidence, even though you would surely rather not have those odd symptoms. The preferred doctor seeks performance support for unusual challenges, rather than for the basics of daily medical practice.

Individuals are expected to be knowledgeable about topics and questions they confront regularly. Only when the inquiry is unusual, unique, complex, or infrequent might a professional refer to sources without his or her professional competence being questioned. People expect others to be "smart," to have their jobs down cold, and to know what they are doing, especially if those others are knowledge workers such as engineers, doctors, management consultants, financial advisors, pilots, psychologists, and school principals. These people and many others are expected to handle *typical* challenges without referring to external sources.

Human resources professionals need to ask, "If a reasonable person sees this individual in the act of referring to external sources, will he question the person's skills or knowledge?" If the answer is that such judgment is likely, then education and training, not performance support, should be used to enhance performance.

When Speedy Performance Is a Priority

What kinds of circumstances necessitate speedy performance? The following situations are most common: (1) when the organization places a very high value on throughput, the processing of a large number of transactions or (2) when life or limb hangs in the balance. Although financial services organizations rely on performance support to bolster retirement advisors, for example, they prefer their people to know many of the recurring aspects of their jobs by heart. Why? They want customer service representatives to be able to do many transactions in short periods of time and to speak with confidence. If most requests for assistance or information necessitate reference, the number of contacts declines, affecting the bottom line.

Speed is crucial during medical or equipment emergencies. If instantaneous response is essential and there is no time to refer for assistance, such as what might transpire during a surgery, then individuals must be educated to perform with fluency and by heart.

When Novel and Unpredictable Situations Are Involved

Performance support is not particularly good as assistance for individuals who confront novel and largely unpredictable circumstances. Such situations demand intangible abilities to handle surprises, stresses, and new challenges. Surgery is a good example, of course. We want fluent performance from a surgeon when the unexpected occurs in the middle of heart bypass surgery.

School districts expect good judgment from employees when they are confronted by parents who are nearly hysterical about their children's test results; the Navy also expects good judgment from pilots when they are subjected to combat situations. Brecke (1982) explored the topic of training to instill judgment in pilots. He provided a useful definition of judgment as the "right stuff" evoked in situations that include uncertainty, lack of complete information, stress, task difficulty, cognitive complexity, and time constraints. Brecke complained that military training in 1982 was characterized by an emphasis on correct completion of prescribed procedures and compliance with rules. Although compliance with procedures can be comfortably supported by job aids, it is not likely to clinch victory in the skies. That victory is the result of good judgment. If good judgment in a topsy-turvy world is a goal, performance support will not be the major player in ensuring the high end of that endeavor.

When Smooth and Fluid Performance Is a Top Priority

World-class athletes, for example, do not use performance support on the field of play. Roger Federer would not turn to his PDA for guidance on handling wind as he attempts to serve out to win the French Open.

Imagine Tiger Woods looking at his PDA as he addresses the ball in a sand trap. Not likely. But imagine if Woods were playing on an unfamiliar course. While strolling to the next green, he could certainly reach into his bag for a small computer that reviews the next hole and others' past approaches and results on it.

Consider Woods' situation, a prima ballerina, a veteran surgeon, or a master teacher. All might and probably should use various forms of performance support in their preparations and to reflect later on how they did. But during crunch time, when performance is expected, they are mostly on their own. Interrupting the flow of such effort to refer to references is preposterous. Successful performance in these cases is dependent on habitual, automatic, flexible, and seamless performance. The tasks are incongruous with reliance on performance support.

When an Employee Lacks Sufficient Reading, Listening, or Reference Skills

The instructional design professional who is considering performance support needs to answer the following questions about the person who will be using the support:

- Is he accustomed to turning to sources outside himself for information? Is he curious? Is he committed to doing the job better?
- Can she read? Does she read? Does she read well enough to use these materials?
- Does he know how to read flow charts, diagrams, charts, and illustrations?
- Is she comfortable with computers and their uses as sources of information?
- How good are his listening skills? Will he take the time to benefit from audio tools?

The *Handbook of Job Aids* stopped there. Today it is important to recognize the immediate aid that can be provided through mobile devices. Consider MP3 players, cell phones, and GPS. Vodcasting (video casting) is now a sidekick to assist the employee who is uncomfortable with the written word. But that individual must want to look to other sources, must be willing to listen, and then incorporate advice. There's no way to get around the fact that people must invite these assets into their work and lives.

When Employees Are Not Motivated

If organizations produce performance support assets, they become valuable only when they are used to accomplish things. Untouched, ignored, unappreciated— well, that's a problem. From time to time, the cause is that the support fails to add value. But other times, lack of use happens because employees would rather not. They're not concerned, interested, focused. Handing them a nifty software tool or reference manual is not likely to help anyone or anything.

REVIEW OF CHAPTER 2

When Would You Use Performance Support?

- When the performance is infrequent.
- When the situation is complex, has multiple steps, or has multiple attributes.
- When the consequences of errors are high.
- When performance depends on a large body of information.
- When performance is dependent on knowledge, procedures, or approaches that change frequently.
- When performance can be improved through employee self-assessment and correction with standards in mind.
- When there is high turnover and the task can be codified.
- When there is little time and few resources for training and development.

When Wouldn't You Use Performance Support?

- When aided performance would damage credibility.
- When speed is demanded.

- When novel or unpredictable circumstances are likely.

- When smooth and fluid performance is a top priority.

- When users lack reading or listening skills.

- When employees aren't motivated.

PREVIEW OF CHAPTER 3

Chapter 3 is the WHY chapter. Why is this happening? Where do job aids and performance support come from? What is the context for the shift to performance support? What does this mean to organizations and to workforce learning professionals?

RESOURCES

Aronson, E. (1999). The power of self-persuasion. *American Psychologist, 54,* pp. 875–884.

Brecke, F.H. (1982). Instructional design for aircrew judgment training. *Aviation, Space and Environmental Medicine, 53*(10), 951–957.

Clark, R.C. (1986). Part I: Task-general instructional methods. *Performance and Instruction, 25*(3), 17–21.

Harless, J.H. (1986). Guiding performance with job aids. In *Introduction to performance technology,* pp. 106–124. Silver Springs, MD: International Society for Performance Improvement.

Hutchins, E. (1995). *Cognition in the wild.* Cambridge, MA: MIT Press.

Rossett, A., & Gautier-Downes, J.D. (1991). *A handbook of job aids.* San Francisco: Pfeiffer.

Rossett, A., & Mohr, E. (2004, February). Performance support tools: Where learning work and results converge. *Training and Development, 58*(2), 35–39.

Performance Support Yesterday and Today

Chapter 3 puts performance support in context. Where does performance support come from? Why is it important now? How does it fit with other options for performance improvement?

We begin this chapter by looking both backwards and forwards with job aids, perhaps the most familiar, conventional, and pervasive form of performance support. Then we'll turn to automated performance support. Where did it come from? How are people thinking and writing about this technology-based approach? Why is performance support appealing today?

JOB AIDS AT THE BEGINNING

Job aids are not new. People have relied on job aids since prehistoric times, when the details of fire tending, skinning, and cooking adorned cave walls.

There are good reasons to appreciate job aids. For example, Duncan's 1985 review of military reliance on job aids between 1958 and 1972 documents their significant and positive contributions to military performance. The military's use of systematic approaches in the design of training (then called the Interservice Procedures for Instructional Systems Development) and reliance on job aids influenced civilian business practices in companies like AT&T and GTE.

Joe Harless (1986), often acknowledged as the father of job aids, stated that job aids can be developed in three to five times less time than it takes to develop equivalent training programs. He also described instances in which the use of job aids diminished the need for training and thus shortened the amount of time that employees were away from their jobs.

Harless was not alone in his certainty that job aids made positive contributions to the bottom line. Duncan (1985) concurred, citing the results of military analyses demonstrating that job aids saved money without jeopardizing work performance.

More Than Money

Job aids, like their automated siblings, relieve individuals of responsibility for storing information in long-term memory. Remember how much you appreciate the shopping list that saves you from impulse purchases. Reliance on a job aid shifts the individual's obligation from repetition over time to searching for information as needed.

That reliance on external resources also creates new responsibilities for the organization. First, they must build or acquire useful resources and systems. Second, they must invest in developing their people to know how to productively search and find the answers and advice they need.

The third organizational responsibility is to create a culture in which reference is encouraged, even honored. Several years ago, a bank teller told me she was going to see if she could find her "cheat sheet" in order to be able to answer a question. Just last week, an executive for a professional association used the exact same words: "Cheat sheet." Neither afforded job aids the respect they deserve. Organizations must move to make it a badge of honor when employees seek what they need.

Schools are beginning to advance that notion. In 1994, Scholastic Aptitude Test (SAT) takers were permitted to bring along their calculators for the big test. And now, according to Gamerman (2006), some middle and high schools are permitting students to look things up online as they take tests and create papers.

Do you want your teller, auditor, auto repair person, dentist, and accountant to look things up when in doubt? Do you want your tenth-grader to check out the spelling of a word or the location of a place? Of course.

Job Aids to Support Procedures and Information

In the early 1970s, job aids were influenced by behaviorism. According to Pipe (1986), individuals often turned to job aids to support them in carrying out a *procedure,* such as securing data in a computer, putting in a new printer cartridge, or mixing a Cosmopolitan. A procedure in this context is a prescribed way of doing something. Procedures mandate a particular course of action in a particular sequence. Job aids that support procedures tell and show actions, order, and results. Job aids have assisted people in all kinds of chores, such as changing the oil in a car, loading a dishwasher, and applying makeup.

Job aids also have a role to play in helping people deal with the challenges associated with the information that surrounds them. Clay Carr (1992) wrote of a 1945 article in the *Atlantic Monthly* in which Vannevar Bush, then director of the U.S. Office of Research and Development, noted an "information explosion." His response was to suggest a "memex," an automated desk that would provide information as it was needed.

Everyone experiences "information overload," "information dump," "information anxiety," and even "information bulimia." What these phrases share is recognition of the profusion of information, the negative effects of being awash in information, the complexity of products and options, and the human and organizational need to make sense of it all. People and organizations need systems that diminish chaos, provide order, and support results-oriented interactions with data. Yahoo's attempt to make the blogosphere understandable and accessible is a good example.

Wurman (1989) claimed that data are not information until they have form and enable knowledge and understanding. A job aid that informs is one that supports people at work by diminishing the uncertainty they experience.

Informational job aids make data useful and become useful themselves when they are accessible and:

- Form a stable repository for facts and concepts that answers the question of *who, what, which, when,* or *where;* and

- Are organized by user frame of reference, function, or content structure.

Thought-Provoking Job Aids

No longer are job aids perceived only as simple stimuli that evoke a response during a task or point to or deliver information. Job aids also have potential to influence the way people think and feel about themselves, their work, their co-workers, their managers, their clients, their products, and their problems. They can be *thought-provoking, as they coach for better performance.* How do we approach an employee who has recently lost a loved one? What about an employee who is chronically tardy? What does the new teacher think about as he reflects on how he taught a language arts lesson?

The combination of cognitive science and information technology thus propel expanded definitions for job aids. These perspectives now dominate:

- Recognition of the importance of how people think about the work;
- Concern with the individual's self-perception, readiness, and confidence;
- Eagerness for the individual to consciously organize information; and
- Belief that performance has roots in thoughts and speech.

Not surprisingly, there is growing interest in using these thought-provoking aids to increase reflection and elevate attention and activity—even for little ones. Figure 3.1 shows FEMA's checklist (www.fema.gov/kids/k_srvkit.htm) to coach children in how to prepare to endure the aftermath of a natural disaster.

Figure 3.1 What Children Should Gather in Preparation for a Disaster

Source: FEMA

Rossett and Gautier-Downes (1991) dubbed this form coaching job aids. Coaching job aids are not limited to deployment at the moment of challenge. An example of this wider window of influence is the job aid that helps managers plan to manifest sensitivity to and congruence with equity guidelines while interviewing potential employees. An hour before the interview, a manager might review company policy, quotes from experts, short examples, and a checklist of things to keep in mind during the different phases of the selection interview. Although the planning job aid might not be in sight during the interview, its influence is felt just before and throughout.

Figure 3.2 provides kids with materials that help them nudge their families to collect provisions in advance of a natural disaster.

Figure 3.2 A Coaching Aid to Help Children Urge Parents Toward Preparedness

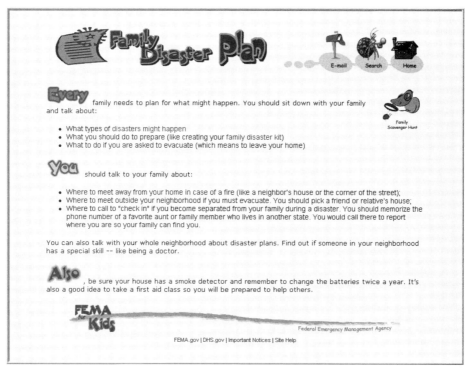

Source: FEMA

Coaching job aids have the following characteristics:

- They answer the question "how," but in a different way than procedural aids do. They tell us "How might I think about or approach that?" They answer the question: "What should I keep in mind?"

- They also answer the question "why," as in "Why would I include those questions in an interview?"

- They articulate quality standards; and

- They encourage a dialog with the user, especially a dialog about reasons, feelings, and approaches.

PERFORMANCE SUPPORT AT THE BEGINNING

Performance support is job aids on steroids.

Revisit Figures 3.1 and 3.2. Job aids or performance support? They are both. The disaster preparation aids are examples of static, familiar coaching job aids that use technology for distribution and update. They illustrate how job aids are a form of performance support.

There you see a little of what happens when technology is added to job aids. In its most basic form, technology enables the desired information to be readily sought, found, used, and tended. And the many people who need it can reach for it simultaneously, across the continent and world. Update is a snap.

There is, however, much more that technology brings to these performance-centered approaches. When technology is combined with information about the user and the context, customized guidance can be delivered when and where it is needed. Treasured benefits derive from the ability of the system to deliver instantaneously, to reside within the context and workflow, to sense needs and personalize information and advice, and to give just what is required.

The disaster aids leverage technology, but not in any way that is even close to what they might contribute. The job aids that reside on the website must be "pulled" by users if they are concerned about their readiness for a disaster and when seeking help in assembling provisions, for example. Technology could add a targeted "push." For example, tailored guidance, directions, and advice about mitigation for wildfires could be targeted and delivered to you because you live in

California, not Louisiana or the Netherlands, and because your region is suffering through a drought.

Meet Gloria Gery

Gery's classic work sketched possibilities for contemporary performance support. She noted that CBT (computer-based training) could be more than a classroom experience delivered on the computer. Throughout the 1980s, 1990s, and into the new decade, Gery (2002) made a case for performance support as faster and cheaper than training because it delivers support where and when needed, in a real-world situation. Her example (p. 4): ". . . rather than send a technical support person to a one-week installation planning course for an upgrade to a mainframe operation system, why not develop a Wizard that guides users through the process?"

Gery's 2000 and 2002 work encouraged support that is there when it is needed. She touted the use of computer software to activate information and to place it next to and within the task. She described what performance-centered tools can do: conditionally guide performers through a process; calculate answers or transform data into a more usable form; and allow individuals to use the tool in several formats. TurboTax was the example Gery used, acknowledging two interfaces, one that interviews the user and solicits data and the other that readies the form for submission.

Integration with the Work

Gery, according to Cavanaugh (2004), identified three ways to parse performance support:

1. **External support**—requiring that users break away from work to refer to the resource;

2. **Extrinsic support**—available within the system, although there is a break in the action to get the necessary information; and

3. **Intrinsic support**—support that is inside the software or system and is indistinguishable from the workflow.

Cavanaugh (2004) acknowledged unresolved questions about the performance support domain and then presented an expanded approach of his own. He called it a spectrum devoted to this goal: "transparency, where there is no distinction between a task and the technological support provided to accomplish that task" (p. 29). Integration with the task was his top priority.

Cavanaugh's "spectrum of support" approach is recapped in Table 3.1: external; extrinsic; intrinsic; intuitive; and intelligent. The "E" words represent, in his view, a lower form of support because they are distinct from work, what Barry Raybould (2000) called stand-alone. Cavanaugh (2004) spoke in favor of integration.

Table 3.1 Cavanaugh's 2E3I Spectrum of Performance Support

2E3I Model	Commentary
External Disconnected and apart from the task Examples: manuals, documentation, support call centers	In Cavanaugh's view, this is the "lowest level of support." In ours, while it is distinct from the work, it provides opportunity to plan, evaluate, reflect, and prepare to do better next time. Integration is one important variable, but not the only one.
Extrinsic Part of the work context, but necessitating a break from the flow of the effort Examples: software's traditional HELP function; interactive map kiosk in a mall; hand-washing directions and exhortations on a bathroom wall	Cavanaugh described this support as embedded but not fully integrated because it must be selected and directed by the user. He sniffs at the lack of integration. We see it as different but valuable.
Intrinsic When needed, the user triggers the support, which is provided in a way that is within the flow of work Examples: Microsoft Word's paper clip assistants, Braille characters on ATM, one-number speed dialing	In Cavanaugh's view, this is "dramatically more useful than extrinsic support." Useful indeed. And we concur with Cavanaugh when he notes that it can be inappropriate and intrusive, as in the paper clip assistant that wants to help when help is not needed.

Table 3.1 (Continued)

2E3I Model	Commentary
Intuitive Support is more seamlessly integrated into the work and task environment Example: Microsoft Word automatically corrects "teh" and turns it into "the."	Cavanaugh favors this form because it compensates for human errors and does so in a less obtrusive fashion. We concur. Who doesn't like it when Microsoft or TiVO make us look smarter than we are?
Intelligent The support is anticipatory and transparent. It knows when you need it and is there, fully integrated into the task. It doesn't jump up and down and point to itself. Examples: Self-launching and self-targeting ordnance, mechanical equipment that will not function unless properly held.	Imagine a physician approaching a patient's bedside. She looks at the chart and chats with the patient, and eventually prescribes a new medication. As she does this, the system responds and reminds her about a possible negative interaction between the new medication and current meds. Who wouldn't like support that is there, knowing it is needed before you know you need it? Great stuff, expensive, definitely a high-value application that is particularly appealing as we move to mobile delivery of performance support (Rader, 2004).

Support for Planning Too

There is obvious appeal to resources that are integrated into the task, support Cavanaugh dubbed intrinsic, intuitive, and intelligent. Surely it is better to know immediately if the medication is contra-indicated, rather than later, after the patient has suffered a grave outcome. Surely it is better to have spelling corrected on the fly, rather than returned a week later by an editor or teacher with a red circle.

But integration, although receiving most of the applause in the published literature, is only one worthy criterion.

In fact, value can come from the absence of integration, from an opportunity to pause and reflect, inspired by expert advice and pithy guidance surrounding the task. An anecdote about Albert Einstein (Schramm & Porter, 1982) is appropriate here. When asked a question about the single event most helpful in developing the theory of relativity, Einstein reportedly responded, "Figuring out how to think about the problem." Performance support can be influential here, as knowledge workers struggle to be, well, more knowledgeable about how to approach the work. And they struggle to do it without committing huge resources to education and memorization.

Les Thurow, former dean of the Massachusetts Institute of Technology's Sloan School of Management, got it. He noted that standards of living rise not because people work harder but because they work smarter and that economic progress represents the replacement of physical exertion with brain power. Performance support, delivered through print and emergent technologies, redefines the phrase, *brain power.* No longer are workers judged competent because they "know it cold." Now workers may express their competence by knowing where and how to access appropriate external resources, even if they know only some of it by heart. What they know is how to find what they need and how to take advantage of their resources. Gamerman's 2006 article in *The Wall Street Journal* documents increasing respect for students who can do this.

This brings us to an expanded model for performance support that honors both integration and planning. As you will see in Chapter 4, we present two kinds of performance support: Planners and Sidekicks. Planner performance support reminds about what to pack for international travel, how to sell the company's product at higher levels in the organization, and what to consider as you look back on a presentation. Sidekicks are there at the moment of need, ready to improve our spelling as we write at the computer. In their GPS (global positioning satellite) form, Sidekicks speak to us as we navigate highways and byways.

State police in Pennsylvania are enjoying a Sidekick in their work. According to a report by Grata (2005), the Motorola Automatic License Plate Reader uses an infrared TV camera to scan passing license plates and compare them to a statewide database where law enforcement agencies post stolen vehicles, fugitives, all-points bulletins, and Amber alerts. Day or night, fog or sunshine, the camera scans passing plates and compares them to the database. Instant information is then delivered to the dashboard—assisting officers in identifying "bad guys" and knowing when back-up is necessary.

The integration that Sidekicks provide is good, but there are even more possibilities for electronic performance support, possibilities that are often overlooked.

Of importance also is the way a tool captures smarts and distributes them before the task or soon thereafter, to assist in planning, making decisions, and reflecting on what has transpired. Let's look at how Planner tools provide support in two very different situations: teachers in training and sales professionals.

A professor of teacher education at San Diego State University described the use of Planners for her aspiring teachers. Their challenge? They want to be able to assess and improve on the practice lesson they just delivered. But they don't know enough to do so. She has developed a checklist of questions for her students to ask themselves. It doesn't matter whether these standards are delivered in print or electronically. What matters is that the novice teachers have access to expert perspectives on quality teaching to refer to as they consider what they did and how they might do it better the next time.

Jack Gordon (2003) commenced an article in elearningmag.com with a story about a pharmaceutical sales rep cooling his heels in a doctor's waiting room. While waiting, the sales rep reaches for his web-enabled personal digital assistant (PDA) and connects to the Internet, "Lo and behold, here is a fresh bulletin from corporate headquarters explaining that the Food and Drug Administration has just changed the prescribing requirements for a competitor's drug" (p. 32). The salesman also turns to the PDA to review notes from a recent course about his company's drug. Once in front of the physician, if all goes as it should, he will display fluency and certainty. Planner performance support helps him prepare himself to make the most of scant moments with the doctor.

Two IBMers, Rae and O'Driscoll (2004), also wrote about the value of information that helps sales professionals plan their approaches. In fact, it solves a likely problem. They told of a sales guy who is readying for a meeting with a client. Such a person, they noted, wants real-time information, on demand. If the organization doesn't provide it, eager sales people will find it as they will, likely by noodling about on the Internet. Does the organization want to shape and authenticate that message or leave each individual to figure it out independently and idiosyncratically?

Front and Center Today

There are many reasons to favor performance support and every reason to recognize growing presence and influence.

Our Purpose Is Performance and Results, Not Education and Training

Have you ever tried to talk to executives about training and development? Mostly, they are not interested. They want to talk about business, results, accomplishments, opportunities, and problems. Their focus is on sales, satisfaction, and operations. Few are riveted by icebreakers, classes, e-learning, or even blended learning. You might have a chance to catch their attention with the phrase "performance support," emphasis on the word performance. Might. Maybe.

In an article in *Training and Development,* Rossett and Mohr (2004) addressed executives who want results, not training:

> Are you willing to send employees to a class so that they can answer customers' detailed questions about insurance policies, cell phone features, or the demographics of Basra or Bimini? *We doubt it.*
>
> After a class about numerous cell phone features, for example, will your employees remember them a week or month later, when queried by a customer? *We doubt it.*
>
> Are you willing to rely on employee memory when critical, complex, or dangerous actions are involved on an airplane or at a nuclear plant? *We doubt it.*
>
> Should the organization do what it takes for employees to learn material by heart—especially when there's much to learn, the content changes often, a mistake is dangerous, and they could take their expertise with them when they leave? *We doubt it.*

It isn't just executives who favor performance over instruction. Employees, in Levy's (2004) view, are "knowledge warriors," too busy for courses, with no need for grades, and with far too much time spent searching for the information they need. Rosenberg (2003) applauded the shift to information and advice on demand, in stark contrast to education and training. His example is his own search for a new automobile. He never took a class, but found exactly what he needed online, in portals that answered questions about advanced features and functions.

Deloitte Consulting executive Nick van Dam (2005) focused on the nature of what he calls the self-service workplace. He said that a growing need for knowledge and skill is occurring in an impatient context, where organizations are less willing to invest in training and development, with concerns about training delivered too early or too late.

Support Where the Work Is Done

Remember Gordon's tale of the pharmaceutical sales rep using his time in the waiting room to bone up in preparation for a short opportunity with a physician? That support is very close to the work, but it can get even closer.

Information Week's 2005 annual survey of five hundred innovations revealed a stunning example of information delivered to the worker and workplace, exactly where the work is done. JM Family Enterprises' Toyota dealership is devoted to cutting the time it takes to repair a vehicle. According to Chabrow (2005), the company is testing a wireless headset with a flip-down screen from Microvision, Inc. Using retinal scanning display technology, pages of an auto repair manual are cast onto the working mechanic's retina. The mechanic searches and changes pages using a belt-mounted touch pad. The technology vice president admitted that mechanics were not initially keen on the idea, but noted that they adjusted swiftly. He anticipated the performance support will increase technician productivity by more than 30 percent because they don't have to stop work, put down tools, and search for what they need in a manual.

Harvey Singh's company, Instancy, develops workflow support and knowledge management applications for web and mobile delivery environments. One example application is field customer service support.

Field customer service representatives must know about products, problems, services, and resources in order to deliver answers while interacting with customers and computers or equipment. Reps are expected to solve problems and answer questions where the needs are, in the field. Figure 3.3 provides an example of PDA-based resources provided to the reps based on Instancy's knowledge-workflow application.

In addition to support for the field reps, the system does two other things. It provides video-based examples that reps can use to educate customers and helps the organization keep track of performance as reps record their efforts, actions, and results.

Gary Dickelman, steward of EPSScentral.info, believes that the challenge confronting us is to aggregate three established disciplines in service to performance: (1) business process improvement; (2) knowledge engineering; and (3) human factors. *Business process improvement* focuses effort on outcomes, standardized processes, customer experience, and a gung-ho commitment to measurement at first, throughout, and continuously. *Knowledge engineering* engages

Figure 3.3 Support for Field Customer Service Representatives

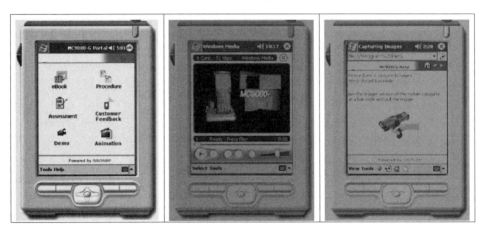

Source: Instancy. Used by permission.

us in collecting, organizing, and distributing the smarts inside an organization. Finally, when concerned with *human factors,* we are attentive to how people interact with work, processes, tools, environments, and technology.

Mobile Support

In October 2005, the city of Philadelphia announced that Atlanta-based EarthLink Inc. will fund, build, and manage a 135-square-mile network to provide it with wireless access. In addition, they will offer low-income residents service for as little as $10 a month. Google, Inc., recently submitted a one-hundred-page bid to provide free wireless Internet access to the city of San Francisco.

Why are these companies doing this? What are city leaders thinking? They are responding to opportunity, of course. City and business leaders perceive high-speed and mobile web access as a basic municipal service like water, electricity, and trash collection. As they look to differentiating themselves from other cities, high-speed mobile access is, they anticipate, something individuals and organizations cannot and will not live without.

All this produces expanded expectations and possibilities. Road warriors have every reason to believe that information and advice will find them, wherever they are. Now soccer moms, too, want information immediately, on the run. Need an

ATM? Your Bluetooth-connected PDA knows their locations. Want to know which way to Mecca or to be reminded of prayer time? That too is available from a mobile phone handset produced by LG of South Korea. Concerned about how the new hardware will synch with a customer's installed base? Connect wirelessly to the company intranet and let it provide more certain answers.

Wildstrom (2005) described what mobile performance support now means to the well-equipped sailor. In the past, boats relied on two-way radio and a depth sounder. Today, the cockpit display integrates several sources of data—radar, sonar, electronic charts, satellite imagery—into an information-rich message. Not only does the system provide protection from collisions and guidance in the fog, but Google-style satellite images allow boaters to discern what is near the dock, to find petrol or a restaurant, and even to make a reservation.

According to eTForecasts (2005), the number of PCs is projected to surpass one billion in 2007, and the number of personal digital assistants (PDAs) is anticipated to reach almost sixty million by 2008, with most enjoying wireless email and web-browsing capabilities. MP3 players are omnipresent. Cell phones too, now at a whopping 1.5 billion and counting, most with FLASH available to provide dynamic displays of information. Cell phones now enjoy nearly universal penetration in Asia and Europe, with the United States lagging behind, but not for long.

People around the world have access to wireless performance support and are no longer tethered to walls and desks for either their jobs or their information and guidance. Internet browser capabilities allow employees to access web-based databases or search engines through their cell phones, PDAs, and PCs. Short text messaging (SMS) can be used to send coaching tips and knowledge checks, or to see whether any new studies have been published. Video clips can provide short examples of desirable performance in areas such as negotiation, while in a cab speeding to what might be a contentious meeting.

The Career Self-Reliant Employee and the Battle for Talent

Bettina Lankard Brown (1996) put her finger on a significant change in the landscape:

> The emphasis on the self-management and self-development of one's career is a reflection of the shift in the unspoken employment agreement between employers and employees over the last three

decades. In the 1960s, the employer-employee relationship was characterized as a parent-child relationship: The organization provided employment in jobs that were narrowly defined, status in the community, and job security in exchange for employee hard work, loyalty, and good performance. Thirty years later, the contract between employer and employee is a partnership. The emphasis in this new contract is on worker employability rather than job security. In this contract, employers provide the opportunities, tools, and support to help employees develop their skills and maintain their employability; the employees have the responsibility of managing their careers, taking advantage of the opportunities they are given. Thus, the employees must be career self-reliant. They must continually update their skills, looking ahead to the future and to market trends as well as to the current demands of the workplace (Collard, Epperheimer, & Saign, 1996). They must have a plan for "enhancing their performance and long-term employability" (Waterman, Waterman, & Collard, 1994, p. 88). The new relationship between employee and employer is described as a contract through which individual needs and those of the organization are balanced.

Brown (1996) speaks mostly of changing expectations for the individual. Hugh McKellar, editor of *KMWorld,* seconded that focus, "KM (knowledge management) is shifting back to individuals, encouraging 'knowledge-conscious behavior,' improving communication, and encouraging enjoyment of the work environment, which we all know improves any organization" (2005).

The organization must change also. The organization that expects career self-reliance of employees must do it in a way that is not perceived by employees as abandonment. In a world in which organizations are concerned about attracting and retaining great people and compete aggressively for talent, leading organizations cannot ignore learning and support. Quite the contrary. The successful organization provides clear expectations for performance, statements about career possibilities, and targeted, diverse resources to enable growth and success.

What kind of resources? Education and training, courses and coaching are fine options. Performance support is another.

There are reasons for organizations to favor providing performance support over conventional learning opportunities. With learning, the investment is in the capacity of the individual. Results are housed inside the individual. Then, that person may elect to depart with his or her smarts. With performance support, more investment is in the development and maintenance of organizational assets, accessible by many when and where needed. Not surprisingly, as ties between individuals and companies have frayed, with individuals joining several organizations throughout their careers, organizations grow more inclined to invest in creating and tending reusable assets, such as performance support. Performance support does not tire, retire, or move on to another organization.

The Need to Know More

While there is some research in this area, more is needed. Intel's Frank Nguyen noted that there are few research studies that practitioners can rely on to provide data-driven guidelines to determine which performance support systems are most effective and when. He expands on this in the accompanying sidebar.

WHAT WE KNOW AND DON'T KNOW

Frank Nguyen

It has been more than two decades since Gloria Gery introduced the concept of performance support systems. Since that time, authors and experts have contributed their thoughts, experience, and advice to guide practitioners in the development of these on-the-job support interventions.

Let's take a quick look at what many *believe* about performance support:

- Implementing a performance support system can cut the amount of necessary training for users (Chase, 1998).

- Highly integrated performance support systems (intrinsic, extrinsic) are better than those that are disconnected (external) from the user's work interface (Carroll & Rosson, 1987; Gery, 1995; Raybould, 2000).

- The type and amount of performance support should vary based on the expertise of the user (Nguyen, in press).

(Continued)

- There are many different ways to categorize performance support systems (Gery, 1995; Ladd, 1993; Sleight 1993).

- We have tools and methods to calculate the return-on-investment for performance support systems (Altalib, 2002; Desmarais, Leclair, Fiset, & Talbi, 1997).

- The field of performance support will converge with training and knowledge management (Elsenheimer, 2000; Rosenberg, 1995; Sherry & Wilson, 1996).

It's important to contrast what we *believe* about performance support to the things that we *know* for sure and certain because research has uncovered these effects.

- Implementing any kind of performance support system, whether integrated or non-integrated, can have a significant effect on user performance and attitudes (Duncan, 1985; Fletcher & Johnston, 1995; Hunt, Haynes, Hanna, & Smith, 1998; Nguyen, Klein, & Sullivan, 2005).

- There appears to be no significant difference on user performance when implementing a paper-based job aid versus electronic performance support system, particularly certain types of non-integrated EPSS (Morrison & Witmer, 1983).

- Users often struggle using search engines to look for support content; linking to content tends to be better (Bailey, 2003; Spool, 2001).

- We can build performance support systems for many different settings: from software applications to factories to educational settings (Brush, Knapczyk, & Hubbard, 1993; Cole, Fischer, & Saltzman, 1997; Dorsey, Goodrum, & Schwen, 1993; Gery, 2003; Kasvi & Vartiainen, 2000; McCabe & Leighton, 2002; McManus & Rossett, 2006; Schwen, Goodrum, & Dorsey, 1993).

- The types of performance support systems corporate employees find useful tend to be extrinsic or external in nature (Nguyen, 2005). In particular, the most highly rated performance support systems are those that are responsive to a user's job role or location in a software system, and then able to deliver appropriate information.

As you can see, what we know about performance support is somewhat less (and perhaps different) than current beliefs or best-known practices. The certainties around performance support are less than one might expect for a field that has seen broad adoption over the last twenty years. More research is needed on topics like the impact of support on time in training and time on task and success in varied settings.

Frank Nguyen is a doctoral candidate in educational technology, focusing on performance support systems. He has managed the design, development, and deployment of enterprise learning management, learning content management, and performance support systems at Intel for the last six years.

REVIEW OF CHAPTER 3

Chapter 3 defines the antecedents for job aids and performance support. We began with job aids and acknowledged their roots on cave walls. We revisited procedural, informational, and coaching job aids—three kinds of performance support that were initially introduced in the *Handbook of Job Aids.*

Then we moved to performance support, defined as "job aids on steroids." We examined the relationship between job aids and performance support, considered the contributions of Gery and Cavanaugh, and noted their emphasis on integrating information with the task. While recognizing the importance of integration, we noted that the lack of integration can also offer benefits. An opportunity to plan and reflect, with support, has potential to improve performance. We looked over the shoulder of a pharmaceutical salesperson who was waiting for a few moments with a physician. He was using performance support that wasn't integrated with the task. It preceded it. It served as just-in-time preparation to take advantage of scant moments with the doctor.

Chapter 3 closed by reviewing trends that are raising the profile and assuring the presence of performance support: the shift from training to performance; on-demand everything; mobility; and career self-reliance.

Then we provided a short review of the literature and encouragement of further research.

PREVIEW OF CHAPTER 4

Chapter 4 introduces Planners and Sidekicks, the two forms of performance support that anchor this handbook. Chapter 3 presented their antecedents. In Chapter 4 we see them at work. What is a Planner? What is a Sidekick?

RESOURCES

Altalib, H. (2002). ROI calculations for electronic performance support systems. *Performance Improvement, 41*(10), 12–22.

Bailey, B. (2003). *Linking vs. searching: Guidelines for use* [Electronic version]. Retrieved January 17, 2006, from www.webusability.com/article_linking_vs_searching_2_003. htm

Brown, B.L. (1996). *Career resilience.* ERIC Clearinghouse on Adult, Career, and Vocational Education. Eric Digest 178. Retrieved October 5, 2005, from www.cete.org/acve/textonly/docgen.asp?tbl=digests&ID=31

Brush, T., Knapczyk, D., & Hubbard, L. (1993). Developing a collaborative performance support system for practicing teachers. *Educational Technology, 33*(11), 39–45.

Carr, C. (1992, June). PSS! Help when you need it. *Training and Development,* pp. 31–38.

Carroll, J.M., & Rosson, M.B. (1987). Paradox of the active user. In J.M. Carroll (Ed.), *Interfacing thought: Cognitive aspects of human-computer interaction.* Cambridge, MA: Bradford Books/MIT Press.

Cavanaugh, T.B. (2004, April). The new spectrum of support: Reclassifying human performance technology. *Performance Improvement, 43*(4), 28–32.

Chabrow, E. (2005, September 19). Wireless revs up vehicle production. *Information Week,* p. 100.

Chase, N. (1998). Electronic support cuts training time [Electronic version]. *Quality Magazine.* Retrieved January 12, 2005, from http://openacademy.mindef.gov.sg/OpenAcademy/Learning Resources/EPSS/c16.htm.

Clark, R.C. (1989). *Developing technical training.* Reading, MA: Addison-Wesley.

Cole, K., Fischer, O., & Saltzman, P. (1997). Just-in-time knowledge delivery. *Communications of the ACM, 40*(7), 49–53.

Collard, B, Epperheimer, J.W., & Saign, D. (1996). *Career resilience in a changing workplace.* Columbus, OH: ERIC Clearinghouse on Adult, Career, and Vocational Education. (ED 396 191)

Desmarais, M.C., Leclair, R., Fiset, J.V., & Talbi, H. (1997). Cost-justifying electronic performance support systems. *Communications of the ACM, 40*(7), 39–48.

Dorsey, L.T., Goodrum, D.A., & Schwen, T.M. (1993). Just-in-time knowledge performance support: A test of concept. *Educational Technology, 33*(11), 21–29.

Duncan, C.S. (1985). Job aids really can work: A study of the military applications of job aid technology. *Performance and Instruction, 24*(4), 1–4.

Duncan, C.S. (1986). Commentary: The job aid has a future. In *Introduction to Performance Technology* (pp. 125–128). Washington, DC: National Society for Performance and Instruction.

Elsenheimer, J. (2000). The performance support bridge to knowledge management [Electronic version]. *Learning Circuits.* Retrieved October 27, 2002, from www.learningcircuits.org/mar2000/elsenheimer.html

eTForecasts. (2005). *PCs in-use surpassed 820M in 2004: PCs in-use will top 1B in 2007.* Retrieved August 20, 2005, from www.etforecasts.com/pr/pr305.htm

Fletcher, J.D., & Johnston, B.R. (1995). *Effectiveness of computer based instruction in military training.* Alexandria, VA: Institute for Defense Analyses.

Gamerman, E. (2006, January 21). Legalized cheating. *The Wall Street Journal* Online. P1. http://online.wsj.com/article/SB113779787647552415.html?mod=home_we_banner_mid

Gery, G.J. (1987). *Making CBT happen.* Boston, MA: Weingarten Publications.

Gery, G. (1995). Attributes and behaviors of performance-centered systems. *Performance Improvement Quarterly, 8*(1), 47–93.

Gery, G.J. (2000). *Attributes and behaviors of performance centered systems chart.* [Online]. www.gloriagery.com/articles/attributesandb

Gery, G.J. (2002). Task support, reference, instruction, or collaboration? Factors in determining electronic learning and support options. *Technical Communication, 49*(4), 1–8.

Gery, G. (2003). Ten years later: A new introduction to attributes and behaviors and the state of performance-centered systems. In G.J. Dickelman (Ed.), *EPSS revisited: A lifecycle for developing performance-centered systems* (pp. 1–3). Silver Spring, MD: International Society for Performance Improvement.

Gilbert, T. (1978). *Human competence: Engineering worthy performance.* New York: McGraw-Hill.

Gordon, J. (2003, January). Learning in the palms of their hands. *Elearningmag.com,* pp. 32–35.

Grata, J. (2005, October 17). License-plate reader gives state troopers instant crime data. *The San Diego Union-Tribune,* p. C1.

Harless, J.H. (1986). Guiding performance with job aids. In *Introduction to Performance Technology* (pp. 106–124). Washington, DC: National Society for Performance and Instruction.

Hunt, D.L., Haynes, R.B., Hanna, S.E., & Smith, K. (1998). Effects of computer-based clinical decision support systems on physician performance and patient outcomes. *Journal of the American Medical Association, 280*(15), 1339–1346.

Kasvi, J.J., & Vartiainen, M. (2000). Performance support on the shop floor. *Performance Improvement 39*(6), 40–46.

Knowledge@Wharton (2005, September). *The upgraded digital divide: Are we developing new technologies faster than customers can use them?* Retrieved October 1, 2005. http://knowledge.wharton.upenn.edu/index.cfm?fa=viewArticle&id=1292

Ladd, C. (1993). Should performance support be in your computer. *Training and Development, 47*(8), 22–26.

Levy, J. (February, 2004). The knowledge warriors. *Training and Development, 58*(2), 47–51.

Levy, J. (2005, March). A parallel universe. *Chief Learning Officer.* www.clomedia.com, p. 13.

McCabe, C., & Leighton, C. (2002). Developing best practices for knowledge work: ISD plus KM, supported by software [Electronic version]. *The eLearning Developers Journal.* Retrieved August 13, 2002, from www.elearningguild.com.

McKellar, H. (2005). Once and future KM. *KMWorld.* Retrieved October 5, 2005, from www.kmworld.com/publications/magazine/index.cfm?action=readarticle&article_id =2129&publication_id=134

McManus, P., & Rossett, A. (2006). Performance support tools delivering value when and where it is needed. *Performance Improvement, 45*(2), 8–16.

Morrison, J.E., & Witmer, B.G. (1983). A comparative evaluation of computer-based and print-based job performance aids. *Journal of Computer-Based Instruction, 10*(3), 73–75.

Nguyen, F. (2005). Oops, I forgot how to do that: A needs assessment of electronic performance support systems. *Performance Improvement, 44*(9), 33–39.

Nguyen, F. (In press). What you already know does matter: Expertise and electronic performance support systems. *Performance Improvement.*

Nguyen, F., Klein, J.D., & Sullivan, H. (2005). A comparative study of electronic performance support systems. *Performance Improvement Quarterly, 18*(4), 71–86.

Pipe, P. (1986). Ergonomics and performance aids. In *Introduction to Performance Technology* (pp. 129–144). Washington, DC: National Society for Performance and Instruction.

Rae, S., & O'Driscoll, T. (2004, August). Contextualized learning: Empowering education. *Chief Learning Officer,* pp. 18–23.

Raybould, B. (2000). Building performance-centered web-based systems, information systems, and knowledge management systems in the 21st century. *Performance Improvement, 39*(6), 69–79.

Rosenberg, M.J. (1995). Performance technology, performance support, and the future of training: A commentary. *Performance Improvement Quarterly, 8*(1), 94–99.

Rosenberg, M.J. (2003, March). Redefining e-learning. *Performance Improvement, 42*(3), 38–41.

Rossett, A., & Mohr, E. (2004, February). Performance support tools: Where learning work and results converge. *Training and Development, 58*(2), 35–39.

Schramm, W., & Porter, W. (1982). *Men, women, messages and media: Understanding human communication* (2nd ed.). New York: Harper & Row.

Schwen, T.M., Goodrum, D.A., & Dorsey, L.T. (1993). On the design of enriched learning and information environment. *Educational Technology, 33*(11), 5–9.

Sherry, L., & Wilson, B. (1996). Supporting human performance across disciplines: A converging of roles and tools. *Performance Improvement Quarterly, 9*(4), 19–36.

Sleight, D.A. (1993). *Types of electronic performance support systems: Their characteristics and range of designs* [Electronic version]. Retrieved January 12, 2005, from http:// openacademy.mindef.gov.sg/OpenAcademy/Learning Resources/EPSS/c7.htm.

Spirgi, H., & Thompson, G. (2005, April). Learning applications: Education in context. *Chief Learning Officer.* www.clomedia.com, pp. 23–27.

Spool, J.M. (2001). *Users don't learn to search better* [Electronic version]. Retrieved April 3, 2005, from www.uie.com/articles/learn_to_search.

Van Dam, N. (2005, April). Creating value through self-service learning. *Chief Learning Officer.* www.clomedia.com, p. 14.

Wagner, E.D. (2005, May/June). Enabling mobile learning. *Educause,* pp. 41–48.

Waterman, R.H., Jr., Waterman, J.D., & Collard, B.A. (1994, July/August). Toward a career-resilient workforce. *Harvard Business Review, 72*(4), 87–95.

Whitney, K. (2005, September 14). U.S. birth rates: Implications for learning leaders. *Chief Learning Officer.* Retrieved October 2, 2005, from www.clomedia.com/content/ templates/clo_article.asp?articleid=1093&zoneid=102

Wildstrom, S. (2005, September 26). Bait, tackle and GPS. *Business Week,* p. 22.

Witt, C.L., & Wager, W. (1994). A comparison of instructional systems design and electronic performance support systems design. *Educational Technology, 34*(6), 20–24.

Wurman, R.S. (1989). *Information anxiety.* New York: Doubleday.

CHAPTER

4

Planner and Sidekick Performance Support

Amy is in charge of mental-health services for a large jail. She supervises seventy-five full- and part-time counselors, psychologists, and social workers. While all have been trained in their professions, situations arise that stump them. She recognizes the potential of performance support for relieving many colleagues' reliance on her. She's also eager to standardize approaches to some very difficult and even dangerous situations in which her people sometimes find themselves.

Alfonso is in charge of customer-service training for a software company. His company demands more expertise from customer representatives, while simultaneously wanting to shrink the hours they spend in training. Alfonso thinks that performance support will help the reps, especially when they are handling questions about a plethora of new products in light of government regulations.

Magnolia is worrying about her progress toward retirement. Will she be able to retire at sixty? Will lack of resources force her to work part-time? And most important, today, fifteen years out, what should she do to assure her goals? Magnolia took a retirement planning class two years ago, but wasn't pleased with the fact that twenty-two others were in the session and she can't now remember most of what was said. What she needs, she thinks, is somebody who can look over her situation and then tailor suggestions to her circumstances. She needs to have questions answered as they come up, but she's no millionaire. Her daughter says that her mutual fund company has online tools that will help answer her questions.

Chapter 4 presents different kinds of performance support with examples of how performance support can and does boost performance. At the close of the chapter, we review the kinds of support by revisiting Amy, Alfonso, and Magnolia and their challenges.

AN EXPANDED VIEW

In *A Handbook of Job Aids,* Rossett and Gautier-Downes (1991) expanded the ways that people thought about and used job aids. That enhancement was based on the nature of the content. To traditional job aids that supported *information* (the Yellow Pages, for example) and *procedures* (documentation that reminded of how to change the message on an answering machine), Rossett and Gautier-Downes added job aids that *coached, advised, and guided decisions.* Is this the right graduate school for me? How do I work with an employee who is often tardy? How do I tailor a presentation for a resistant audience?

While those remain fertile distinctions, what we see today is that effective performance support often *brings the three together in one automated program.* For example, a performance support program for an individual contemplating graduate education might include a database of possible university programs and prerequisites; procedures for applying; and self-assessment checklists to help potential applicants determine readiness and preference for one program or university over another.

How then will we parse the topic of performance support here? We will do it by focusing on two dimensions. The first dimension is the degree of **integration** of the support into the task. Is the performance support inside or outside of the task? Is it like TiVo or is it like the earthquake preparedness materials displayed in Chapter 3? TiVo coaxes automatically, as you power it up for the first time. The earthquake support site provides checklists that help each family assess readiness to deal with an earthquake. TiVo support is inside, integrated into the task. The preparedness guidelines stand apart; they nudge you to print them out to help you figure out what to do to prepare and to help you examine the quality of your mitigation efforts.

The second dimension for performance support is how much **tailoring** the support offers. Is the support standard for all or actively tailored to your situation? Does it know you and act differently as a result of that knowledge? Is it a mass mailing from your city government about cleaning up open spaces to reduce fire dangers *or* a notice sending you to a website because the system recognizes that your home is on a canyon and you must do special kinds of cleanup to mitigate fire danger?

INTEGRATION, TAILORING, AND PIZZA DELIVERY

Let's use a typical football game day activity—calling the local pizza joint for an extra-large double-meat, triple-cheese pizza—to illustrate these kinds of performance support. How do you get the pizza to the house, where friends and family eagerly await it?

1. You might pull the Yellow Pages out of the drawer and leaf through to the pizza section to find your favorite place, Oscar's Pizza. After you've found the number, you head over to the phone and dial.

2. You might glance at the Oscar's Pizza magnet that adorns your refrigerator. Then, standing near the fridge, you dial.

3. If you order from Oscar's *every* Sunday, no matter the sports season, you probably have the number programmed into speed dial. Push one button, speak a few words, and thirty minutes later, hot pizza is at your door. Figure 4.1 illustrates the degree of both *integration* and *tailoring* for each pizza delivery alternative.

Integrated?

The Yellow Pages is only slightly integrated with the task. It requires you to find the book and then find the number *before* dialing the telephone. The fridge magnet is more integrated with the task. You refer to the number as you dial the phone. Speed dial is the most integrated with the task. You don't even have to read the number or dial the phone; speed dial makes this happen for you.

Figure 4.1 Using Performance Support for Pizza Delivery

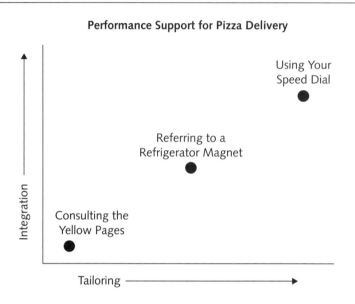

Performance Support for Pizza Delivery

Tailored?

Yellow Pages are not active or personalized for an individual. True, they represent your geographic area, but the tailoring is slight. Your fridge magnet is more tailored. It suggests that you've ordered from Oscar's before and will likely order from them again. There's only so much fridge real estate; choices must be made. The speed dial feature knows you most of all. You've taught it about yourself, your relatives, your friends. Although others may have an Oscar's magnet on their fridges, no one else will have a speed dial programmed just as you do. And again, limited space in phone memory suggests that Oscar's Pizza is important to you.

INTEGRATION, TAILORING, AND FINDING YOUR WAY

A familiar task provides another example of integration and tailoring. Imagine that you have an important appointment across town, at a place you have never been. Table 4.1 presents alternative support systems to get you to your destination.

Table 4.1 Using Performance Support to Reach a Destination

Ways of Reaching an Unfamiliar Destination	Commentary
Consult the **city map** you have pinned to your wall before you leave.	The map is a job aid, but is not insinuated into the task and is not tailored for you. It doesn't know where you are going or offer guidance on the best way to get there. It will not adapt to your twists and turns as you travel.
Go to **MapQuest** and enter your address and the destination address. Print the results. Refer to the results as you drive.	Here we see the blending of computer-based performance support and job aids. The online tool is used prior to undertaking the challenge. It is preparation for it. What results from the planning effort is a conventional print job aid that is insinuated into the task, albeit precariously. As you negotiate the highways and byways, a trusty piece of paper points the way.
Another alternative is to **ask your brother for directions** as you head out the door. He generously provides them.	This may get you there if you have a good memory and your brother is reliable. But insinuated with the task? Definitely not. And when you get distracted and turn left instead of right, his directions will not adjust to your errant ways.
How about this? Hop in the car. Dig through the glove box. Pull out a map. **Read the map while you drive.**	This job aid is insinuated into the task. It is there when you need to decide *right or left.* While integrated into the task, you have to tailor it to you, and at some risk.
Better? Hop in the car and fire up the **GPS.** Key in the destination address. A sultry voice tells you how to get there, no matter where you start or how you diverge from the original path.	The GPS support is identified with the task. While there is a display with directions, the directions are little more than comfort because a voice is anticipating what you will need do and then prompting you to do it. Most interesting is how *active* the system is, how it adjusts to your location and actions. When you refuse or skip guidance, new advice is calculated for you, tailored to your current location. GPS is tailored *and* integrated.

Table 4.1 illustrates the two key dimensions of performance support. First, the amount of integration into work and life. MapQuest, as an online trip planning tool, is not integrated. It is performance support that exists outside the task and is used prior to it. The printed output from MapQuest, however, is integrated. It is inside the task. A glove box map is also inside, perhaps dangerously so.

The second dimension is tailoring. Is the tool offering up a standard, consistent message or one that is customized to your situation? This is a question about the activity level of the tool. Does the tool adjust to you? Does it know you? Does it care which mutual funds you hold, what products you sell and in which geography, or whether you just by-passed the verbal suggestion to turn left at Albatross Street? Does it reach out and nudge and remind about goals? Does it provide a statement of operating procedures or model approaches to customers' objections? The Yellow Pages and Technorati's searchable blog directory are standard, worthy, and passive resources. You go there to find information on mockingbirds or local veterinarians that specialize in farm animals. Those resources wait and serve.

Schwab.com and Quitnet.org are different because they actively focus on you. They "know" you and your goals. In both cases, they know your situation too. Schwab will help you reach financial goals. Quitnet is there to help the individual who wants to stop smoking turn away from a cigarette after a long, hard day at work.

Please look again at Table 4.1. The paper map in the glove box or the map on the wall does not know you. MapQuest, on the other hand, is customized, but nowhere near as much or as immediately as a GPS that knows where you are, recalibrating directions to match every move, patiently acknowledging location, and telling what to do to reach your destination.

Figure 4.2 portrays guidance options along both dimensions.

Technology Marches On

Just as we applauded ourselves on these examples, technology tossed a curve ball. MapQuest, not one to stand on its laurels, launched more integrated and tailored products and services, MapQuest Find Me and MapQuest Mobile. Find Me, not surprisingly, increases tailoring. It finds you and guides accordingly. MapQuest Mobile delivers targeted messages and advice to cell phones. The new MapQuest services are all about tailoring and integration. Now the market

Figure 4.2 Using Performance Support for Reaching a Destination

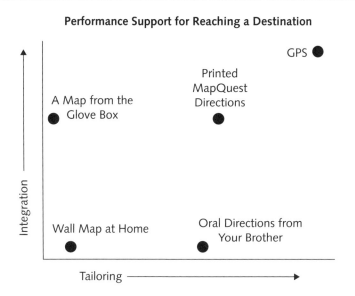

Performance Support for Reaching a Destination

gets to decide how important that level of support is. Are people willing to pay for it?

The Flip Side of Integration and Tailoring

These examples make integration and tailoring look awfully good. And they are.

There are, however, things to say in favor of less integration and not so much tailoring. Really. Let's look at integration first.

Support for Planning and Reflection

The opposite of integration is not disintegration. In this case, it is planfulness, readiness, a reflective stance. It is information and advice consulted in advance of performance. How can we use delivered knowledge to prepare, to mitigate, and to make better decisions about what to do next? Performance support of this type stands just before or after performance, rather than in the midst of it. Hurricane Katrina raised motivation to turn to such tools. Figure 4.3 provides an example. Californians use it to prepare themselves and their families for a disaster.

Think of a continuum with education and training at one extreme, providing experiences just in case someone needs memorized knowledge to do something.

Figure 4.3 Disaster Planning for Parents

PREPAREDNESS TIPS   *California Governor's Office of Emergency Services*

Tips for Preparing Children

Children need to be prepared for a disaster as much as adults, if not more.

Infants and Toddlers

For infants and toddlers, special emphasis should be placed on making their environment as safe as possible.

☐ Cribs should be placed away from windows and tall, unsecured bookcases and shelves that could slide or topple.

☐ A minimum of a 72-hour supply of extra water, formula, bottles, food, juices, clothing, disposable diapers, baby wipes and prescribed medications should be stored where it is most likely to be accessible after an emergency. Also keep an extra diaper bag with these items in your car.

☐ Store strollers, wagons, blankets and cribs with appropriate wheels to evacuate infants, if necessary.

☐ Install bumper pads in cribs or bassinettes to protect babies during the shaking of an earthquake or explosion

☐ Install latches on all cupboards (not just those young children can reach) so that nothing can fall on your baby during an earthquake or explosion.

Be Smart
Be Prepared
Be Responsible

Preschool and School-age Children

By age three or so, children can begin to understand what earthquakes are, as well as fires and floods, and how to get ready for them. Take the time to explain what causes these types of emergencies in terms they'll understand. Include your children in family discussions and planning for emergency safety. Conduct drills and review safety procedures every six months.

☐ Show children the safest places to be in each room when an earthquake hits or explosion occurs. Also show them all possible exits from each room.

☐ Use sturdy tables to teach children to Duck, Cover & Hold during an earthquake or explosion.

☐ Make sure that children are ready to protect themselves with Stop, Drop and Roll during a fire. Also make sure that you practice emergency exit drills in the house (EDITH) regularly.

☐ Teach children what to do wherever they are during an emergency (at school, in a tall building, outdoors).

☐ Make sure children's emergency cards at school are up-to-date.

☐ Although children should not turn off any utility valves, it's important that they know what gas smells like. Advise children to tell an adult if they smell gas after an emergency.

Source: California Governor's Office of Emergency Services

At the other extreme is integrated performance support. It is the GPS that advises how to get to that appointment while traversing highways and streets. Somewhere between the two points is support that is experienced just prior or after performance, as the individual prepares or reviews. In lieu of immediacy is the opportunity for reflection. There are benefits to thinking before acting, of course. Consider what goes into getting ready for a wedding or a performance review. Who wouldn't benefit from collected expertise on standards for anticipating, planning, and reviewing?

The Personalization Myth

That's what Jupiter Research called it in a 2003 study that found only 8 percent of respondents reported that personalization increased their visits to web content. Think about that. This number contrasts with 54 percent of consumers who stated that basic site improvements would encourage more visits—54 percent cited faster-loading pages, and 52 percent cited better navigation as greater incentives.

Personalization sounds good, but is it as good as it costs? A single, standard message costs far less to produce and maintain. With the cost of personalization estimated at four or more times basic costs, Jupiter Research and respondents favored attention to usability over a tailored experience.

While time and money are well spent in settling on the message, once it is hatched, the cost is sunk. Modern technologies make it easy to distribute and update. Will many elect to pay for MapQuest delivered to their cell phones, for example? Just how important is personalization to the individual, moment, and place? Jupiter suggests it is less critical than assumed. It remains to be seen.

There are reasons beyond cost to appreciate a standard message well delivered. Pat Weger, then vice president for learning at ATT Broadband, noted that her priority was messages delivered in a standardized fashion, tirelessly, swiftly, repeatedly, in the many places they were needed. Not surprisingly, Weger was not keen on a do-your-own-thing approach to installation and maintenance. She wanted to be able to speedily distribute consistent operating procedures and lessons learned to people in the field. When updates appeared, as they often did, she wanted to be able to ship immediately and to know the workforce had received her messages.

Regulatory content is also an issue. The pharmaceutical industry receives government approvals for what they may say about medications. One way of controlling the content, of making certain that there is no gap between intended message and received message, is to craft, codify, distribute, and track standard content.

A fourth reason to appreciate standardization is the bonding that occurs when there is one, clear, articulated approach to what is said about gnarly topics. How do we handle this customer complaint? What are we saying about the closing of these stores or plants? Why are we replacing this software with a new version? How do we explain reorganization to global partners?

What does this mean for how we think about and produce useful support?

PARSING PERFORMANCE SUPPORT

Performance support is an information-rich asset that a nurse, teacher, parent, mechanic, taxpayer, pilot, or auditor turns to for help in getting things done. Performance support appears in many forms, from notes on scrap paper to well-worn documentation, to automated SOPs (standard operating procedures) to posters to ehelp.com and GPS.

Because there are so many possibilities, we've tamed the domain into two kinds of performance support: Planners and Sidekicks. Planners are in our lives *just before or after* the challenge. They help us to decide whether Avian Flu should alter trip plans or to reflect on how we could have improved the presentation offered at the sales meeting. Figure 4.3, the disaster planning tool for communicating with kids about disasters, is a good example of a Planner.

Sidekicks are at our side *during* the task. The quick food cook reads the job aid as she creates the new food product. The quarterback glances at his wrist in the huddle. The writer pecks away and smiles at how Wikipedia sports a red line under it in this sentence. Sidekicks vary in how close they are to the task. They might be next to the task, as is the case with the cook and quarterback, or integrated into it, as is the spelling checker.

Consider Figure 4.4. Integrated supports are Sidekicks. Other options, with little or no integration, are Planners.

Tailored supports for reaching a destination are presented to the right in Figure 4.5. GPS directions and guidance given to you, based on where you are commencing the trip, are there. More uniform options are presented to the left. Nothing special for you there. This is standard content for everybody who lives in Brockton, Melbourne, Hyderabad, or Escondido.

Figure 4.4 Parsing Integration into the Task

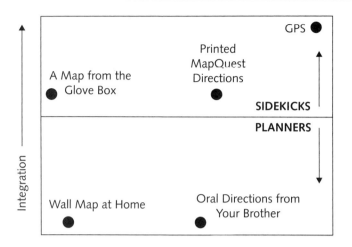

Figure 4.5 Parsing Tailoring

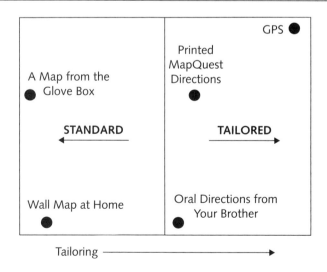

When we put it all together, we have a useful way of parsing the topic of performance support, which we'll use for more elaborate examples in Chapters 5 and 6. With full recognition that integration and tailoring reside on a continuum, Figure 4.6 categorizes jobs aids and performance support to advance consideration of the possibilities.

Table 4.2 presents examples of each kind of performance support. In Chapters 5 and 6 we present extended examples of each kind. Examples in Chapters 5 and 6 are bolstered by interviews with the people who developed and used the performance support initiatives.

Performance Support Is Delicious

There is debate about the *real* purpose of performance support. Gustafson (2000) raised this issue: Does performance support exist to help users accomplish a task or to help them become more capable and able so that they will not need such external assistance? He recommended that professionals determine whether the goal is what he dubbed "black box," supporting performance without increasing the user's skills, or "glass box," increasing a user's internal skills and knowledge.

Figure 4.6 Kinds of Performance Support

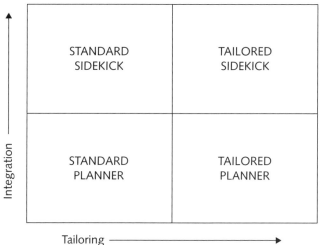

Table 4.2 Examples of Kinds of Performance Support

Performance Support	Standard	Tailored
Planners: They are there when we get ready to act and afterward, when we reflect on our efforts	This is a print or automated program that reminds a salesperson what to keep in mind when selling at higher levels in the organization. This same program reminds of what to consider afterward, as the salesperson reflects on the success of the interaction.	This is an automated program that seeks data about a potential customer, qualifies the customer, and then informs the salesperson of the size loan for which he or she will qualify. The amount and rationale are provided to the salesperson to aid in targeting a proposal and countering objections.
Sidekicks: They are with us in the work, as we act.	Here the customer and salesperson look at a PC and examine a table that compares a recommended product to the competitors' products.	When the customer picks a product configuration, the salesperson identifies the customer and the system details compatibility with the customer's current installed base and what it will take for successful installation of the new product.

McManus and Rossett (2006) took on the issue. What about spelling? Black or glass box? Must people learn to spell better in a world with spell checkers built into word processors? Shouldn't the salesperson know by heart how to compare her company's product with a competitor's? But isn't there a case to be made for the saleswoman and her customer looking together at an authoritative and current source?

Consider the topic of sexual harassment. Many of the mundane and frequent actions involved in creating a productive and sensitive culture should be committed to memory. But what exactly should the manager say in an interview with an employee who is distressed because she thinks she is being harassed? Doesn't it make sense to have support to turn to, for planning, just so the response is both sensitive and congruent with organizational policy, and perhaps even as a Sidekick, during the interaction, so no stone goes unturned? Wouldn't it make sense to have a series of questions for reference, both for the manager and for the associate?

Reasonable individuals will tussle over the question of investing in memory versus investing in assets that provide external support. And most will settle on a combination of black and glass box solutions. Quick-food establishments provide an example of preference for a combination. Employees rely on performance support when they commence their efforts; soon repetitions and expectations reduce and eliminate the need to refer. Figure 4.7 is just such a resource. Jack in the Box introduces many new products to many new team members. This standardized Sidekick assures that you get exactly what was ordered, no matter the restaurant or location.

Chefs create the burger from the bottom up, just as it is represented here, in two distinct stacks. The separate stacks are assembled and wrapped when finished.

Figure 4.7 Jack in the Box New Product Sidekick Performance Support

Original Ciabatta Burger

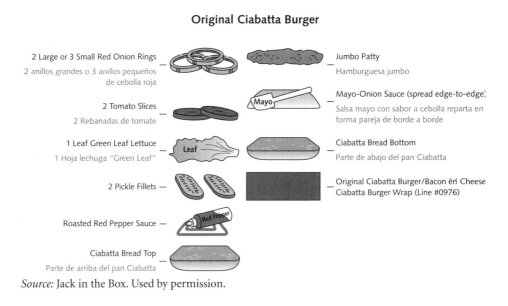

Source: Jack in the Box. Used by permission.

Douglas and Schaffer (2002) put the question of memory versus support in the context of changes buffeting the profession. As was discussed in Chapter 3, there is a shift from instruction-centric training to more results- and performance-centric initiatives. Think again about the sexual harassment challenge. There is both much to know by heart plus benefits to be derived from external resources. Both are operative here and in many situations.

What matters are results in the workplace—for managers, individuals, and the organization. HR employees, for example, do not want to struggle with HR screens, to reflect on their enterprise resource planning system, or to appreciate the value of performance support. They want to pay someone, track something, or notify someone.

E & E, based in Berlin, Germany, makes that point with an example. Their ESCRIBA product is performance support for global software system giant SAP. The challenge? To create documents within the context of SAP.

Most SAP-supported processes end with a document, such as a letter of confirmation, contract, or inventory list. Creating these documents can be burdensome. Picture an HR employee as she attempts to use SAP to do something mundane and important. First, she searches on the local or central file storage for a similar document created in the past and which she hopes to re-purpose for this situation. What then follows is a series of copy, cut, and paste steps in which she goes back and forth between SAP, old files, and the new file in order to create a document that works. Success is when the new document possesses necessary data, text blocks, and other structuring elements, such as footers and headers. Figure 4.8 maps this typical, clunky process.

Now let's envision the same process with ESCRIBA. When the HR employee reaches the point in SAP to create the new document, ESCRIBA automatically extracts required data from SAP. If some data are not available, the HR employee is presented with a series of wizard-like questions to capture the missing information. ESCRIBA combines these two sources and automatically creates the finished document. It is readily editable. Compare the rectangle in Figure 4.9 with the one in Figure 4.8. Note that a previously cumbersome process has become more efficient.

ESCRIBA is also an example of the convergence of instruction, performance support, and performance-centered design. For the typical SAP user, the document is generated automatically—no prior training required. The logic for assembling the relevant data through the automatic extraction from SAP and the

Figure 4.8 Document Generation Without ESCRIBA

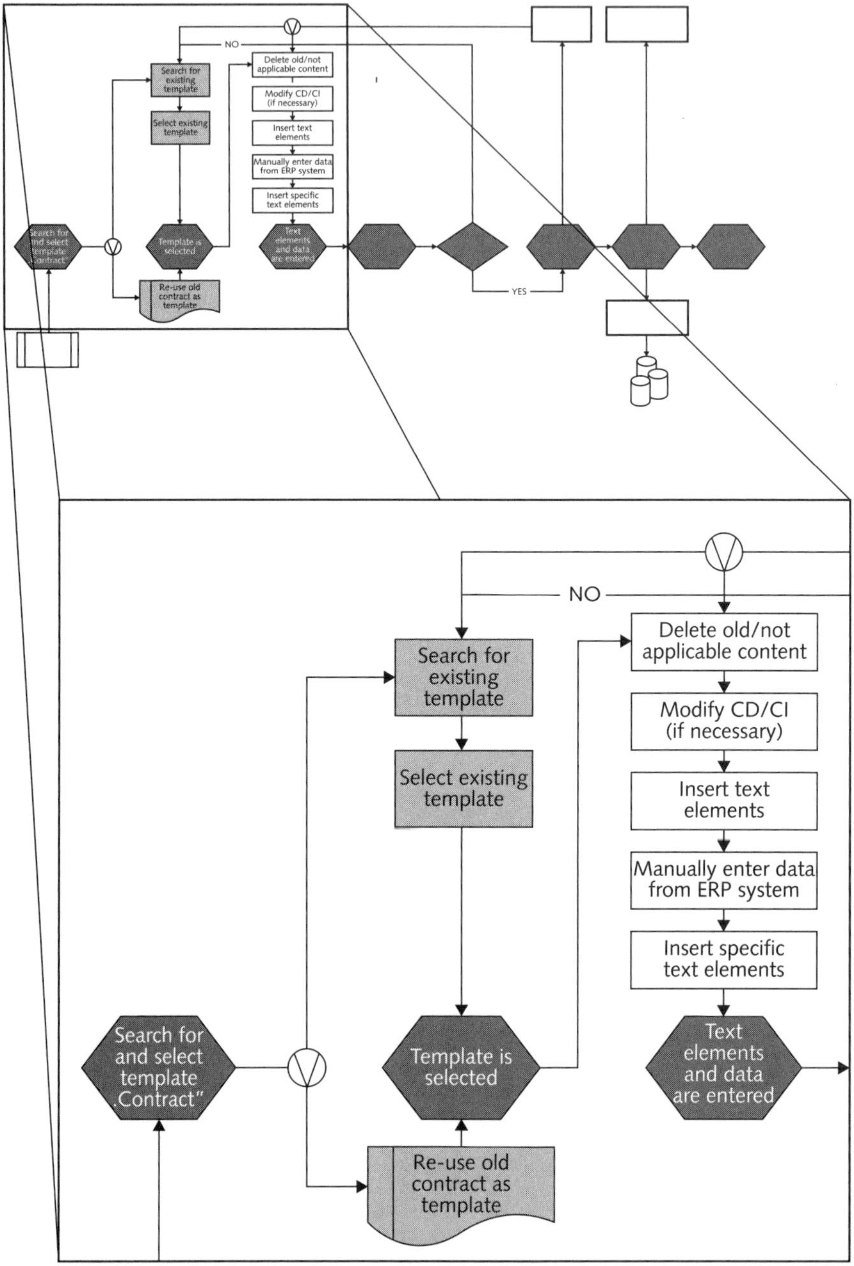

Source: E&E information consultants AG. Used by permission.

Figure 4.9 Simplified Document Generation Process with ESCRIBA

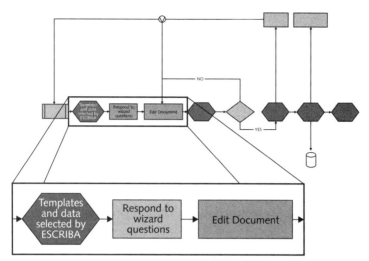

Source: E&E information consultants AG. Used by permission.

Wizard questions is established in advance by a small group of business experts. They do not require specific IT skills either, but receive guidance on using a separate ESCRIBA component to prepare the data templates and wizard modules later used by standard SAP users.

Much effort is invested in a small, targeted group of qualified experts. They are trained and coached to make certain that the templates, tools, and systems deliver what is needed. The standard users require little training, instead, they rely on performance support as a Sidekick to enable them to do what they need to do with SAP.

Planners and Sidekicks have a long history and a bright future as we labor to plan effective meetings, spell correctly, satisfy customers, stock the house for nutritious eating, and make good and fair decisions about whom to hire.

REVIEW OF CHAPTER 4: ADVISING AMY, ALFONSO, AND MAGNOLIA

This chapter opened with the challenges confronting three people. Let's use Tables 4.3 through 4.5 to make recommendations for Amy, Alfonso, and Magnolia. That is how we'll review Chapter 4, the kinds of performance support.

Table 4.3 Performance Support for Amy's People at the Jail

Performance Support	Standard	Tailored
Planners: They are there when we get ready to act and afterward, when we reflect on our efforts.	Amy creates standard operating procedures so that new people have a clear map of what is expected of them. As Schmid and Gerlach (1990) found, there is value in representing information in ordered and sparse detail.	The same difficult and infrequent situations cause problems. Amy decides to produce checklists which can be stored in PDAs that are keyed to these situations: Confronted with a person in distress, say this, do this, request this, and so on and so forth. She works with experts and legal counsel to assure the quality of her advice. Amy practices with the staff so that they can find the guidance they need.
Sidekicks: They are with us in the work, as we act.	Amy produces a pocket guide with phone numbers appropriate to circumstances and facilities. Armed guard? Ambulance?	Amy wants to develop a standardized online intake tool that will ask questions of new inmates, collect answers, and then tailor proper placements and cautions for each new inmate.

Table 4.4 Performance Support for Alfonso's Software Company

Performance Support	Standard	Tailored
Planners: They are there when we get ready to act and afterward, when we reflect on our efforts.	Alfonso invests in creating an online system that shows current customers' installed hardware and software bases.	Based on that and the new software the company is rolling out, he and two engineers produce a program that shows likely customer problems and strategies for handling them, given the customer's circumstances. The system allows reps to prepare in a targeted way for calls they make and receive.

Table 4.4 (Continued)

Performance Support	Standard	Tailored
Sidekicks: They are with us in the work, as we act.	Alfonso produces a basic guide to the company's products. Organized by likely customer questions, the guide presents comparisons with prior products and competitors and, because it is online, it allows for ready search and access while the rep is on the phone.	Alfonso also invests in creating an online system that shows current customers' installed hardware and software bases. Based on that and the new software the company is rolling out, he and two engineers produce a program that shows likely customer problems and strategies for handling them, given the customer's circumstances. Because the reps have prepared in advance, using the Planner, they now select a button and a summary of the information pops up, highlighting key points. That authoritative information is shared with the customer, on the spot, or sent in an email.

Table 4.5 Performance Support for Magnolia's Retirement Planning

Performance Support	Standard	Tailored
Planners: They are there when we get ready to act and afterward, when we reflect on our efforts.	Magnolia looks to her mutual fund company. At their website, she finds many resources that press her to consider her goals, IRA, tax deferral, automatic deposit program, and how to handle the money matters associated with a potential job change.	Magnolia's company provides her with a tool so that advice is tailored to her situation. They ask her scores of questions, all of which result in advice geared to her risk tolerance, current asset allocation, years to retirement, and likely historical yield. The program is direct and specific.

(Continued)

Table 4.5 Performance Support for Magnolia's Retirement Planning (Continued)

Performance Support	Standard	Tailored
		She now knows that, given prior patterns, she must save more or take on more risk if she is going to be able to retire at sixty with >$5,500 per month for twenty-five years.
Sidekicks: They are with us in the work, as we act.	Magnolia is considering who should be the executor of her will. She and her daughter go online and find a checklist to take with her as she talks with potential candidates. She needs support on this because these are family members and feelings could be hurt. Also, she wants to be systematic and serious about the choice.	Magnolia's mutual fund company understood her needs and now tailors a message for her each month. As she examines her monthly report, this message is designed to help her track her progress toward goals and to provide ideas about ways of reviewing and questioning results.

PREVIEW OF CHAPTER 5

Chapter 5 provides extended examples of Planners. Planners are performance support tools that help people figure out what to do and help them determine how well they did it and what they might want to try next. Chapter 6 will do the very same thing for Sidekicks.

RESOURCES

Aronson, E. (1999). The power of self-persuasion. *American Psychologist, 54,* pp. 874–885.

Douglas, I., & Schaffer, S. (2002). Object-oriented performance improvement. *Performance Improvement Quarterly, 15*(3), 81–93.

Gustafson, K.L. (2000). Designing technology-based performance support. *Educational Technology Magazine, 40*(1), 38–44.

Jupiter Research (2003, October 14). Jupiter Research reports that website "personalization" does not always provide positive results. Retrieved October 17, 2005, from www.jupitermedia.com/corporate/releases/03.10.14-newjupresearch.html

McManus, P., & Rossett, A. (2006, February). Performance support: Value delivered when and where needed. *Performance Improvement.*

Rosenberg, M.J. (2003, March). Redefining e-learning. *Performance Improvement, 42*(3), 38–41.

Rossett, A., & Gautier-Downes, J. (1991). *A handbook of job aids.* San Francisco: Pfeiffer.

Rossett, A., & Mohr, E. (2004, February). Performance support tools: Where learning work and results converge. *Training and Development, 58*(2), 35–39.

Schmid, R.F., & Gerlach, V.S. (1990). Instructional design rules for algorithmic subject matter. *Performance Improvement Quarterly, 3*(2), 1–14.

Examples of Planner Performance Support

Planners support performance *just before or after* the challenge. They provide information *in advance of* performance so that expectations, requirements, or goals are set and then met. They provide information *afterward* to enable reflection and planning for future improvements. To find examples of Planners, you need look no further than the Internet. Planners are busting out all over the Internet. For example, online traffic sites reveal current traffic jams and highway speeds to help determine the fastest route from where you are to where you want to go. Google Earth allows you to see that the second home you were favoring in Colorado is in close proximity to the airport. Maybe it wouldn't be quite right for you.

No task is too mundane to be supported by a Planner. You can glance at a well-worn list to make sure you've gathered the essentials for international travel. You can virtually arrange furniture to see whether it will fit in a new condo. You can look at next weekend's football schedule and construct a shopping list.

More lofty concerns are also supported by Planners. The IRS provides a tax withholding calculator so that income taxes are neither over- nor under-withheld throughout the year. That planning calculator can be used at the beginning of the year to change withholding allowances and can also be used throughout to determine whether adjustments are necessary. The living to 100 calculator (www.agingresearch.org/calculator/) helps individuals self-assess and thus plan to make choices with promise for helping to live a long life.

Chapter 5 presents the stories of five Planner support tools. The examples include commentary about the original need and what was done to meet that need. You'll read about the reasons for the chosen format and about lessons learned.

A RUBRIC FOR TEACHERS
Background

In 1998, Grant Wiggins and Jay McTighe introduced the concept of *backward design* for creating classroom teaching units. Their book, *Understanding by Design* (UbD), was about strategies devoted to achieving more results-oriented teaching. The premise—help teachers start with a focus on the desired results and then work backward to the teaching strategies. Christianna Alger, assistant professor of education at San Diego State University (SDSU), described how this helps teachers to "not look at a bunch of activities, but think about the evidence."

These concepts were the subject of study for teachers enrolled in a master's level graduate education course at SDSU. The teachers in the course worked with the UbD concepts to complete the main assignment for the course—design of a curriculum unit. The instructor for the course, Dr. Alger, wanted to provide the students with a tool to help guide them through the assignment and provide opportunities for them to review their progress in light of her goals for their effort. For this purpose, Dr. Alger developed a *rubric* for the students to use.

A *rubric* depicts quality work by presenting criteria, typically on a continuum from excellent to poor, in order to help neophytes "get" the differences between poor and excellent effort. Rubrics include detailed characteristics of performance as expected for each level of quality. While rubrics are often used for student evaluation, so that they will know on what they are being judged, the focus here is on the use of a rubric as a *Planner* to improve work, on a way to help aspiring teachers understand the essence of effective effort.

Reflecting on Performance

The *Understanding by Design Unit Rubric* (see Table 5.1) was created to help the teachers focus their efforts for the course project—creating a curriculum unit using the principles of UbD. This Planner included specific criteria to help students meet the requirements of the project. Through the rubric, students gauged their performance against teacher expectations. For example, in Stage 1 of the UbD model, curriculum designers must identify what is worthy of understanding. What are the desired results of the unit? By reading across the row of the rubric, students can discern that identifying what learners should know and be able to do is not enough. They must also identify the "big idea" of the unit and develop engaging questions that guide the curriculum. A rubric clearly distinguishes levels of performance to help students guide their own efforts. It has implications for them as they design their curriculum and, just prior to turning it in, as they look at the rubric and tighten the match between their efforts and the criteria on the rubric.

The rubric also is at the heart of evaluation for the assignment. Dr. Alger explained how the students themselves complete the rubric as a self-assessment. They rely on the "scores" across the top and are pressed to determine how well they have reached these unusually specific criteria. Alger commented that the rubric is helpful to them as they work on their assignments and "they know what is weak and what is strong." As a Planner, the rubric not only details the end result, but provides vivid criteria for reflection, with the intent to improve performance on their next curriculum design.

An Ironic Twist

In an ironic twist, Dr. Alger described how the process she went through for development of the rubric followed the UbD procedure. First, she identified the desired results. Then she determined what the acceptable evidence of performance would be and determined degrees of quality for each of the criteria. Last, she determined what she needed to teach students during the course in order to obtain the desired results.

Dr. Alger commented that one of her challenges was to "make sure the rubric and assignment mesh." As with any job aid, the support provided must advance performance and, according to Dr. Alger, you also must confirm that "what you are asking them to do is doable."

Table 5.1 The UbD Unit Rubric to Help Students Create Curriculum

CATEGORY	7 - 8	5 - 6	3 - 4	0 - 2
Stage I Desired Results	Author has identified the big Ideas in the unit and used these to develop essential questions to guide the unit. What students will know and be able to do as a result of the unit is clear and coherent. Unit questions support the essential question. The essential question is engaging to students.	Essential question is loosely tied to big ideas. Identification of what students will know and be able to do is less developed. May or may not have unit questions.	Author has identified what students should know and be able to do, but has not developed an essential question to guide the unit.	There is little evidence to suggest the author understands Stage I of backward design.
Stage II Acceptable Evidence	There are strong connections between the performance task and desired results. The performance task is well developed and includes supporting documents and a nuanced rubric with appropriate criteria for evaluation. The assessment provides an opportunity for students to self-assess.	There is some connection between performance tasks and desired results. The performance is somewhat developed and the author has included some of the resources needed, The rubric lacks nuance. There is a component of student self-assessment.	There is little or no connection between the performance assessment and desired results, The PA seems more like an activity rather than an assessment May or may not Include student self-assessment.	There is little evidence that the author understood Stage II of backward design.
Stage III Learning Experiences	Teacher clearly understands the scaffolding that will be necessary for the student to achieve the desired results and this is reflected in the day-to-day lesson plan. Teacher uses a variety of resources and teaching strategies. Another teacher could implement this unit.	Teacher has scaffolded some of the learning, but there are holes in the content or skills students will need to achieve desired results, Lesson plans are incomplete.	Lesson plans appear to be a series of activities rather than a cohesive whole. Some skills and knowledge necessary to achieve desired results may be missing. Plans are sketchy. Another teacher could not implement these plans.	There Is little evidence that the teacher understood Stage III of backward design.
Reflection	Teacher has completed the Design Standards survey and written an analytical, thoughtful, insightful reflection of both the unit and the process.	Teacher has completed the Design Standards survey and written a reflection. However, the reflection lacks analysis.	Either the reflection or the Design Standards is missing.	Little evidence of reflection.
Writing	Unit format is pleasing to the eye, well-organized, complete, and the writing is sophisticated with appropriate grammar, spelling, and usage.	Unit is well-organized, complete, and the writing has few grammar, spelling, and usage errors.	Unit is poorly organized, and has several grammar, spelling, and/or usage problems.	The unit is disorganized and lacking in parts.

Source: C. Alger. Adapted from Wiggins and McTighe (1998).

When Dr. Alger was ready to actually create the format, she called on Rubistar to help her do it. Rubistar (http://rubistar.4teachers.org/index.php) is itself online Sidekick performance support. The site provides templates for generating rubrics. Numerous formats and models are provided. Is your effort more like a newspaper article, digital storytelling, or video pre-production?

As a Planner, the rubric improves performance by stating and clarifying expectations. The rubric format influences two key audiences. First, the designer is pressed into significant thought to get clear about what really counts and, second, the rubric helps students or employees fine-tune their efforts when they reflect on their experiences in light of articulated expectations.

CALCULATOR FOR LIFTING OPERATIONS
Background
Preventing back injuries is a major challenge for workplace safety professionals. According to the Bureau of Labor Statistics (BLS), 43 percent of the 1.3 million workplace injuries and illnesses in 2003 were sprains and strains, most involving the back. Many of these injuries stemmed from overexertion in lifting in occupations such as labor and material movers, heavy and tractor-trailer truck drivers, and nursing aides, orderlies, and attendants (Bureau of Labor Statistics, 2005). In addition to pain and suffering, the compensation claims associated with back injuries cost billions of dollars. According to a study cited by the U.S. Department of Labor (n.d.), the use of better job design or ergonomics could prevent up to one-third of compensable back injuries. How might performance support assist professionals to evaluate jobs and prevent back injuries?

Simplifying a Complex Assessment
The Washington State Department of Labor and Industries faced just this question. Due to ergonomics rules put in place in 2000, the department was required to develop easy ways for employers to understand and abide by the new safety regulations, including identifying and reducing workplace lifting hazards. Rick Goggins, an ergonomist with the department, was a member of the team charged with the development of a tool for analyzing lifting operations. The team knew the tool should be based on the National Institute for Occupational Safety and Health (NIOSH) Lifting Equation (www.cdc.gov/niosh/94–110.html), a well-known

science-based equation familiar within the safety industry. The equation involves precise measurements, many variables, reference tables, and calculations.

While relying on the theory behind the equation, Goggins' group determined that the tool had to be simple enough to complete a quick ergonomic assessment with relatively easy mathematical operations. A firm requirement was that the tool must fit on one page. The design was supposed to be such that anyone could make the initial assessment, even if he or she lacked a background in safety. Safety professionals and ergonomists could also use the calculator as a quick screening tool, and then do more complex assessments like the NIOSH equation if they required more accuracy.

Goggins said that a team of ergonomists created the initial design of the calculator for analyzing lifting operations, "and then kept simplifying." For example, rather than requiring the user to measure exact inches as required in the NIOSH Lifting Equation, the new calculator simply uses *zones,* as shown in Step 2 of Figure 5.1. The evaluator enters data related to the lifting task, such as the weight of the object, the position of the body during lifting, and whether the person twists during the lift. Some simple calculations then result in a determination of whether the lift is a hazard or not. If so, the safety specialist has a number of ways to alter the lift to make it safer for the worker. Goggins reported, "One of the benefits to using it, more than just the weight limit it provides, is some indication of what the root cause of the lifting hazard might be. For example, if the weight limit shown in the posture diagram in Step 2 is low, then the location of the lift is one of the primary issues, and so solutions should focus on bringing the load close to the body and between knee and shoulder level. If the multiplier in Step 3 is low, then the lifting duration or frequency is an issue, and solutions such as job rotation, mechanization, and reducing unnecessary lifting should be considered."

The team also worked with web experts to develop an online version for those with Internet access. Figure 5.2 shows how the online interface makes the calculator even easier to use in assessing risk and danger. If a risk is identified, a popup suggests actions to take.

Because of the regulatory environment, the department was required to solicit comments from the public and experts in the field prior to using these planning tools. Goggins mentioned that the tight delivery schedule precluded

Figure 5.1 The Paper-Based Calculator for Analyzing Lifting Operations

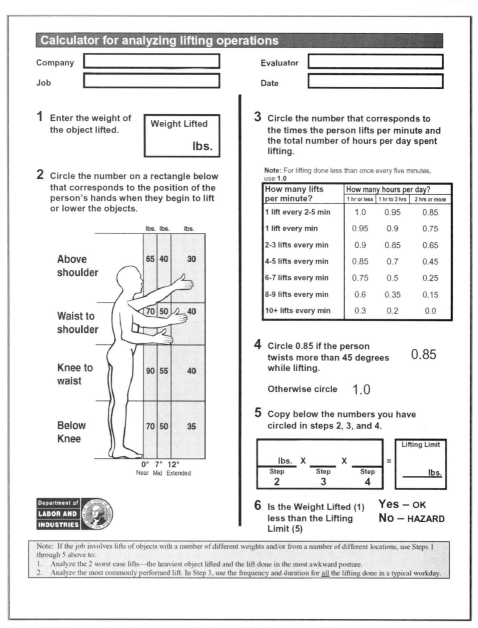

Source: Washington State Department of Labor and Industries. Used by permission.

Figure 5.2 The Online Calculator Does the Math for You

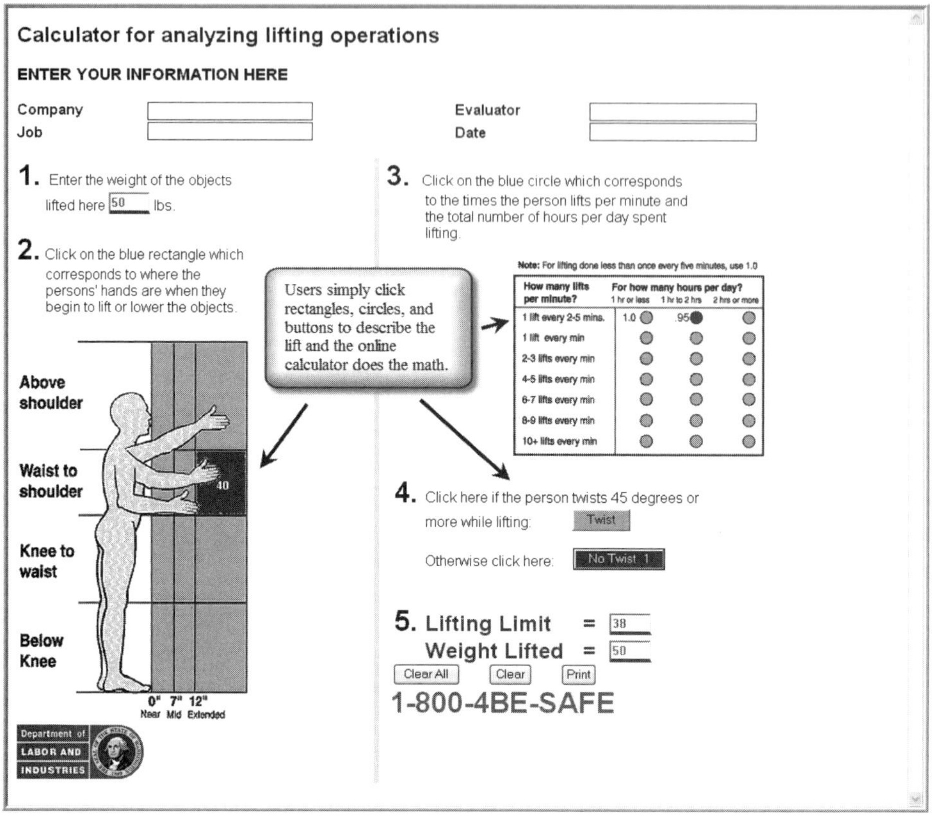

Source: Washington State Department of Labor and Industries. Used by permission.

having an opportunity to step away from the effort and then returning with "fresh eyes" to improve on it. Although the print version remains the same, the online version has been tweaked since its original introduction—primarily by reducing the jargon and making it more readable.

Current Use

Although the regulations that prompted the development of the calculator have been repealed, the calculator for analyzing lifting operations continues to be popular with safety and human resources professionals and with line employees, such as safety committee members. The calculator is included in a workshop delivered by the Department of Labor and Industries and is included on a CD that contains related materials. Goggins noted that the calculator is used by safety training professionals throughout the country and Canada and has been adapted for use by military, aviation, and many other organizations. It is also freely available on the Internet (www.lni.wa.gov/Safety/Topics/Ergonomics/ServicesResources/Tools/default.asp) in print and electronic versions.

As a Planner, this tool supports performance by aiding assessment of a task (lifting) either before or after performance. The calculator is used to determine whether there is a hazard and to point to changes that can be made to the lifting procedure to mitigate the risk of injury. After adjustments are made, the Planner can be used again to determine whether the problem was resolved.

By its nature, the performance support tool takes a complex cognitive activity and renders it do-able. Ease of use and visual appeal encourage individuals to leverage the tool to improve workplace safety.

SALES REP INCENTIVE TOOL
Background

In 2001, Eli Lilly and Company was faced with a challenge. In response to conditions in the marketplace, they decided to significantly alter their compensation incentive plan for salespeople. Not only did they consolidate two separate plans into one, they also changed the pay mix, or how much of an employee's pay would come from incentives versus guaranteed base. Sales reps would now have a greater opportunity for more sales incentives. With that potential for more money came more risk.

Lilly human resources professionals and line management recognized that communication about the new plan was critical. Employees would naturally be apprehensive about any potential changes to their compensation. It was important for employees to understand how the new plan would work and what their pay would look like under different selling scenarios. Since each salesperson's pay varies with base salary and sales performance, the information conveyed to each employee required some personalization. Miscommunication or misunderstanding could lead to a situation in which a rep might not be motivated to sell—the opposite of what Lilly was trying to accomplish. How could Lilly provide reassuring and accurate information about looming changes in compensation?

Not Just Content, But Delivery

Curtis Gifford, manager of compensation design, is no stranger to developing training sessions and support tools to handle the sensitive topic of pay. Although not a "training" person, Gifford is a whiz at developing focused desktop performance support tools that provide information in a clear, concise format. To address the new incentive plan challenge, Gifford not only built a performance support tool for employee planning, he also embedded it in a communication system meant to calm fears about the forthcoming change. Here is what Gifford did.

Based on the mechanics of both the old and the new incentive plans, Gifford built a tailored Planner to enable sales reps to tinker with the numbers. His intention was for them to get to know the new incentive plan by running what-ifs on their sales performance and its effects on compensation.

The tool itself is only part of this performance support story. Instead of just sending the tool to employees or having them grab it off the company intranet, Lilly decided to distribute it through sales managers. The new plan was rolled out at a national sales meeting, and the tool was distributed on a CD with related support materials. Once back within their territories, managers were expected to sit down with employees and work through the mechanics of the new incentive plan using the tool as a guide. The manager could explain the new program and ease lingering concerns. Together, the sales rep and manager could perform a variety of "what if" scenarios based on the rep's own base salary and level of sales accomplishment. They could then compare results under the new and old plans.

Using past performance as a guide, the rep anticipated what sales performance would be as a percentage of quota for each quarter. The manager entered the numbers into the calculator, along with base salary information. Figure 5.3 illustrates how these data would be input and displayed in the tool. The tool calculated incentive payments under both the current (old) and new plans. The totals at the bottom presented a clear comparison for discussion. Since the current (old) plan had two components, one of which was not based on individual sales performance but on overall corporate performance, the manager could enter differing performance data to demonstrate how increasing individual performance in the new program yielded more incentive compensation.

Figure 5.3 Planner Support for Transitioning to a New Sales Incentive Plan

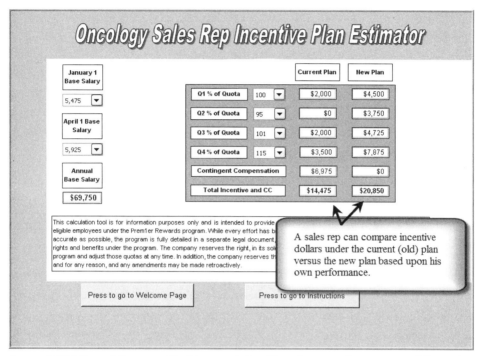

Source: © Eli Lilly and Company. Used by permission. Data shown are for purposes of illustration only.

Performance Support for Influence

Accurate, personalized information enabled reps to forecast their situations and assured them that performing well would be rewarded well. Through education, information, and conversation, Lilly influenced how sales reps responded to the new incentive plan.

ELECTRONIC REFERENCE LIBRARY

Background

With more than two thousand restaurants in seventeen states, Jack in the Box is a growing hamburger restaurant chain in the United States. Running these restaurants requires thousands of pages of reference materials for everything from how to assemble a Ciabatta Burger to how to fix the fryer to food service safety checklists. Historically, reference materials were contained in manuals and updates were mailed to restaurants. As you might expect, the updates did not reliably make it into the manuals and the materials were sometimes outdated or incorrect. Every few years, Jack in the Box republished the manuals and distributed them to the restaurants. Alas, of course, soon something was out-of-date. Like many businesses in many industries, Jack in the Box wanted out of "the paper business" for its reference materials.

A Team Effort for Developing the Performance Support System

Jack in the Box recognized early on that a partnership between the training group and the information systems (IS) department was critical if the new system was to succeed. Roles were defined. Roger Salvatore, director of multimedia development for Jack in the Box, described his group as content managers. They served as librarians for the reference materials and their conversion to electronic documents. IS, on the other hand, was responsible for determining the "best way to get it out there" and developing the interface. The best way, in this case, was for each restaurant to have accessible computers mounted on the wall. A touch screen system was created for employees to quickly find the reference materials they sought without having to worry about learning how to use a mouse or other pointing device. Figure 5.4 shows one screen within the system. It lists reference manuals for the many pieces of equipment restaurant.

All documents in the library are Adobe Acrobat pdf files and can be viewed or printed in preparation for a task. For example, a new employee may need to learn how to clean the shake machine. The employee can search for the information on the shake machine, quickly access the materials, review them, and use them as reference as he or she cleans the shake machine for the first time. A more experienced employee might consult the online shake machine manual if it isn't working properly and troubleshooting is required. An illustration of the shake machine documentation is shown in Figure 5.5.

Real-World Limits and Adjustments

All the original reference materials were converted to pdf file format, which resulted in what Salvatore called "very fat" files. Because many of the restaurants have bandwidth limitations, it became apparent that some documents were slow to load. In response, Salvatore's group targeted a limit of 20 to 50K on file size by

Figure 5.4 Jack in the Box Reference Materials

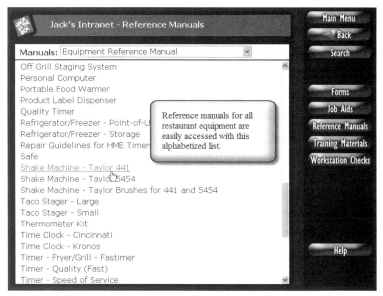

Source: Jack in the Box. Used by permission.

Figure 5.5 Documentation for the Shake Machine

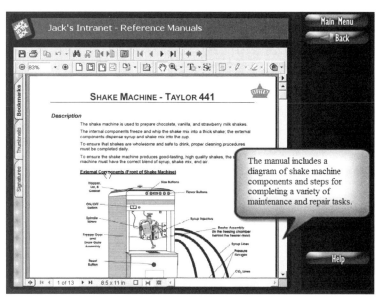

Source: Jack in the Box. Used by permission.

reducing colors, simplifying graphics, or breaking a large document into several smaller documents. In the future, as infrastructure improves, Salvatore acknowledged that they hope to deliver not only text-based materials, but different kinds of media, including video.

The Start of Something Even Bigger

Although the performance support system started with deployment of electronic reference materials, the system has grown dramatically. With a "send feedback" feature on the main menu, employees and managers have been actively suggesting forms and job aids to add to the materials. It is also part of the broader computer-based training platform based at each restaurant that provides crew-level training for new employees or introductions to new products and procedures. Management training modules are also available and are integrated in a blended solution that includes classroom training. See Figure 5.6.

Figure 5.6 The Jack in the Box Computer-Based Training Main Menu

Source: Jack in the Box. Used by permission.

Impact of the Conversion to an Electronic Library

According to Salvatore, the biggest impact of the system is that "all restaurants have immediate access." Rather than digging through old manuals or searching for materials that often cannot be found, employees now have instant access to the information they need to do their jobs. When there is a procedure or process change, Salvatore's group installs the new materials on the server and current information is instantly "available for everyone."

Salvatore reported that the system saves time and money. It has improved the efficiency with which employees can find needed information, while also reducing costs associated with producing and shipping the paper-based manuals and documents.

CLO DASHBOARD™

Background

Learning executives, sometimes dubbed chief learning officers (CLOs), require information to make strategic decisions. How fast are we bringing new employees up to competence on the new software? Is the e-learning initiative having an impact on sales performance? Are associates in the different regions fulfilling compliance requirements? Is our safety program making any difference in the field, where it matters? Are enhanced efforts with employee training improving retention in the finance division? Are we taking advantage of the licenses we have with vendors? To what extent are we using the programs we have purchased? How satisfied are far-flung employees with access to our library of e-learning modules?

Not surprisingly, data needed to answer these and other questions reside in disparate systems in silos throughout the organization. How then can learning executives be certain that their efforts are in alignment with organizational strategy? How can they effectively monitor their learning initiatives and quickly access information to make critical decisions and adjustments?

Strategic Data (At-a-Glance)

CLO Dashboard™, a product offered by Zeroed-In Technologies, is what Chris Moore, their chief executive, calls a performance dashboard devoted to helping chief learning officers to answer questions about use, satisfaction, results, and impact. CLO Dashboard™ aids CLOs as they align goals and objectives with corporate strategy through what Zeroed-In Technologies call *key learning indicators* (KLI), metrics that define the outcomes associated with specific goals. To generate the information for the KLIs, the system captures and analyzes data at a detailed work-process level and then displays the metrics in a graphical dashboard. That dashboard is a performance support Planner. It supports the CLO by capturing past performance, highlighting trends, and drilling down to determine the root causes of successes or problems.

Let's look at CLO Dashboard™ at work within the fictitious company, Dynametrix. Figure 5.7 displays how a CLO might view the status of initiatives related to three KLIs that her organization has identified—sales performance, sales readiness, and operational excellence. The intent of this main scorecard is for the executive to be able to grab a snapshot of progress toward goals and to

Figure 5.7 CLO Dashboard™ Displays the Overall Health of an Initiative

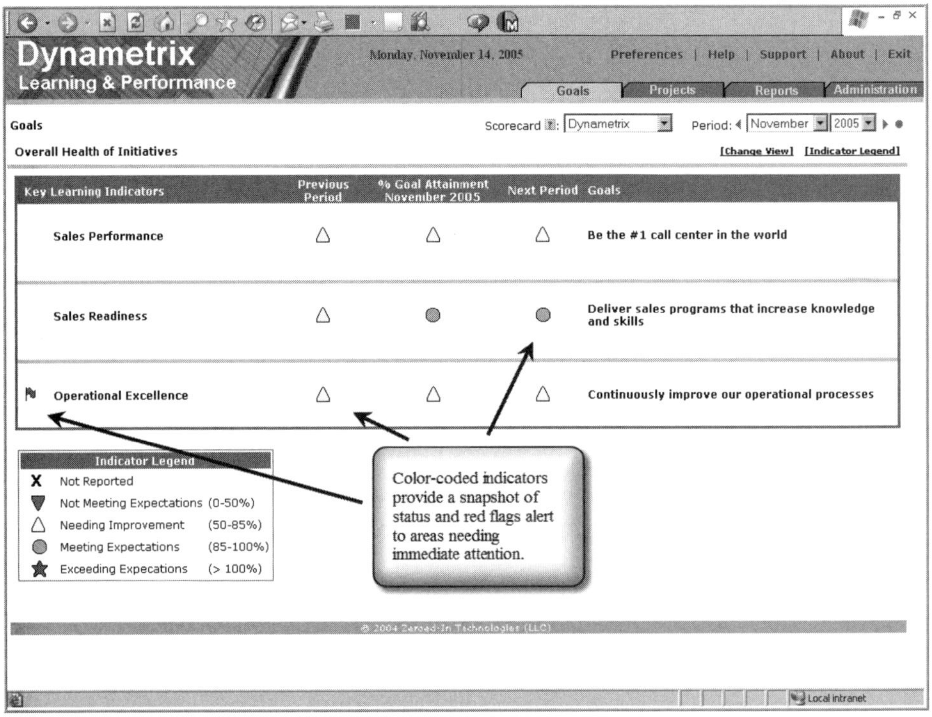

Source: Zeroed-In Technologies. Used by permission.

flag where corrective action might be required. In this example, the red flag was generated by a trigger indicating a measure either lags or exceeds predefined thresholds. Of course, the challenge is in defining and setting meaningful indicators and thresholds.

Not surprisingly, the CLO wants to know more. The first level of drill down is shown in Figure 5.8. This illustrates actual progress against targeted progress for the indicator's composite measures. In this example, ratings for learner satisfaction with the course and post-training exam scores are high, but the percentage of the salesforce that has been trained is below target.

The CLO can drill down further to see the status of individual tasks and the responsible person or team. In this example, the development of a new program for competitive sales tactics is under scrutiny. Figure 5.9 shows that the project is on time, but appears off the mark on budget. After further investigation within

Figure 5.8 Key Measures for the Sales Readiness Indicator

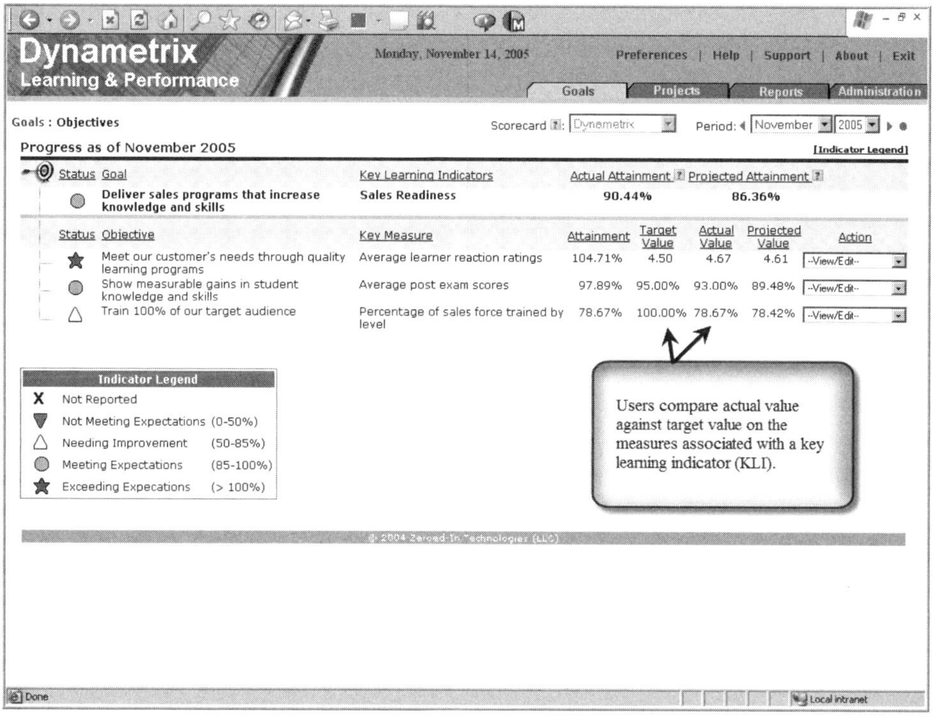

Source: Zeroed-In Technologies. Used by permission.

Figure 5.9 Drilling Down into Details at the Task Level

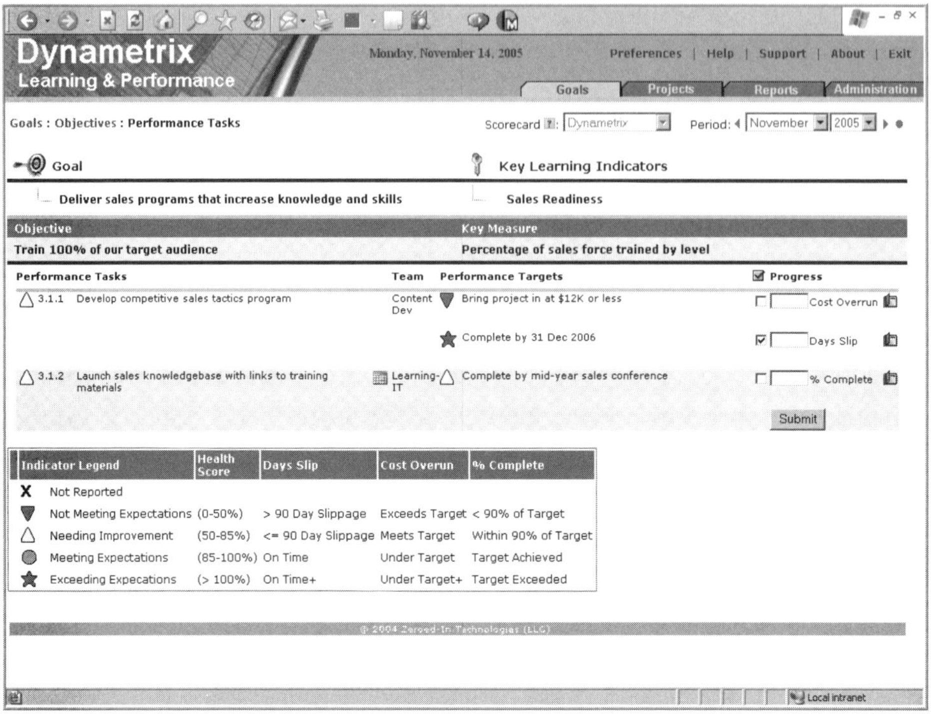

Source: Zeroed-In Technologies. Used by permission.

the system, the CLO recognizes that, even though actual costs are exceeding projected costs, this is happening because the project is ahead of schedule, and thus costs have been accrued in advance of projections.

Impact

Chris Moore, president and founder of Zeroed-In Technologies, described CLO Dashboard's™ work on behalf of NCR Global Learning. Moore spoke of improved communication between the management of the learning unit and the leaders of other business units. Why? Business data were now influencing learning services and programs. Immediate access to information about the past, present, and future enabled more timely decisions and robust discussions.

CLO dashboard had an impact at NCR by providing answers to specific questions. For example, how can we optimize expenses through better utilization of training facilities? By monitoring the *volume and distribution of employees traveling out-of-country to attend training,* the dashboard revealed which locations could serve as centralized hubs for training. The ability to drill down into the data exposed some underutilized European facilities that were targeted for consolidation. As a result of the analysis, there has been a dramatic reduction in facilities costs and travel expenses. According to Moore, without CLO Dashboard™, it is conceivable that they might not have fully understood which locations were best suited for their instructor-led training programs.

Ready to Drive?

Are all organizations ready for an executive dashboard? Moore says that successful use depends on the maturity of the learning organization. He continued, "There is a lot of talk about measurement, but very few people doing it." Defining metrics and measures are a challenge. Several of the learnings from the NCR case study revolved around the definition of indicators, including ensuring agreement between units and including a "metrics friendly" training manager in the project. Another challenge is the availability of the data. Does the organization have the data? If so, is it *readily* available? Are business units amenable to sharing?

Moore pointed out that the shift to more measurement and dashboards is predicated on relationships, trust, and eagerness to improve. He noted, "Learning executives don't always have the relationships needed to get data to measure impact." So it is a two-fold question. What is the *organizational* readiness for a dashboard? What is the *data* readiness for a dashboard?

The decisions supported by this Planner will be as good as the data and measures that underpin the system. While many will be initially excited about this nifty computer-based visual support tool, the development process and associated revelations strike us as most important.

DIGITAL DASHBOARDS

Dashboards support performance by pulling data together from several sources to use for strategic decisions. The intent is to enable speedier, better decisions by providing easy access to the information needed to figure out what to do in a fashion that is aligned with the strategic goals of the organization. That has

---

(Continued)

implications for CLOs, of course. It also has the potential to influence sales-people, customer service reps, investors, and many others.

Dashboards use data visualization and graphical presentation to offer a snapshot analysis of a wealth of data, often from many and varied sources. Information is displayed using tables, charts, and graphs. Gauges and dials are used to chart performance. Dashboards typically include a time element so users not only see an analysis of past performance and current progress toward a goal, but projections into the future. They include alerts to problems or communicate when critical figures meet thresholds. Imagine a sales executive viewing an interactive map of the world with countries color coded to represent market share of a new product. She can drill down to a country, state, city, or perhaps even a zip code. She can see where sales are booming, where they are falling behind forecast, and trends for the future. A graphical alert notifies her that there is a distribution problem in a specific location. The ability to drill down allows the executive to quickly identify areas for concern and kudos, gather supporting data for a decision, and react quickly—without going to twenty people or thirty different spreadsheets, people, or systems.

Dashboards evolved from the executive information systems of the 1980s and are used today by many who are not yet executives. Kopcke, chief technology officer at Hyperion Solutions Corp., told *ComputerWorld* (Betts, 2003), "What we're seeing today are management dashboards, which have been pushed down through the organization, providing relevant information to a particular manager. At Southwest Airlines, they call them cockpits, and they're specialized, so that the guy in charge of putting peanuts on airplanes gets a different view than the guy who's in charge of purchasing jet fuel. But they all see what planes are flying where." Convio, an online service provider for nonprofit and higher education institutions, offers a dashboard for non-profit fundraising administrators. The Constituent Information Dashboard is a graphical one-page summary of system use and online giving.

For more information about dashboards, see articles cited in the resources section of this chapter or visit the websites of providers such as Zeroed-In Technologies, Hyperion Solutions Corporation, Business Objects, iViz Group, Corda Technologies Inc., or Visual Mining.

REVIEW OF CHAPTER 5

Planners

- Planners are called on just before or after a challenge.
- When referred to before performance, they provide information that helps clarify what is to be done or what will happen.
- When used after performance, they provide information to reflect on success and plan for future adjustments or improvements.

Examples of Planners Demonstrate

- Planners help us reflect on our performance with the intent to improve.
- Planners can provide information to us just before or after a task, such as a lifting operation or using a milkshake machine.
- As seen with the lifting calculator, Planners can make complex tasks much simpler and help users perform smarter.
- Delivery methods and content presentation can encourage collaboration and influence attitudes, such as with the incentive plan calculator.
- The incentive plan calculator demonstrates how Planners can be tailored for users and provide personalized information to encourage and guide performance.
- Planners, such as the electronic reference materials, provide help when help is needed within the user's environment.
- Planners can save time and money.
- Planners, such as dashboards, make information accessible to decision-makers. They also encourage collaboration and are tied to the planning that goes into achieving business objectives.

PREVIEW OF CHAPTER 6

In Chapter 6, we'll take a look at more real-world examples of job aids and performance support systems. This time we'll provide examples and commentary for Sidekicks, those tools that are used to boost performance *during* the challenge.

RESOURCES

Betts, M. (2003). Management dashboards becoming mainstream. [Electronic version]. *ComputerWorld.* Retrieved November 14, 2005, from www.computerworld.com/databasetopics/data/story/0,10801,80189,00.html

Bureau of Labor Statistics. (2005). *Lost-worktime injuries and illnesses: Characteristics and resulting days away from work, 2003.* Retrieved October 13, 2005, from www.bls.gov/iif/oshwc/osh/case/osnr0022.pdf

Kirtland, A. (2003). Executive dashboards. *Boxesandarrows.* Retrieved November 14, 2005, from www.boxesandarrows.com/archives/executive_dashboards.php.

Schiff, C. (2004). Maximize business performance: Industry dashboards to the rescue. *DMReview.com.* Retrieved November 14, 2005, from www.dmreview.com/article_sub.cfm?articleId=1007643

U.S. Department of Labor. (n.d.). *Back injuries—nation's #1 workplace safety problem.* Retrieved October 13, 2005, from www.pp.okstate.edu/ehs/training/oshaback.htm

Washington State Department of Labor and Industries. (n.d.). *Evaluation tools.* Retrieved from www.lni.wa.gov/Safety/Topics/Ergonomics/ServicesResources/Tools/default.asp

Wiggins, J., & McTighe, J. (1998). *Understanding by design.* Alexandria, VA: Association for Supervision & Curriculum Development.

Examples of Sidekick Performance Support

While Planners support performance *just before or after* the challenge, Sidekicks are right there *during* performance. They coax, remind, direct, and inform about what to do at the time of need. The map in the glove box and the GPS are Sidekicks that help as we travel. The step-by-step instructions on the sign within the voting booth help cast votes. A salesperson refers to a sticky note with product codes affixed to the side of his computer monitor. An application programmer uses a wizard to upgrade a database.

Sometimes Sidekicks provide temporary support. The sticky notes with product codes will disappear if the codes are repeatedly used and moved into memory. Others will always be useful when there is too much to know or because the task is performed infrequently or changes often. There will always be a need for voting Sidekicks due to infrequency and changing technology.

Chapter 6 provides the stories of four Sidekicks used for everything from carwashes to football to salesforce automation. As in Chapter 5, the examples include commentary about the need for performance support and how that need was addressed. While all Sidekicks are integrated to some extent with the task, they vary in their degree of "embeddedness." We will start with the least integrated support and move through examples that culminate with a performance support *coach* that is one with the task.

MIKE'S EXPRESS CARWASH POSTER
Background

With thirty-four locations in Indiana and Ohio, Mike's Express Carwash is considered large within an industry dominated by small, mom-and-pop companies. Mike's is the fifth-largest carwash company in the United States. Salty, slushy streets during snowy winters create high demand for Mike's Express Carwash. A holiday gift appreciated by many in central Indiana is a "Works" book of carwashes at Mike's Express, a coupon book good for five carwashes with extra services termed "the works."

Mike's offers impeccable and friendly service. Attendants are neatly dressed and prepared for the many aspects of their jobs. They learn how to wash cars, maintain equipment, and provide exceptional customer service at Mike's own university. In a business reliant on repeat customers, the company emphasizes great service at a price that is considered a good value.

But mistakes and damage do happen. A bumper doesn't come clean or an antenna is broken. Bill Dahm, president of Mike's Express Carwash, told the *Indianapolis Star,* "Such incidents are defining moments. Instead of fussing about your fault or my fault, we want to take care so the customer comes back. Some of our best customers are people who might have a little incident, but they tell their friends they are happy with the way they were treated" (Smith, 2005).

Although only .001 percent of Mike's customers have any form of damage to their vehicles, about four years ago Mike's noted an increase in what they call "preventable damages" to customers' vehicles. After an analysis of the problem, Mike's Express Carwash determined there was a need for improved attendant training. They also determined that training alone would not be sufficient because there were too many special attention items or vehicle restrictions for an attendant to memorize. Solving the problem required several approaches, including a Sidekick for reference as the vehicle approaches the carwash.

A Blended Solution

Joe Rice, director of HR and training for Mike's Express, described how Mike's solution for reducing preventable damages:

- The initial training was enhanced. Attendants' initial training now includes the manager walking them through a computerized slide slow of the different vehicle restrictions. This initial training also includes a self-guided test.

- On-the-job training was restructured to allow plenty of time on the carwash lot. During the on-the-job training, attendants evaluate each vehicle that enters the lot and discuss potential problems with their training managers.

- "Meeting refreshers" were developed. The refreshers are structured activities that location managers use during team meetings to refresh attendants on vehicle restrictions and the associated customer communications.

- A three-panel poster was created for the offices at all locations. The three posters, each measuring 11 inches by 17 inches, include information about vehicles Mike's cannot wash and items requiring special attention. They also include instructions about how the attendant should respond to a customer with one of these items.

The first three approaches build *awareness* about preventable damages and vehicle restrictions. They also help build *knowledge* about the kinds of potential problems that arise, such as antennas, ladders, and luggage racks. The fourth method, the poster, provides the just-in-time *support* needed for attendants to pair concerns, requirements, and parts with specific makes of automobile. This blend of approaches, from initial training to refresher training to poster Sidekick support, helps attendants handle mundane and infrequent challenges.

The Sidekick at Work

A truck with tripod mirrors drives into the carwash lot. The attendant notices the mirrors and alarm bells sound in his head from his previous training. He rushes into the office and checks the Vehicle Restrictions poster (see Figure 6.1).

Figure 6.1 Panel 1 of Mike's Express Vehicle Restrictions Poster

Source: Mike's Express Carwash. Used with permission.

Unfortunately, permanent tripod mirrors are on the "we can't wash" list. The attendant returns to the customer and politely explains that the mirrors pose too great a risk for damage. The truck is turned away. Damage is avoided. The poster (and the training) assured the attendant's performance.

In some cases, when a risk is identified, such as a cracked windshield, the attendant may give the driver an option to proceed or halt the wash. If the driver elects to proceed, Mike's will not be responsible for any further damage. The poster in Figure 6.2 helps attendants explain the customer's options.

In another case, a van with running boards approaches the carwash. An alert attendant is unsure whether this vehicle will go through the wash safely. As Figure 6.3 shows, attendants need to deactivate the "brush" for vans with running boards in order to minimize the risk of damage. The attendant takes proper action, and the van comes out clean and damage-free.

Figure 6.2 Panel 2 Displays High-Risk Items

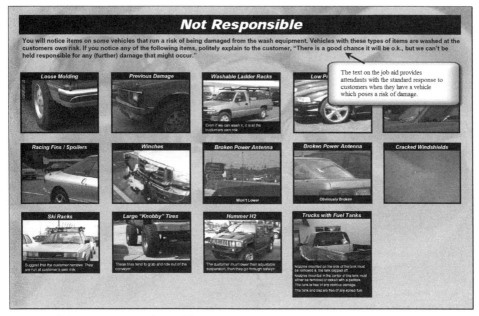

Source: Mike's Express Carwash. Used by permission.

Rice said that it is typical for an attendant to refer to the poster a couple of times each day. Although that sounds infrequent, he added, "But that potentially saves us thousands of dollars each day." In fact, the implementation of the Vehicle Restrictions poster and the associated training elements has reduced preventable damages by 25 percent.

In addition to saving customer grief and company money, Rice reported that *managers* love the posters. He said, "I've had numerous comments from managers about how such a simple tool has made their jobs easier and helped save them money—personally. A high percentage of our managers' compensation is tied directly to the profitability of their locations." Managers also described how attendants review the poster during slow periods or between customers. Rice said, "They don't like to be caught off guard by any updates or changes to our vehicle restrictions."

Figure 6.3 Panel 3 Shows Items Requiring Attendant Attention

Source: Mike's Express Carwash. Used by permission.

Humble and Effective

The poster does its job in a straightforward way. Each year when new vehicle models create a new set of restrictions and procedures, the poster is updated. Rice recounted, "The poster has also been a great tool for communicating these updates and changes to our associates." He remarked that Mike's Express Carwash is considering posting the restrictions on their website so that *customers* can view the information too.

The attendants at Mike's do carry custom handheld devices for entering services, scanning coupons, and swiping credit cards. Rice concedes, "Handheld availability [of vehicle restrictions] would be great, but is currently not available with our technology." While delivery of vehicle restrictions information through a handheld would be a more integrated solution, the poster remains an effective Sidekick, even if it does require a twenty-five-foot jog into the office to view it.

LIBRARY OF CONGRESS ONLINE LEARNING CENTER DEMONSTRATIONS

Background

Many people in the field of learning love to learn. Some have bookshelves full of course binders, reference books, and industry journals. Others dedicate a portion of their hard disks to articles, white papers, and templates. Most can manage these materials with a good "spring cleaning" every few years or when the purchase of a new computer presses them to revisit, categorize, and even discard old files.

But imagine if your library included 530 miles of bookshelves with more than 130 million items. Then envision being in the process of "superimposing a digital, virtual library on top of [this] library formed of objects—books, maps, periodicals, and films" (James Billington, Librarian of Congress, in Whitney, 2005). This is the task of the Library of Congress, the world's largest library and the nation's oldest federal cultural institution.

Terry Bickham, director of the office of operations management and training, and chief learning officer for the Library of Congress, said, "A lot of that information doesn't come to us in hard-cover books. It comes to us in unfiltered, chaotic electronic media, and somehow the Library has to develop a deep scholarly expertise that will enable us to filter and navigate and analyze and interpret all of this stuff for the Congress and the nation" (Whitney, 2005). How does the Library of Congress develop its workforce for the digital age, noting and respecting the demographics of library employees? The average worker is over fifty years old, and the average tenure is more than twenty years. Lisa Dawes, chief of training operations with the Library of Congress, described employees who are "real experts in their fields but don't necessarily use computers."

As part of their efforts to develop employees, the Library of Congress has implemented a Pathlore learning management system (acquired by SumTotal Systems, Inc., in October 2005) to help employees and their managers build individual development plans, administer all Library training, and serve up six hundred online courses. Dawes explained that employees will "ultimately use the tool to capture competencies and tie courses to those competencies."

As the Library of Congress made plans for the rollout, they "recognized the need to have 'help' content" for their audience to help them "get over the initial hurdle." In addition to offering traditional help, they wanted to provide support that went a step beyond by offering tools through which users could actually *see* how the LMS works. Their solution was to embed *Show Me* animated help screens within the LMS to support employees who are not strong computer users.

Show Me How

Dawes and her training operations team identified three areas in which they could add support for the LMS users—searching for and enrolling in courses, managing individual development plans, and viewing transcripts. For each of these areas, a two- to three-minute demonstration was developed to illustrate the actions required to complete the task. Figure 6.4 illustrates the menu from which an employee can obtain the support. After clicking on the link, a new window opens with the *Show Me* demonstrations. Each demo can be played, paused, and rewound.

The Show Me How to Search for Training demonstration simulates the task with both audio and screenshots. The screenshots are enhanced with animation to mimic the clicks, entry, and selections employees will make. In addition, bubbles with instruction (see Figure 6.5) or information (see Figure 6.6) appear.

Figure 6.4 Access to Show Me Support

Source: Library of Congress. Used by permission.

Figure 6.5 Bubble Text Documents Necessary Steps

Figure 6.6 Text Within Bubbles Provides Definitions

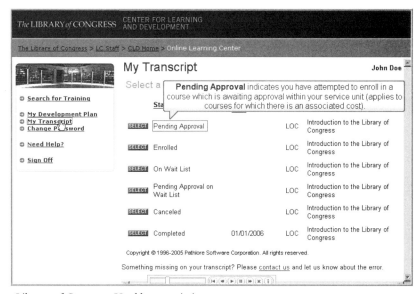

Using Technology to Streamline Development

Mark Hoffmeyer, the developer of the Show Me demonstrations, used Macromedia Captivate (formerly RoboDemo and now an Adobe product, since the acquisition of Macromedia by Adobe) enabled Hoffmeyer to record onscreen actions to create Flash demonstrations. Additionally, the software provided the functionality to add the text captions and audio narration. No programming was required. Hoffmeyer worked with two instructional designers who scripted the help content. He then used Captivate to create the demonstrations. Hoffmeyer reports that this work was accomplished in a couple of days. Never having used Captivate before, Mark described it as "very, very easy to use, user friendly, and very powerful." In fact, the use of Captivate was such an immediate success that another group at the Library resolved to use it.

The team tested the Show Me demonstrations with twenty individuals in conjunction with the usability testing of the new LMS interface. Dawes said the results were very "affirming of the value of the demo." Testers reported that the demonstrations made the LMS easier to use.

Rollout

The demonstrations are just one way the Library is supporting users of the new LMS. The rollout includes a half-day of classroom training for basic computer skills and an orientation to the LMS. Additionally, a computer lab is available to those employees without computers. To encourage success, there is much communication with supervisors and managers, who are expected to emphasize the benefits of the courses and the importance of individual development plans.

As this book is being written, the new LMS and the Show Me demonstrations are being rolled out to approximately 4,500 employees of the Library of Congress. Time will tell how the Show Me demonstrations influence use of the LMS and ease library employees' anxiety with this technology.

FOOTBALL WRISTBANDS
Background

Remember playing the game of "telephone" when you were a kid? A group of people gather in a circle and one person whispers to the next. That person carries the message on to her neighbor and so forth until the message arrives—often garbled—at the end of the circle. If you aren't a football aficionado, you may not realize that a similar telephone game occurs when plays are called. In the NFL, an offensive coordinator will call a play to the signal-caller on the sideline, who then passes it to the quarterback. The quarterback then passes the call to his teammates on the field. With some plays tagged with fifteen-word titles, teams seek ways to call plays more expeditiously while reducing errors. Many think the answer is wristbands. They are Sidekick performance support—job aids worn on players' wrists.

How Wristbands Work

The job aid is a laminated paper slid into a sweatband with clear compartments that are fastened to the sweatband with Velcro. Figure 6.7 shows a typical wristband.

Figure 6.7 Sidekick Support for Football Plays

Source: Cutters. Used by permission.

Note how each play is assigned a number. To make calls more efficient, the offensive coordinator tells the signal-caller a number, rather than the complete name of the play. The signal-caller then relays the number to the quarterback. He uses the wristband to identify the play and calls it aloud in the huddle. Packers coach Mike Sherman told *The Sporting News* (Pompei, 2005), "Using the wristband, all I have to say is 'two' instead of 'Red right switch split right two U corner halfback flat.'"

Mistakes still happen due to the small type and bands that are occasionally ripped off wrists. Opponents may even try to pull the wristbands off to create some short-term havoc, but they still won't know which play is coming next. Since the numbers change every week, the wristbands are quickly rendered obsolete.

Some teams rely on them heavily. Others don't use them at all because they have too many play variations. Still others use them as backups to headset communication systems.

Sometimes they are intended to help overcome obstacles to performance, such as a noisy crowd of football fans. After the September 2005 upset of Michigan by Notre Dame, Notre Dame Coach Charlie Weis told the *South Bend Tribune*, "I wanted to take the crowd out of the game . . . All the skill guys had wristbands on, so all we had to do was signal the play out and then [quarterback] Brady [Quinn] could pass it on to everyone from there. But it was just so that we could take the noise out of the game" (Hansen, 2005).

As a Sidekick, wristbands are embedded in the world of the user. Actually *worn* by the quarterback, they reduce cognitive load and lessen the chance of error. They improve efficiency. They provide just-in-time support right where it is needed—in the middle of a huddle in the middle of a football field.

SALESFORCE.COM'S INTERACTIVE COACH
Background
Customer relationship management (CRM) and its associated software are hot topics in the sales and marketing arena as more companies adopt customer-centric strategies to maintain or improve their competitive advantage. CRM

technology, such as Salesforce.com, has brought on-demand hosted software to even the smallest of companies eager for comprehensive customer information. Companies turn to CRM tools, such as Salesforce.com, to help salespeople handle customer information and close more deals while devoting less time to administrative duties.

Hal Christensen, a partner in Christensen/Roberts Solutions, explained how hosted CRM solutions help organizations be more competitive. Although sold on the benefits of hosted CRM solutions, Christensen admitted that there are some sticky problems associated with CRM implementation. The Salesforce.com Interactive Coach, developed by Christensen/Roberts Solutions, addressed those concerns. Christensen described the purpose of the Salesforce.com Interactive Coach in their entry for the 2005 PCD (Performance-Centered Design) Awards: "Misalignment between the process and the application and the inefficiency of poorly prepared users have been the major reasons why well over half of all CRM implementations have failed to achieve the anticipated results" (Christensen/Roberts Solutions, 2005).

Salesforce.com Interactive Coach won that 2005 PCD Award, presented each year by EPSSCentral (www.epsscentral.info/knowledgebase/awardssamples/). The Salesforce.com Interactive Coach won in the category of embedded/intrinsic solutions because they are "embedded in the task context and focus on task completion—not learning—without breaking the task context or flow." The essence of performance-centered design (PCD) is to create tools and systems that have knowledge of the task and workflow baked in. Wrap it all up in an intuitive interface and you've enabled users to proceed with little or no prior training. The Salesforce.com Interactive Coach provides an integrated example of Sidekick performance support.

Highlights of Embedded Support

The Coach works right along with the user in real time. It is the salesperson's Sidekick. As the user goes about a task, context-sensitive information guides, prompts, informs, corrects, or hastens. Procedures are inside the software, definitions pop up, business rules actually rule. No training required.

No Training Required?

Christensen described how one of the challenges of CRM implementation is user adoption. Salespeople, the primary users of CRM, frequently ask, "Why do I have to do this?" They'd rather be out selling, in the field, with customers, not entering data or planning efforts in a CRM system. One of the ways to combat this resistance, Christensen said, "Is to get them immediately up and running." He remarked that his goal was to make the system so easy to use that they can get in, do their thing, and get back to selling.

The Coach, like its human counterpart, senses what the user needs and acts as a guide throughout the task. Support is delivered via an ActiveGuide Toolbar, which serves up menus of options based on the user's location in the sales process. As users choose a task, they may even select their desired level of assistance—general information about a screen, step-by-step coaching through the task, or no assistance at all (see Figure 6.8).

Figure 6.9 shows how the Coach begins to walk a user through creation of a new selling opportunity with a pop-up informational box and red outlining around the menu item to highlight location. As the Coach and user move forward, the system, shown in Figure 6.10, also informs the user why this information is required.

Figure 6.8 Users Select a Preferred Level of Support

Source: Christensen/Roberts Solutions. Used by permission.

Figure 6.9 The Coach Points to Action to Take

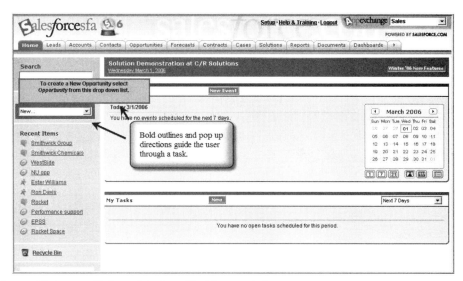

Source: Christensen/Roberts Solutions. Used by permission.

Figure 6.10 The Coach Providing Task Guidance *and* Context

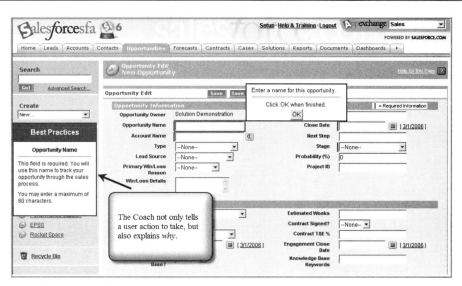

Source: Christensen/Roberts Solutions. Used by permission.

Figure 6.11 demonstrates how the Salesforce.com Interactive Coach helps users avoid entering an incorrect account name. The Coach enables the user to follow the sequence without having previously studied the field definitions or learned the steps. Christensen reflected, "[The Coach provides] the ability for someone who has not worked with the software to work right away, the right way, without prior training."

Tailoring the Off-the-Shelf Solution

As is typical in many hosted applications, Salesforce.com is challenged by being "all things to all people," while also allowing for customization. To companies with limited capacity for such tailoring, the software provides what feels like too many options. The Coach steps in here. The support offered by the Coach enables users to ignore options they don't need by providing access to just what they do need.

Figure 6.11 The Coach Endeavors to Reduce the Chance of Error

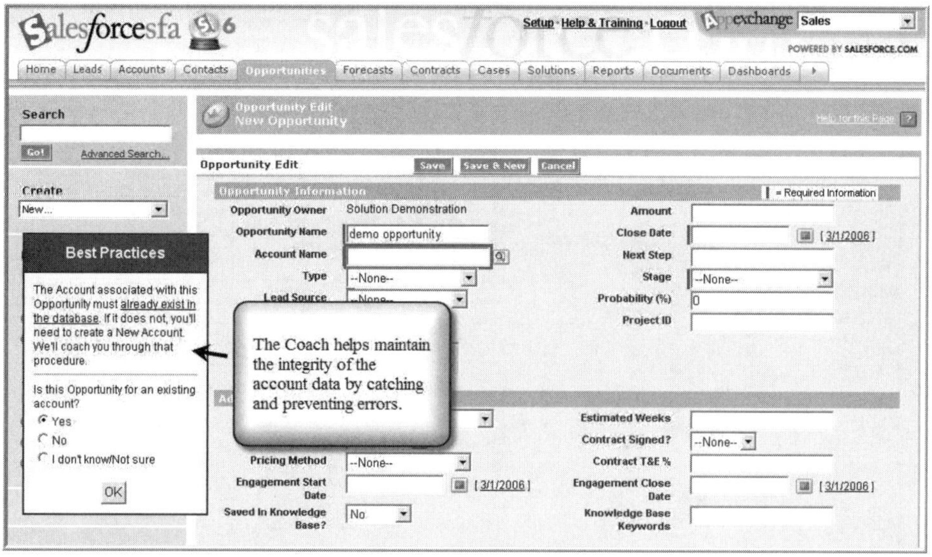

Source: Christensen/Roberts Solutions. Used by permission.

Let's consider an example. The Coach makes it easy to change the default names of sales opportunity stages to names tailored to the company's unique sales process. Figure 6.12 shows how the Coach nudges the manager to set up Salesforce.com with opportunity stage names for typical sales processes so sales reps within the company will see terminology familiar to them.

Automation of Tasks

The Coach takes over to complete what is a multi-screen, time-consuming process within Salesforce.com, reducing over seventy-five steps to five. Christensen estimated that changing the opportunity stages to match the company's sales process could take three to six hours, including training and trial-and-error, without the Coach. With the Coach, this same task would require from fifteen to thirty minutes.

Figure 6.12 The Coach Helps Users Tailor the Application

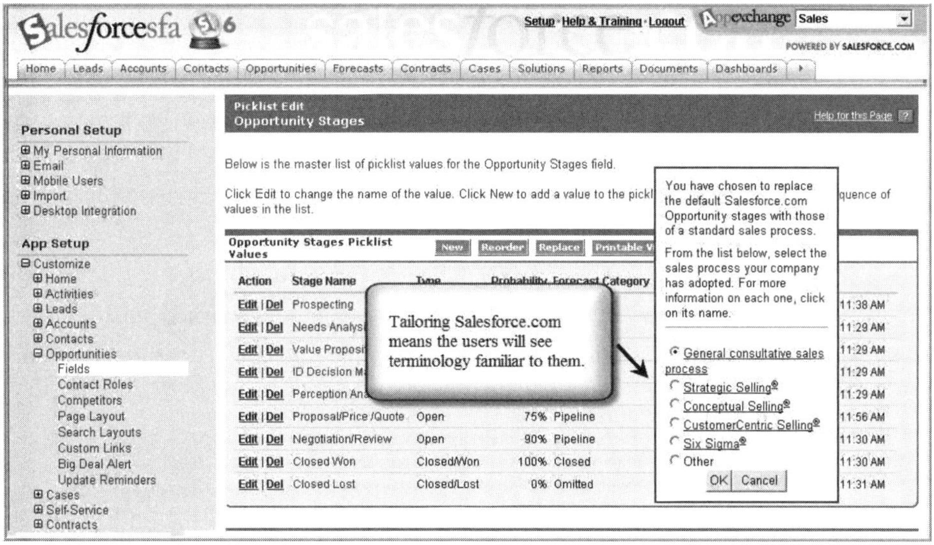

Source: Christensen/Roberts Solutions. Used by permission.

Creating the Sidekick Support

The Salesforce.com Interactive Coach was developed using Rocket Software's ActiveGuide Web Studio (see www.rocketools.com/). ActiveGuide enabled the developers to create the JavaScript file, which controls the support interface. Christensen/Roberts Solutions (2005) described the structure of the support. The JavaScript file acts as a "layer of intelligent support between the user and the application. This layer . . . manipulates and monitors all of the application's controls, as well as all of the user's actions within that application." The scripts can be modified from a central server. In addition, the support runs independently from Salesforce.com. Thus, no changes are required to the Salesforce.com application for the support to run.

Compare this Sidekick to the Library of Congress' demonstrations. While the library's program provides beneficial support, of course, the Coach is more integrated into tasks confronting a Salesforce.com user. The Coach actually creates *interactions* between the user and the application—guiding input, catching errors, and prodding the performer forward in real time.

Like the Library of Congress' Captivate developer, Christensen said users of the ActiveGuide tool "don't have to know programming," but added they would be more efficient if they knew a little html or JavaScript. The small team for development of the Salesforce.com Interactive Coach included Christensen, one staff member, and assistance from ActiveGuide. He spoke of the easy-to-use drag-and-drop and toolbar features within the software, but acknowledged that there was some learning curve associated with the product. Christensen added that it would be most effective to separate the storyboarding from actual development in ActiveGuide. (This would be a more similar process to the one described for the Library of Congress, in which designers worked on the script and a developer worked with the software tool.) He advises designers to really "think it through, map it out, plot it out." We will discuss that in Chapter 7.

A New Mindset

While there may be some challenges when learning new software tools or techniques for performance support, Christensen emphasized that the biggest obstacle to Sidekick solutions such as the Salesforce.com Interactive Coach is the mindset of individuals in traditional training and development roles. He described it simply as a "different way of thinking." Their traditional mindset focuses on content—what do learners need to *know* to do this task. The goal of embedded performance support, as Christensen described it, is to "create a user experience." Designers should be asking, "How can I augment the interface to make it easier to complete the task *with the skills they already have*?" Performance support is about the task. Christensen emphasized, "We're trying to make someone *immediately competent.*"

The beauty of effective Sidekicks is the power to support performers in real time as they go about their business. They navigate new tasks or complex software without blinking. That leads to lower training costs and fewer errors. The Salesforce.com Interactive Coach is a nifty example. For another, visit ThinkSmart Performance Systems at www.thinksmartps.com.

REVIEW OF CHAPTER 6

Sidekicks

- Sidekicks are called upon *during* a challenge.
- Sidekicks provide information, reminders, directions, and warnings right when they are needed.

Examples of Sidekicks Demonstrate

- Sidekicks can be tightly or loosely integrated with a task. They may require we run a few feet, or they may appear automatically before we even call on them.
- Sidekicks help us avoid mistakes and costly errors.
- Sidekicks are sometime just one element of a blended solution to a performance problem.
- Sidekicks often offer advice and help performers comply with business rules or best practices.
- Time and money can be saved with the use of Sidekicks.
- Sidekicks increase the speed or accuracy of tasks.
- Sidekicks may be temporary or permanent supports, depending on whether the information is learned through application or not.

- Sidekicks can be delivered very simply, such as with a poster or a laminated card affixed to a wrist.

- Delivery of Sidekicks may *look* complicated (as in the Salesforce.com Interactive Coach), but tools exist to streamline development of automated Sidekicks.

- Sidekicks can help performers complete a task without prior training.

- Sidekick development requires a new mindset.

PREVIEW OF CHAPTER 7

In Chapter 7, we encourage you toward performance support solutions. The chapter includes information on clarifying the opportunity and making sure performance support is really appropriate. We'll talk about formats, media, technology, and software. We also explore initial development steps and options and considerations for choosing to use a vendor.

RESOURCES

Christensen/Roberts Solutions. (2005). *PCD Awards 2005 Submission Form.* Retrieved December 15, 2005, from www.crsol.com/home/pss/pcd/CRS_2005_PCD_Concept_Form/CRS_2005_PCD_Concept_Form.htm

Hansen, E. (2005). Big house arrest: Irish stun Michigan in its own backyard. [Electronic version]. *South Bend Tribune.* Retrieved September 13, 2005, from http://www2.southbendtribune.com/stories/2005/09/11/sports.20050911-sbt-MARS-D1-Big_House.sto

Library of Congress. (n.d.). *About the library.* Retrieved December 27, 2005, from www.loc.gov/about/

Pompei, D. (2005). Wristbands take sweat out of calling plays. [Electronic version]. *The Sporting News.* Retrieved November 1, 2005, from http://msnbc.msn.com/id/8162171/print/1/displaymode/1098/

Smith, B. (2005). Firm builds business 1 clean car at a time. [Electronic version]. *Indianapolis Star.* Retrieved April 13, 2005, from www.indystar.com

Whitney, K. (2005). Terry Bickham Jr.: Cataloging learning at the Library of Congress. [Electronic version]. *Chief Learning Officer Magazine.* Retrieved December 27, 2005, from www.clomedia.com/content/anmviewer.asp?a=1134&print=yes

Getting Started with Performance Support

It is time to move from enthusiasm about performance support to action. This chapter is devoted to helping you move forward with performance support.

The chapter has four sections.

1. The first section focuses on clarifying the opportunity. What are you attempting to do? For whom? In what situation? Is performance support going to work here?

2. The second section presents formats. What might the support look like?

3. The third section is all about media and technology. What are your options? How do you decide?

4. And the fourth and final section supports you in your initial development steps. Will you develop the program, or will you turn to a vendor? How do you select a vendor? What software tools can be helpful?

CLARIFY THE OPPORTUNITY

The first step in developing a performance support solution is to reflect on the opportunity. What are we trying to accomplish? Better service? Higher output?

More accurate results? Less time spent in training? In Chapter 6, Mike's Express Carwash conducted an analysis to figure out why damages to vehicles had increased. Uncovering the nature of the problem enabled them to develop a targeted and blended solution—including performance support—for reducing preventable damages. *First Things Fast* (Rossett, 1999) is a source of detailed information about analysis. The website associated with the book (www.jbp.com/rossett.html) suggests sources and questions to enable lean analysis.

What information do you need as you plan performance support efforts? Here we look briefly at questions in three domains: the audience and their context, the task or content, and the organization.

Questions About the Audience

Who *are* these people? Do they drive trucks from Brussels to Barcelona? Or are they knowledge workers tethered to a desk in Boston, eager for access to business intelligence? Are they baristas promoting a new latte at Starbucks? Are they seniors stymied by Medicare regulations?

Here are questions to consider with regard to the *audience and their setting:*

What Skills and Habits Do They Possess? Are they new to the job or do they need orientation to the work, programs, or products? Do they know what is expected of them? Are they able to read and understand the language in which materials will appear? Do they know related vocabulary? Are they eager to do better?

Are They Comfortable with Technology, Fearful, or Somewhere in the Middle? Have they relied on their computers or mobile devices for support in the past? Can they use a mouse? Are they fond of the classroom or eager to reclaim time closer to their work challenges or home life? Would they know how to perform a search online? Do they tend to search for answers anywhere at all?

What Is the Working Environment? Where will the support be used? When it is needed, will the individual be in a position to seek support? Is the employee at a desk, in the car, or hiking in a national park with a group of sixth graders?

Think context here. Is there a way to meld support into the workflow? Will this be an apt solution for a person whose hands are tied up fixing a sink, working in the dark, or at a computer terminal? Are there competing tasks and interruptions? Can the employee search for support when customers are watching her efforts? Is speedy response important? What access to technology does the employee enjoy? At Jack in the Box (see Chapter 5), their solution for electronic reference materials was adjusted to match store limits on bandwidth.

Where Will the Support Reside? Cavanaugh (2004) offered guidance in thinking about the performance support. Please revisit Chapter 3, Table 3.1, and review Cavanaugh's 2E3I spectrum of performance support. Must the support be one with the work or can it reside nearby? Will it be integrated into the task, the software, and the context or will it be in close proximity, hailed when needed, perhaps used as a Planner? Is it hidden until called on by the performer or always visible?

Does the Performer Want to Do This? Job aids and performance support are not appropriate means for erasing resistance caused by doubts about the effort. Why? They won't elect to use the support. They will not glance at the poster, printout, or software. They will do as they typically do, unaided, not becoming interested just because performance support has appeared.

Questions About the Task

Data collection for performance support should follow the natural progression of the job or task. Observe the task from start to finish as it is performed in the work environment. While watching, press the performer to share what he or she is thinking about in order to perform the job. Why this act? Why that choice? What did he consider as he decided? What does she do or think about and in what order? Does every performer follow the same order? Does it matter? Are there times when the performer must do things differently? Why? Do people get hurt here? Could sales or scrap be affected?

What distinguishes an effective from ineffective approach to the matter? Chapter 8 provides examples of how IBM used ethnographic research to define what great performance looked like and used that intelligence to define their performance support.

Before: *What does the performer need to know, do, or possess when commencing his or her efforts?* Begin by watching a worker *prepare* to carry out the task. Is location important? Tools? Reflections? Collaborations? Forms?

What are the similarities and differences in how novices and experts prepare? Should the preparation stage be included within the performance support, or should it be supported by an additional job aid, by training, or by coaching from a supervisor? Do workers need to *know* something about performance support before they begin using it? As we will discuss in Chapter 9, performance support is often implemented as a blend. Instruction is the anchor and the performance support is introduced in an abbreviated class. Insurance adjusters, for example, are taught to use software on their portable PCs to estimate the company's response to claims. They attend short classes that prepare them to use the software in stressful environments, sometimes while customers circle, asking questions and debating settlements.

During: *What is done? Are there special circumstances or safety considerations?* How does the performer do what needs to be done? What are the major steps or skills needed? How does it typically happen? What information is required? Does the employee require codes or decisions or approvals in the midst of the effort? Where are errors made? What stymies people? Are others involved in the effort?

Technology is of growing importance here. Wouldn't it be divine if the data captured during analysis could transform itself into performance support, with minimal coding and fussing? Gary Dickelman pointed to Instancy and Briteworks as tools to facilitate that transfer. See Table 7.3 for more examples.

After: *What does the performer need to do upon completion?* What does the performer do once the widget is assembled or the order is placed or the performance appraisal is completed? Are there any special precautions, reminders, or standards of excellence? When reviewing the order, proposal, or appraisal form, what should the employee consider?

Questions About the Organization

Is the organization ready for performance support? Stone and Villachica (2003) urged an environmental scan to assess readiness for electronic performance support and e-learning initiatives. Are line managers ready to understand and advance performance support? Are they ready for workers who *know* less, even if they *perform* better?

Take a close look at the culture. What habits and preferences surround classroom training? Coast Guard officers have been responsive to this issue. When they select performance support solutions, as Rossett and Mohr (2004) reported, Coasties typically retain a role for the classroom, if only to introduce performance support and provide a rationale for it. Rossett and Frazee (2006) introduced the idea of an anchor blend, where the topic *and* the approach to learning and support are first introduced in the classroom.

We expand on organizational readiness in Chapter 9.

FORMATS FOR SUPPORT

Once you have clarified the audience, content, and context, consider what support will look like. In 1991, Rossett and Gautier-Downes built on the work of Harless (1988) and defined seven *formats* for job aids. Recently, technology has added both value and complexity to the matter. In this section we've grouped formats according to their purpose—as they support procedures, decision making, and retrieval of information.

Formats That Help DO IT

Most people are familiar with performance support for procedures. There is a new cordless telephone to program, a computer table to build, a delivery truck to load, or a sales estimate to calculate. *Procedures* dictate the steps in a particular order to complete those tasks. There are two support formats that help with procedural *do it* tasks: the step format and the tailored-step format. Both enable orderly performance. Both can be delivered through print or technology.

The Step Format

When people think of job aids, they often think of the step format. The step format, as its name suggests, presents information, directions, and activities *in sequence.* It is used for procedures that consist of steps that must be performed in a specific order with one defined outcome. The step format does not ask for user input or provide choices. For instance:

a. Lift tab.

b. Peel back.

This surprising and insulting little job aid is on the metal seal of a tennis-ball can and is bolstered, just in case you still don't get it, by a graphic representation of the procedure.

Parents worldwide lament step format "support" materials as they labor to assemble a bicycle, ping pong table, or electronic toy robot. Ehow.com provides a treasure trove of step supports for topics from cleaning paint off carpets to advising a friend who gets arrested in the middle of the night. Employees use step formats to create a new style in Microsoft Word or change the fax cartridge.

The Tailored-Step Format

The tailored-step format is also characterized by steps performed in sequence. It differs from its sibling, the step format, by *requiring the user to provide input* in order to continue through the steps to the goal. The tailored-step format is personalized; the guidance or outcome varies with inputs from users. The Calculator for Analyzing Lifting Operations profiled in Chapter 5 is an example of a tailored-step format delivered in print and electronic versions. The tailored-step prompts the user for orderly information to complete a task—in this case, determination of the physical risk associated with a lifting activity.

In its most sophisticated form, the tailored-step format is an integrated wizard that guides the user through the steps of the task without the employee breaking stride. If you have purchased electronics or software lately, you have experienced it firsthand.

Formats That Help INFORM and DECIDE

Sometimes there are no steps to follow. The goal is to provide access to information or expertise in response to an actual or implied question. What is the product code for the new model? What is Agnes in Accounting's phone number? What do I need to consider before I select that person to hire? Now that I have hired him, what bases must I touch to make sure that he is appropriately oriented to our unit? Formats that provide information and decision-making support include lists, coaches, graphical representations, quizzes, and decision tables.

The List Format

The product list. The employee directory. The list of customers who have purchased a product within the last sixty days. A listing of possible flights for an upcoming international trip. They are lists.

Lists get their meaning from organization and formatting that makes sense to users. A listing of flights can be sorted and evaluated by cost, city of origin, times, or by connecting flights. Let's illustrate with a non-example. Many years back some graduate students were building an online tool for a professor in the

English department. It was intended to help undergraduates with poetry. How did they propose to structure the interface for the tool? Alphabetically, by the titles of the poems. Good idea? No. That was not a particularly meaningful way to do it. Better would be the theme or chronology or the presence or absence of poetic devices. The first letter of the first word of the title of the poem did not provide meaningful scaffolding for students who knew few or none of the poet's works.

The Coach Format

Coaches are *guides* to help knowledge workers deal with uncertainty. They help in areas people consider "gray." How do I approach this client? What do I want to consider as I put the proposal together? They light the way with gentle (or not so gentle) nudges about corporate rules or best practices. They help catch and correct errors. They help people think about things in more robust ways by reflecting on guidelines, standards, or rules. Pop-ups, context-sensitive toolbars, and assistants are all performance support *coaches.* The Salesforce.com Interactive Coach, profiled in Chapter 6, uses the coach format.

The challenge is to prompt mindfulness, consideration of many factors, most with the freedom to skip one element or another. Typically, the savvy user needs only a reminder or a prompt to keep the factors or heuristics in mind. Jakob Nielsen lists ten guidelines for user interface design (www.useit.com/papers/heuristic/heuristic_list.html) in Figure 7.1. As "rules of thumb," they are an example of a coach that nudges designers toward better interface design.

The Graphical Format

Figure 7.1 is straightforward. No graphical magic there. It makes sense, but sometimes more is necessary. The graphical format strives to make support more intuitive by presenting information visually. The goal is clarity and elegance. Tables, charts, graphs, and other devices enable us to quickly discern information and trends and to solve problems. The CLO Dashboard described in Chapter 5 is a good example.

Meet Dr. John Snow. During the 1830s and 1840s, Dr. Snow contended that cholera outbreaks were being transmitted via contaminated water, even though it was commonly believed at that time that diseases were transmitted by inhalation of vapors. After a severe epidemic in 1853, Dr. Snow plotted deaths from cholera in Central London with dots on a map. The map showed that the majority of

Figure 7.1 A Coach for Interface Design

Ten Usability Heuristics

by *Jakob Nielsen*

These are ten general principles for user interface design. They are called "heuristics" because they are more in the nature of rules of thumb than specific usability guidelines.

Visibility of system status
    The system should always keep users informed about what is going on, through appropriate feedback within reasonable time.
Match between system and the real world
    The system should speak the users' language, with words, phrases and concepts familiar to the user, rather than system-oriented terms. Follow real-world conventions, making information appear in a natural and logical order.
User control and freedom
    Users often choose system functions by mistake and will need a clearly marked "emergency exit" to leave the unwanted state without having to go through an extended dialogue. Support undo and redo.
Consistency and standards
    Users should not have to wonder whether different words, situations, or actions mean the same thing. Follow platform conventions.
Error prevention
    Even better than good error messages is a careful design which prevents a problem from occurring in the first place. Either eliminate error-prone conditions or check for them and present users with a confirmation option before they commit to the action.
Recognition rather than recall
    Minimize the user's memory load by making objects, actions, and options visible. The user should not have to remember information from one part of the dialogue to another. Instructions for use of the system should be visible or easily retrievable whenever appropriate.
Flexibility and efficiency of use
    Accelerators -- unseen by the novice user -- may often speed up the interaction for the expert user such that the system can cater to both inexperienced and experienced users. Allow users to tailor frequent actions.
Aesthetic and minimalist design
    Dialogues should not contain information which is irrelevant or rarely needed. Every extra unit of information in a dialogue competes with the relevant units of information and diminishes their relative visibility.
Help users recognize, diagnose, and recover from errors
    Error messages should be expressed in plain language (no codes), precisely indicate the problem, and constructively suggest a solution.
Help and documentation
    Even though it is better if the system can be used without documentation, it may be necessary to provide help and documentation. Any such information should be easy to search, focused on the user's task, list concrete steps to be carried out, and not be too large.

Source: Jakob Nielsen. Used by permission.

deaths were clustered around a water pump on London's Broad Street. The map convinced authorities to remove the handle from the pump, ending the epidemic in London and supporting Snow's contention that cholera was transmitted via contaminated water. Figure 7.2 is a portion of Snow's 19th Century map. Note how the dots clustered around the Broad Street pump.

Dr. Snow's map in Figure 7.2 is rudimentary by contemporary standards. You can now find a map on the Internet with color coded states indicating the extent of influenza throughout the United States (www.weather.com/maps/activity/coldandflu/index_large.html).

Graphical formats are used to convey large amounts of information via a drawing, a chart, map, or even color coding. When assembling an artificial Christmas tree, the illustration of the rows of branches and their associated color codes makes the job a breeze. Target pharmacies use colored rings around the neck of prescription bottles so families can readily distinguish prescriptions within families. Fundraising drives use the ubiquitous temperature gauge

Figure 7.2 Snow's Map of Cholera Deaths

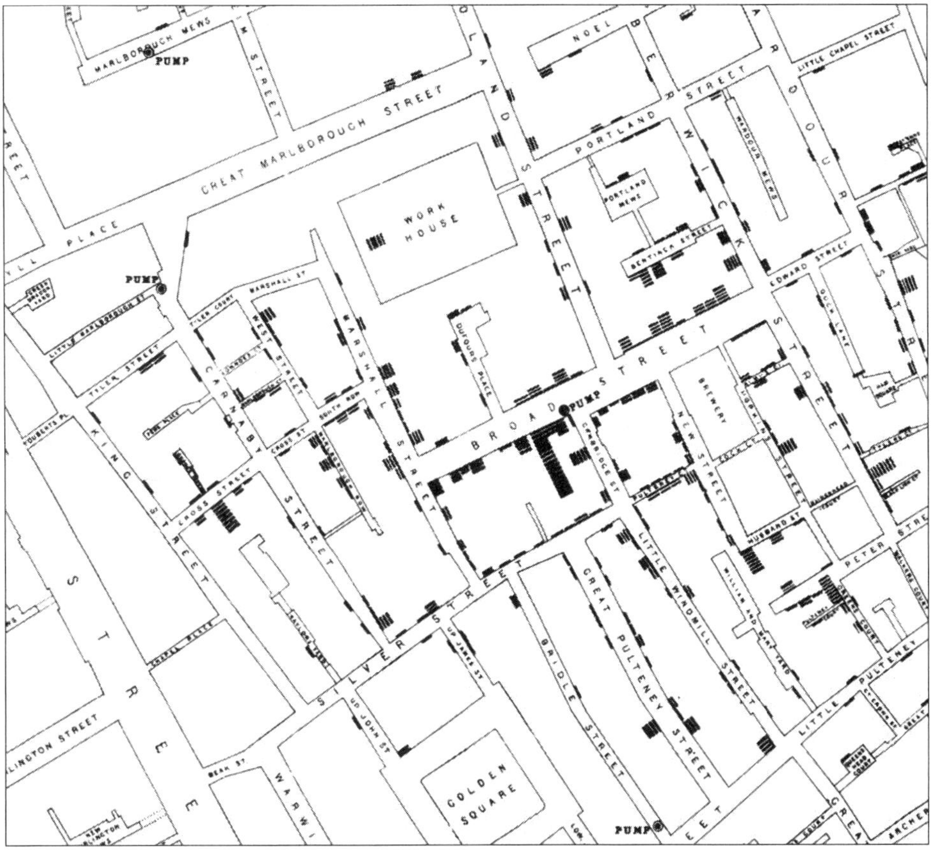

Source: Snow, 1855

graphic to illustrate the amount of giving versus the goal. See Chapter 10 for Intel's workflow diagrams as springboards for performance support.

The Quiz and Decision Table Formats

The *quiz format* is used when a solution or conclusion is derived from a series of questions and answers. The quiz format is used to prompt a process for considering many variables before deciding. The quiz format is based on give and take between the performance support tool and the user.

The Purina dog breed selector at purina.com is a good example of the quiz format. To select a dog breed from more than 180 options, an individual could read books, talk with pet owners, and interview veterinarians. Or that same person could go to the Purina website (www.purina.com/dogs/puppies/Choosing.aspx) and come to a thoughtful choice in ten minutes. The quiz format asks the person to reflect on dog size, energy level, and hairiness. The potential dog owner then indicates how strongly he agrees or disagrees with statements such as "My dog is my best friend." After the user responds, the tool presents recommendations about appropriate breeds based on personal preferences and what experts know about the breeds (this one is more likely to bite, shed, or eat voluminously, for example). The breed recommendations are presented in a decision table, with four suggested breeds compared by weight, size, grooming, and exercise needs.

Figure 7.3 is an example of the quiz format. What is educational technology, and is it right for you? Really right? SDSU's Educational Technology program "quizzes" you to make sure, at edweb.sdsu.edu/edtech/wha_is/selfassess.htm.

Decision tables allow users to identify and compare potential solutions. The decision table format is used when several conditions or variables influence the choice or choices. Order is not a factor. Several choices make sense. It is up to the individual to weigh the possibilities in light of critical variables. Figure 7.6 is an example of a decision table depicting college savings options.

Formats That Help LOCATE Information

The formats discussed so far are about the ways in which information can be presented. But what do we do when tremendous amounts of information are available? How do users find what they need? In this section, we present formats that help cope with abundance. These formats are about support for the *hunt,* more than the prey. They help sift and sort via navigation schemes and search options.

The Navigation Format

The navigation format helps with the hunt by actively pointing to what the user is likely to need. By asking who you are or giving an opportunity for you to indicate what you need, the site configures itself to serve your likely priorities. This might mean hiding what is *not* needed and providing easy access to what *is.*

Portals, menus, widgets, and dashboards are examples of navigation formats that provide access to information, resources, or services. Do you Yahoo!? With a click you can view the latest entertainment news, access a mapping tool, or use a messenger or mail service. You can even tailor the page to display weather in your area, stocks you follow, and current, local movies. The employee considering an MBA can go to her company's human resources portal to review educational

Figure 7.3 What the Heck Is EDTEC?

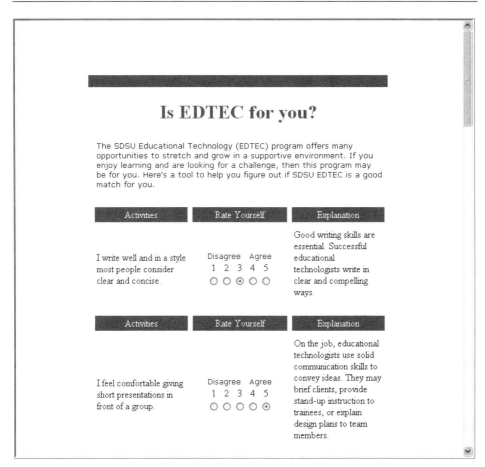

Source: Active Decisions. Used by permission.

reimbursement policies. Aba.com serves up financial news, regulatory informa-tion, and resources for individuals in the financial services industry. Widgets, downloadable tools, deliver tailored tidbits of news, weather, sports team news, or other information, to the desktop.

The Search Format

Imagine that Sara needs to convert dollars to francs. She goes to Google™, types in "currency conversion," and *voila,* she has several online converters at her fin-gertips. Leonardo is working on a report for his boss and uses his employee database to list all employees in the organization who possess Ph.D.s in math, science, and technology. And then there is Sheila. Sheila is always looking for that perfect job. She's the queen of advanced search on Monster.com.

Could she target her search more effectively? Delaney (2005) tested Monster against Simply Hired in a search for accounting jobs near Portland, Maine. Monster found six; Simply Hired yielded seventy-four, and with subsequent filtering for size, Simply Hired narrowed the quest to twenty-nine with revenues over $500 million.

The power of the *search* format is epitomized by Google. Their mission is "to organize the world's immense (and seemingly infinite) amount of information and make it universally accessible and useful" (Google, 2005). While Google indexes over one billion images, if you type in "missing front tooth," your search is narrowed to 185. Type "missing front tooth + girl" and you are down to two. Talk about performance support!

The search format is used when a savvy individual confronts vast amounts of information, but wants just a fraction of it. "Vertical" search formats are emerging to give Google and Yahoo competition. They specialize in industry-specific domains so searchers spend less time with less relevant links. For example, sidestep.com focuses on travel. Lawcrawler is all about the law.

IBM has developed abundant performance support options for its sellers and leaders. This abundance has led to the development of performance support to increase the value of performance support. Chapter 8 presents examples of how IBM helped leaders and sellers find tailored company resources.

Combining Formats

Most performance support requires several formats. Some United States federal tax forms are examples of *combination support.* The primary format used for the 1040 form is tailored step. The guidelines that accompany the 1040 are in a step format. When complex decisions must be made, lists and tables help taxpayers figure it out. If online tax software is used, coaches help you in the form of pop-ups and context-sensitive toolbars and menus.

Let's look at another example of combination performance support. This one has special meaning for one of the authors. If you search for "college planning calculator" on the Internet, you will find a plethora of tools to help parents of college-bound children anticipate and deal with college expenses. Here we have mocked one up so you can get a flavor for the support they provide. These data are not real and are for illustration purposes only.

Many of the college planning tools start with a *tailored-step* format to gather information about from the user about the family, student and desired college or university. The output from this is a number (see Figure 7.4)—the amount required for each year of college. Some of the tools then gather information about the parent's anticipated savings (*quiz* format) and predict how those savings will grow over time (*graphical* format).

The eye-opener is the *graphical* display in Figure 7.5. It shows the shortfall—YOUR shortfall. This picture is more illustrative than a paragraph of text explaining that you are missing the mark by almost $30,000. With that information in hand, parents can explore *decision tables* to compare investment vehicles on a variety of criteria, such as tax treatment and age limits.

CONSIDER MEDIA AND TECHNOLOGY OPTIONS

Remember the football players who relied on job aids attached to their wrists? Do you recall the story of the Coast Guard officers who used a red line on a gauge to indicate a threshold? How about those Library of Congress employees who use online simulations for guidance? Performance support happens in many ways from the sublime to the considerably less sublime.

Will a print job aid suffice? Should the print be delivered in an unusual size, shape, location, or be laminated to avoid blood spatters? Would technology provide additional opportunities for delivery where needed or to accommodate personalization?

Figure 7.4 The First Step in a College Planner

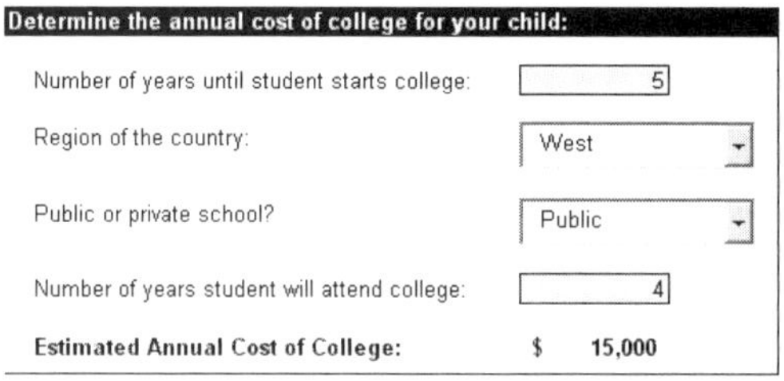

Determine the annual cost of college for your child:		
Number of years until student starts college:		5
Region of the country:	West	
Public or private school?	Public	
Number of years student will attend college:		4
Estimated Annual Cost of College:	$	15,000

Figure 7.5 Graphical Display of College Savings Shortfall

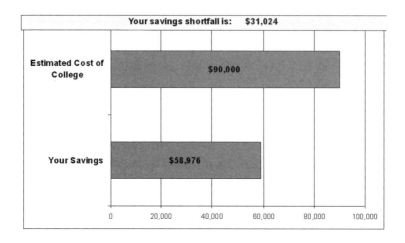

Figure 7.6 A Decision Table of Savings Options

Features	529 Plan	UGMA/UTMA (Custodial Account)	Coverdell Ed. Savings *Not offered by Fidelity	Taxable (Brokerage) Account
Any earnings grow tax-deferred and qualified distributions are federal income tax-free[1]. See Income Tax Benefits	✓	Part of investment earnings may be tax-exempt	✓	
High annual exclusion transfer tax limits. See Gift and Estate Tax Benefits	Up to $55K per Beneficiary in a single year ($110K per married couple)[3] See details	Standard $11K annual ($22K per couple)	$2,000 annual account contribution limit	
Beneficiary can be changed[2]. See Ownership and Control	✓		✓	
Parent (account owner) maintains control over distribution of assets. See Ownership and Control	✓		✓	✓
Contributions not limited by the income of the parent (account holder). See Ownership and Control	✓	✓		✓
No age limit for beneficiary (child). See Contribution Limits and Other Features	✓			✓
Low impact on financial aid. See Effect on Financial Aid	✓		✓	✓
Choice of investments. See Investment Management	A choice of Portfolios managed by professional fund manager	Owner (Custodian) researches and chooses investments	Owner researches and chooses investments	Owner researches and chooses investments

Source: Fidelity Investments. Used by permission.

Consider the example about readiness to finance a child's college education. All that expertise about investment and savings takes on meaning within the context of *your* savings, earnings, debts, and other requirements. And all are best explored in the privacy of your home. Technology is a plus here because it can do the things presented in Exhibit 7.1.

When Is Technology Appropriate?

While there is much to like, technology isn't always the answer. Mike's Express Carwash (see Chapter 6) found that a print poster was the best way to deliver information to carwash attendants. On the other hand, performance support baked into software applications presents enormous advantages when using that software.

How much "smartness" is required? Table 7.1 presents five levels of "smartness" and how to use the levels to think about media and technology for performance support.

Consider *smartness* for dieting. Remember the era when dieters consulted a 3-by-3-inch calorie book tucked into a purse or briefcase? That small book worked—it was there with a number for a food item when needed. Print recipe books and cards provide sequential information to support hungry dieters as they create meals.

Exhibit 7.1 What Technology Offers to Performance Support Solutions

- Technology enables personalization, as it adapts to your needs and circumstances by relying on a database that is based on your circumstances and the collected wisdom on the matter.

- It can provide a consistent, stable message.

- It allows for immediate and ready access, often to large quantities of information.

- It is scalable, as many in Broward County, Florida, can look up how to prepare the house for a hurricane at the same time.

- It is a great way to update information everywhere simultaneously.

- It delivers the smarts where the work challenge is, from a flight deck, to a mine shaft, to hotel reception.

Table 7.1 How Smart Must the Performance Support Be?

Smartness	Comments and Examples
1. Information Only	Information is factual. • Product codes • A dictionary
2. Sequential Information	There is a specific order or sequence to the information. This information would be used to complete a task or procedure. • Steps to secure data on your company's intranet • Procedural instructions for completing and submitting an insurance claim
3. Decision Support	The information coaches or provides guidance in decision making. • A product sales sheet comparing a product to its competitors • What to consider as you prepare for an international trip to a country where bird flu has been reported
4. Tailored Decision Support	The information adjusts to the user/situation and input. *Technology will usually be required at this level.* • A tool for determining the appropriate watering schedule for *your* lawn and the time of year • Suggestions about your readiness to retire and what to do to improve readiness • Advice on which colleges you might want to attend based on your answers to questions
5. Knowledge Generation and Targeting	Information is captured, combined, and reused in new ways. *Technology will be required to deliver this level of guidance.* • Amazon.com sends you an email about a new book you may want based on your previous purchases. • iTunes *learns* your music preferences based on your purchases. Pandora.com provides you with music and then, based on your ratings, determines what they call your *music genome.* • An insurance model tracks claims and calculates risks of lending to one family or business versus another.

To get even smarter, we turn to technology. Weight Watchers Online dieters have access to calculators and options for charting progress. They calculate POINTS® earned for exercise by entering weight, duration of exercise, and activity level. Weight Watchers On-the-Go™ offers tools for your mobile handheld device to bring tailored information to you wherever you are and whatever you might be thinking about eating. As you stand in line at Taco Bell, for example, your handheld reminds you of progress on your diet today and helps you choose the beef taco over the seven-layer burrito.

What is the volume of information? Smartness and volume are two different things. You can have a simple list of ten numbers or a list of ten million numbers. While ten numbers could be presented on a sticky note, ten million could not. But what about thirty or one hundred? This one question alone could lead to or eliminate a medium for performance support. A dieter may keep a paper list of Weight Watcher POINTS® values on the fridge for the twenty foods he most frequently eats. A tasty alternative is WeightWatchers.com, where the dieter can go to find POINTS® for over 27,000 foods. As volume and variables increase, and tricky relationships exist, more is gained from investing in technology.

How dynamic is the information? Do the data become stale quickly? High school chemistry students can rely on a poster of the periodic table of elements because the elements change rarely. On the other hand, stockbrokers and investors need real-time pricing information. The New York Stock Exchange (NYSE) has invested more than $2.5 billion in the past twelve years in technology to accommodate "virtually every investor order and trading strategy, enabling market participants to enjoy the superior pricing, transparency, depth, and liquidity that are NYSE hallmarks" (New York Stock Exchange, 2005). What is more dynamic than the equity markets?

Will the benefits of automation justify costs? The roots of technology are in automation of tasks and calculations. Will automated calculations reduce errors? Does the task require complex algorithms to make proper decisions? Will an automated solution save money by increasing volume of transactions or accuracy? Would it improve compliance by combining user input with business rules in a back end database?

Is the challenge all about software? Are employees being asked to leverage a new database or employee resource planning program? Consider the potency of information and guidance infused into software, baked in as the software is baked, rather than bolted on later, as an afterthought.

Think about the electrician who comes to your home to provide an estimate for service. He probably hand-writes the estimate using a small calculator (or his head) to figure the total. Compare this to what you might experience with a cross country move. The moving company estimator shows up with a slick performance support system on a handheld personal digital assistant. As he walks through the house, he uses the touch screen to select rooms, pieces of furniture, their shape and size. He then enters the origination and destination for the move so the system can compute the costs. The result is a report containing an approximate total weight, number of pieces of furniture, number of boxes, and the dollar estimate for the move. This is a cool tool, right? But it is even more than that. In that competitive industry, moving companies typically provide "not to exceed" estimates. Any miscalculation results in losses. An accurate estimate is paramount. Anticipation of hidden costs and problems is essential. Additionally, data gathered during the estimate is used to select the type of truck for the move and to alert the movers to the need for mitigation and special item handling. The tool helps movers be more savvy and anticipatory than they actually are.

Do not forget the audience. How large is the audience? Where are they? How frequently do they access the information? Do they need that information to obtain the desired results? If only two people in the world were trading on the NYSE, investing $2.5 billion would be unwise. But there are 1.46 billion shares traded on an average day by the members of the exchange and the investors they represent (New York Stock Exchange, 2005). It makes more sense for the NYSE to invest in technology than for the owner of a small firm with three plumbers at work in Bangalore or Binghamton.

EMBARK ON DEVELOPMENT

This section is about what to consider as you embark on the development of performance support. Do you develop the solution in-house or contract with a vendor? What should you think about as you consider a vendor? What development tools might contribute to the effort?

Choosing to Develop In-House or to Outsource

In a survey of *Chief Learning Officer* magazine's Business Intelligence Board, almost two-thirds of respondents reported that they outsourced training activities, at least to some extent (McStravick, 2005). Some of this effort was the outsourcing of asset development. What would inspire an organization to outsource development of a performance support solution? Organizations outsource for these reasons:

- To reduce costs;
- To gain access to expertise;
- To remain focused on core competencies;
- To impose discipline and control scope creep (Braue, 2005);
- To reduce false starts, to get it right fast; and
- To decrease development time.

On the other hand, organizations that elect *not* to outsource have concerns about loss of control, higher costs, security and intellectual property, vendors that do not "get" their business, and providing opportunities for internal staff to be engaged in new approaches. Table 7.2 looks at outsourcing.

Selecting Vendors

In a survey of senior training executives, International Data Corporation's McStravick (2005) concluded, "Clients look first to those providers who can demonstrate that they know the company's business and can provide training efficiency for a reasonable cost." Kruse (2005) had the following to say about finding qualified partners:

> Many training companies say they do multimedia; and many new media companies say they do training. But the field narrows considerably when you look at companies that truly place an equal emphasis on both instructional design and technology.

Table 7.2 Thinking About Outsourcing for Performance Support

Issue	Considerations
Do you have talent and staffing for this effort?	Do you possess the talent and staffing to build, test, deliver, and maintain the performance support system? Do you have the resources to deliver in a timely manner? Is this the best use of your internal resources?

Is your talent current? Are they familiar with the possibilities? Emergent tools? Are they keeping pace with the latest technology? If you outsource this project, are you missing an opportunity to invest in critical skill sets that may be required in the future?

Is internal IT keen on this effort? What are their preferences regarding in- and outsourcing? Will they provide direction regarding extant databases and IT architecture to internal or external partners? |
| Do you have time for development? | Will outsourcing reduce development time, as Braue suggested above, or do you have tight internal controls for development? Are you confident that your people know what they are doing and will avoid false starts and costly errors? Is scope creep a chronic problem? If so, who manages it better—you or your vendors? What is your history of delivering on time? Can a vendor do this job better? |
| Do you have the necessary resources? | Where will this money come from? What are the costs of the initial development effort? What about maintenance? Upgrades and enhancements?

What about tools? Can you purchase tools and training so that our internal people can use the tools?

What do vendor fees include? Are they charging based on developer time and materials? Are they including any licensing fees? Will they develop internal staff and enable them to maintain the program? |

Table 7.2 Thinking About Outsourcing for Performance Support (Continued)

Issue	Considerations
Does outsourcing suit you?	This is about cultural fit. Is information held closely or shared? Are employees accustomed to working with vendors? Have such relationships been productive in the past? Do security measures make outsourcing a monumental task? Does your organization embrace outsourcing in order to stay focused on its core business? Does your organization already have guidelines for determining when to outsource? Is there a preferred vendor program?

Add performance support to the mix, and things grow more rarified. Here are some suggested providers of performance support. We are not endorsing them, of course, but are encouraging you to consider them:

- Ariel Performance Centered Systems, Inc. (www.arielpcs.com)
- Christensen/Roberts Solutions (www.crsol.com)
- E&E information consultants AG (www.ee-consultants.de/)
- EPSScentral (www.epsscentral.net)
- Intrepid Learning Systems (www.intrepidls.com)
- learningguide (www.learningguide.co.uk/)
- SI International (www.si-intl.com)
- Upstream Development LLC (www.upstreamdev.com)

Ask hard questions of these and other vendors:

- What is the vendor's commitment to **quality**? Do their demonstrations illustrate this commitment? Have they received awards or published articles? Can they point to results with organizations similar to yours? Look at Chapter 8. Do the demonstrations possess many of the eight attributes presented there?

- Can the vendor meet your **time and cost** requirements? What is their history of on-time delivery? How do they handle scope creep or cost overruns? What are their fees? What do fees include? Is pricing reasonable and competitive? Are contract terms well-defined, yet flexible? What do they propose for maintenance agreement terms and conditions?

- What **expertise** does the vendor possess? Do they know your business or industry? Do they have the appropriate resources? What tools do they use? Who will be on the team? What experience do team members possess? What partnerships do they rely on? How willing are they to share their expertise with internal people?

- What **questions** do they ask you? Does their inquisitiveness suggest that they know where problems and potholes lurk? Do they anticipate problems and work around them?

- What will the **relationship** with this vendor be like? Have you worked with them before? Will the cultures mesh? Do they describe repeat relationships with prior organizations?

- How well do they **understand your requirements**? What is their proposed solution? Does it reflect understanding of the objectives of the project and your priorities? Do they understand how corporate politics might influence this project? Are they ready to develop a low-cost pilot and then to improve based on the results of that smaller effort? Have they included several key deliverables in their proposal rather than one final delivery?

- What is the **viability** of the vendor? How long have they been in business? Do they rely on a single client? Are they about to be gobbled up by a competitor? Is litigation pending? In essence, are they dependable and able to see you through to completion of the project and beyond?

- Do **references** sing their praises? What is the vendor's reputation? Do references attribute success, in whole or in part, to the vendor? What was their experience with this vendor? Did they deliver on their promises? Ask references about all of the above factors—every single one of them.

Tools for Building Performance Support Tools

There is software that helps to build performance-centered tools or complete performance support solutions *without reliance on IT, without the need to have access to application source code, and without writing code.* The Library of Congress simulations profiled in Chapter 6 are examples of performance support built without coding through the use of Macromedia Captivate. Gary Dickelman (see epsscentral.net and epsscentral.info) described how software tools have evolved to the point where performance-centered solutions no longer require custom programming. Current performance support software development tools themselves enable key elements of software lifecycles. He elaborated:

> "Some tools rapidly scavenge and catalog assets from the target environment that enable thorough analysis, solution design and quick generation of prototypes, proofs-of-concept, and even complete deployable solutions. There are others that obviate the development activity entirely, where the design specification itself is sufficient to create the solution. Others add or compress functionality to meet the needs of workers, but without explicitly commingling the solution with the application's code. In essence, the software enables the collection of information during analysis and design and the speedy conversion of that information into a prototype."

Table 7.3, provided to us by Dickelman, lists valuable tools. Take them for test drives. Note, please, that new tools continuously emerge, of course.

REVIEW OF CHAPTER 7

Clarify the Opportunity

- *Ask questions about the audience.* What skills and habits do they possess? What is the working environment? Where will the support reside? Does the performer want to do this?

- *Ask questions about the task.* What does the performer need to know, do, or possess *before* commencing his or her efforts? What is done *during* performance of the task or job? What does the performer need to do *after* completion of the task?

- *Ask questions about the organization.* Do executives and managers support performance support? Is the organization married to classroom training or open to solutions converging learning and work?

Table 7.3 Software for Performance Support

Issue/Need	Tools	Discriminators*
Model-driven content development to capture maximum number of assets from target system(s)	Macromedia Captivate	Object recognition
	OnDemand	Enterprise class (vs. desktop only)
	Epiplex	
		Configuration management
Programs optimize content development via auto-generation and maximal use of subject-matter expertise	RWD InfoPak	SCORM/AICC conformance
	Datango	
		Extensibility to other forms of performance support
	Outstart	
Content includes animation, simulation, procedural documentation	Firefly	Formative evaluation tools
		Cross-application
		Application types (legacy, client-server, web)
		XML stores and metadata
Content is contextualized	Epiplex	Object/transition recognition
Support is embedded into the task context	RWD InfoPak	Independent of application source code
	OnDemand	Independent of IT resources
	2Work!EPSS	
	Assistware	Security
	ActiveGuide	Content push vs. pull
	Centra Info Guide	Passive, web-based delivery
		Thin or no client
		Repurpose and contextualize third-party content
		Ease-of-use/speed of development and maintenance

Source: Contributed by Gary Dickleman

*Tools listed in the table may or may not reflect all of the corresponding discriminators. Only a very few tools reflect all.

Table 7.3 Software for Performance Support (Continued)

Issue/Need	Tools	Discriminators*
Process capture, analysis, modeling, and continuous formative evaluation	Epiplex MeasureLive Knoa Various business activity monitoring (BAM), business process reengineering (BPR) and steady-state simulation products (e.g., Lombardi)	Focus on actual end-user actions Addresses both human competency and business process simultaneously Time to capture and analyze Model inference (vs. brute-force attribute capture and building)
Comprehensive workflow-and-knowledge infrastructure providers (learning, content and knowledge management systems)	Outstart Instancy Xegy SumTotal Plateau Saba Centra ProCarta	Powerful/flexible portal architecture Fast/easy custom configurations Includes web services and web parts interfaces Single-source authoring for both web and mobile devices Supports Flash-based content output (and any other ubiquitous standard) Incorporates both learning and performance support capabilities SCORM 2004 (or latest) Implementation of sequencing and personalization rules Built-in performance management ASP option

WHAT'S THE VALUE OF PERFORMANCE SUPPORT?

Gary Dickelman

The performance support imperative becomes clear when couched in business terms. That is, the investment in performance-centered methods and tools reap huge returns. It is no longer a matter of evaluating tools by feature, function, and price. Rather, it is a matter of estimating and measuring the return on investment. An organization might easily invest up to $1 million in performance support, knowing confidently that the effort will give an $18 million return, for example. It is no longer valid to simply compare the prices of tools that have similar functionality from the developer and end-user perspectives. One must dig deeper into the architecture and complete lifecycle to assess a tool's ability to manage development, deployment, and maintenance, and then make meaningful business measurements, like total costs of ownership (TCO), time to competency, the net-present value placed on time to competency, and return on investment (ROI). For example, two model-driven content development tools may differ in price by as much as $200,000, while appearing to have the same features and functions. The real difference is that the more expensive tool might have a robust content management and configuration management system, replete with workflow notification, versioning, and therefore be capable of supporting large, geographically disbursed development teams. The cheaper tool, on the other hand, is simply a desktop tool with no such supporting infrastructure. If used for a large project, the huge cost of management and enterprise deployment quickly becomes apparent. In other words, the "cheaper" tool really has hidden costs that might ultimately exceed that of the expensive one in practice. You must therefore measure or estimate TCO to truly compare the tools.

Gary Dickelman is one of the original thought leaders in performance support. For over twenty years he has been passionate about creating work-enabling systems that human beings can actually use. Gary is the founder of EPSSCentral (www.epsscentral.net).

Consider Many Formats

- Two formats help with *procedural* tasks—the step format and the tailored-step format. The tailored-step format, a more personalized approach, *requires the user to provide input.* The system adjusts to input.

- Formats that provide *information and decision-making* support include lists, coaches, graphical representations, quizzes, and decision tables. These formats enlighten performance by providing recommendations and advice.

- The search and navigation formats help performers deal with a profusion of information. These formats are about the hunt, more than the prey. They help performers *locate* information via navigation schemes and search options.

Ponder Media and Technology Options

- There is much to like about technology for performance support. Among other things, it enables personalization. It is scalable and allows access to large quantities of data. It delivers the smarts where the work challenge is.

- While there is much to like, technology isn't always the answer. As you consider whether technology is needed to deliver the performance support, ask the following:

  - How "smart" must the support be?
  - What is the volume of information?
  - How volatile is the information?
  - Will the benefits of automation justify costs?
  - What is required to reach your audience at work?

Embark on Development

- Weigh the pros and cons of developing in-house versus looking for an emperical vendor.

- Look for vendors with skills in instructional design *and* performance support technology *and* your vertical domain. Can they meet your time and cost requirements? Do they understand your business? Are they committed to quality?

- Whether or not you decide to outsource or develop internally, there are software tools to build performance support prototypes.

PREVIEW OF CHAPTER 8

In Chapter 8, we look at the *essence* of effective performance support. What makes for effective performance support? How is one company striving for quality in performance support?

RESOURCES

Active Decisions. (n.d.). *Find the right dog for your lifestyle.* Retrieved December 8, 2005, from http://sy.adiho.com/ASA/Controller?adi_hasScript=1&_AD_195R22=111&adi_scriptSID=1CEC67AE5D85D3BD5897A7AA226C35FD&sysid=4&appid=9901

Braue, D. (2005, February). Buy vs build: The pendulum swings. *Technology & Business.* Retrieved December 12, 2005, from www.zdnet.com.au/insight/business/soa/Buy_vs_build_The_pendulum_swings/0,39023749,39181961,00.htm

Carr, C. (1992, June). PSS! Help when you need it. *Training and Development,* pp. 31–38.

Cavanaugh, T.B. (2004, April). The new spectrum of support: Reclassifying human performance technology. *Performance Improvement, 43*(4), 28–32.

Centers for Disease Control and Prevention, Division of Bacterial and Mycotic Diseases. (2005). *John Snow.* Retrieved December 8, 2005, from www.cdc.gov/ncidod/dbmd/snowinfo.htm

D'Agostino, D. (2005, May). Customized outsourcing: The latest on rentable software. *CIO Insight.* Retrieved December 12, 2005, from www.cioinsight.com/print_article2/0,1217,a=152003,00.asp

Delaney, K. (2005, December 19). Beyond Google. *The Wall Street Journal,* p. R1.

Dickelman, D.J. (Ed.). (2003). *EPSS revisited: A lifecycle for developing performance-centered systems.* Silver Spring, MD: International Society for Performance Improvement.

Driscoll, M., & Hynes, C. (2002). Back to fundamentals: The business realities of funding for performance support projects. *Technical Communication, 49*(4), 458–466.

Gery, G.J. (2000). Attributes and behaviors of performance centered systems chart. [Online]. www.gloriagery.com/articles/attributesandb

Gery, G.J. (2002). Task support, reference, instruction, or collaboration? Factors in determining electronic learning and support options. *Technical Communication, 49*(4), 1–8.

Google. (2005). *Corporate information.* Retrieved from www.google.com/intl/en/corporate/index.html

Harless, J.H. (1988). *Job aids workshop.* Paper presented at Job Aids Workshop by Harless Guild and Associates, Atlanta, Georgia.

Huber, B., Lippincott, J., McMahon, C., & Witt, C. (1999). Teaming up for performance support: A model of roles, skills, and competencies. *Performance Improvement, 38*(7), 10–14.

Kruse, K. (2005). Finding e-learning vendors. *e-learningguru.com.* Retrieved December 12, 2005, from www.e-learningguru.com/articles/art6_2.htm

McNeil, S. (2005). *The visual representation of information: John Snow.* Retrieved December 8, 2005, from University of Houston, Instructional Technology Program website: www.coe.uh.cdu/courses/cuin7317/students/class02/snow.html

McStravick, P. (2005, September). Taking the pulse of training outsourcing. *CLO Magazine.* Retrieved December 12, 2005, from www.clomedia.com/content/templates/clo_article.asp?articleid=1062&zoneid=13

New York Stock Exchange. (2005). *Technology.* Retrieved from www.nyse.com/about/technology/1091792165957.html

Raybould, B. (2000). Building performance-centered web-based systems, information systems, and knowledge management systems in the 21st century. *Performance Improvement, 39*(6), 32–39.

Rossett, A. (1987). *Training needs assessment.* Englewood Cliffs, NJ: Educational Technology Publications.

Rossett, A. (1999). *First things fast.* San Francisco: Pfeiffer.

Rossett, A., & Frazee, R.V. (2006). *Blended learning opportunities.* American Management Association Special Report. Retrieved from www.amanet.org/blended/index.htm

Rossett, A., & Gautier-Downs, J.D. (1991). *A handbook of job aids.* San Francisco: Pfeiffer.

Rossett, A. & Mohr, E. (2004, February). Performance support tools: Where learning work and results converge. *Training and Development, 58*(2), 35–39.

Sherry, L., & Wilson, B. (1996). Supporting human performance across disciplines: A converging of roles and tools. *Performance Improvement Quarterly, 9*(4), 19–36.

Snow, J. (1855) *On the mode of communication of cholera* (2nd ed.). London, England: John Churchill. Retrieved January 24, 2005, from University of California, Los Angeles, Department of Epidemiology website: www.ph.ucla.edu/epi/snow/snowmap1_1854_lge.htm)

Stone, D.L., & Villachica, S.W. (2003). And then a miracle occurs! Ensuring the successful implementation of enterprisewide epss and e-learning from day one. *Performance Improvement, 42*(3), 42–51.

The Elements of Effective Performance Support

Have you grown keen on performance support? Do you see the potential in Planners and Sidekicks? We hope you are intrigued with what can be done with print, and that you recognize that even more is possible via technology. You have notions about the people, challenges, and tasks you want to support. You are ready to go forward to design performance support programs and to improve the ones you already have.

This then is a good time to consider the attributes of effective performance support. What design elements should be included? What do we hope to deliver to users? What about the user experience? If you're thinking about making a purchase or establishing a contract, what is desirable? In this chapter we answer these questions.

THE LOOK AND FEEL OF QUALITY

Craig Marion (2002) acknowledged that there are two ways to parse what constitutes quality in performance support: by looking at the results of the support programs OR by analyzing extant systems. We've favored the latter approach in part because it is difficult to lay hands on data about accomplishments within organizations associated with most interventions. Performance support is no exception.

Another good reason to focus on successful efforts, seconded by Craig Marion, is that system designers need to know what goes into effective programs. That comes from looking under the hood.

We've examined many tools, taken test drives, and talked to users. We've built support tools. We've read articles about quality in information, performance, and decision support. And we've borrowed generously from the international awards program for performance-centered design (PCD) and related writings (Dickleman, 2001; Gery, 1991; Marion, 2002). The performance centered design (PCD) website, www.epsscentral.info, and their criteria for selecting award winners influenced the way we answered the question: What does good performance support look like?

IBM BRINGS IT TO LIFE

We decided that the best way to illustrate these concepts is through examples.

But where would we find such a treasure trove? IBM On Demand Learning stepped up. Robert Weintraub, who has responsibility for "work-embedded learning" in IBM, worked very closely with us on this chapter. He helped develop the principles and selected and commented on the IBM examples.

IBM has used performance support for many years. They explained that their company's breakthroughs came more recently, when they combined IBM's On Demand Learning strategy with intranet technology. In essence, IBM has developed a new place for people in key roles to go in order to do much of their work, called the IBM On Demand Workplace. The On Demand Workplace, or ODW, is not only becoming the focal point for work, but the place where IBM Learning "embeds" Planners and Sidekicks, to increase the performance, knowledge, collaboration, and skills of the IBM workforce.

Partnership between the Learning and ODW organizations has been fundamental to the performance and learning environment IBM is forging. In fact, it has become clear to IBM that the new world of "role enablement" and "work-embedded learning" requires a mixture of capabilities from across the business: instructional designers, information architects, user-centered design experts, IT architects, performance-centered design experts, workflow experts, and content-management experts, just to name a few. Such cross-functional teams are brought together to enable key IBM roles.

In this chapter, we focus on two critical roles in IBM: "sellers" and "leaders." We picked them because everybody reading this chapter has a sense of what sellers and leaders do. No doubt you can imagine their challenges and their opportunities.

The IBM Seller's Workplace

The IBM sales community is the group primarily responsible for generating revenue for the company. The company is eager to enhance their productivity and help them generate more revenue—as well as build their skills and make their lives a little easier. To do so, IBM created the "Seller's Workplace" on its intranet. The primary goals of the Workplace are to give salespeople more time to spend with their clients and the knowledge, skills, and aids to make that time more productive. Through "work-embedded learning," IBM brings sales methods, applications, tools, and resources together for sellers in a customized On Demand Workplace. Seller's Workplace is an integrated "home" for IBM sales professionals.

Seller's Workplace is comprised of four integrated and contextualized portlets:

1. *My Opportunities* presents personalized views of salespeople's revenue pipelines and the opportunities they and their entire sales teams are managing through those pipelines. As they delve deeper into the workplace and start working on particular accounts, sellers are presented with specialized support to help them do their work. Increasingly more specific content is delivered based on the profiles of the users and the workflow tasks in which they are engaged.

2. *Teams and Experts* displays contact details and single-click access to those working on the opportunity or with the client, along with pertinent industry experts. A single click also provides access to Seller's Connection, where questions can be posted to a global network of sales experts.

3. *Sales Navigator* offers context-specific work-embedded learning in the industry or stage in the sales process for the particular opportunity.

4. *Working Knowledge* delivers personalized news and information from internal and external sources, based on a continually updated, personal profile.

Figure 8.1 depicts the main page of the Seller's Workplace with the portlets targeting a specific opportunity.

Figure 8.1 IBM's Seller's Workplace

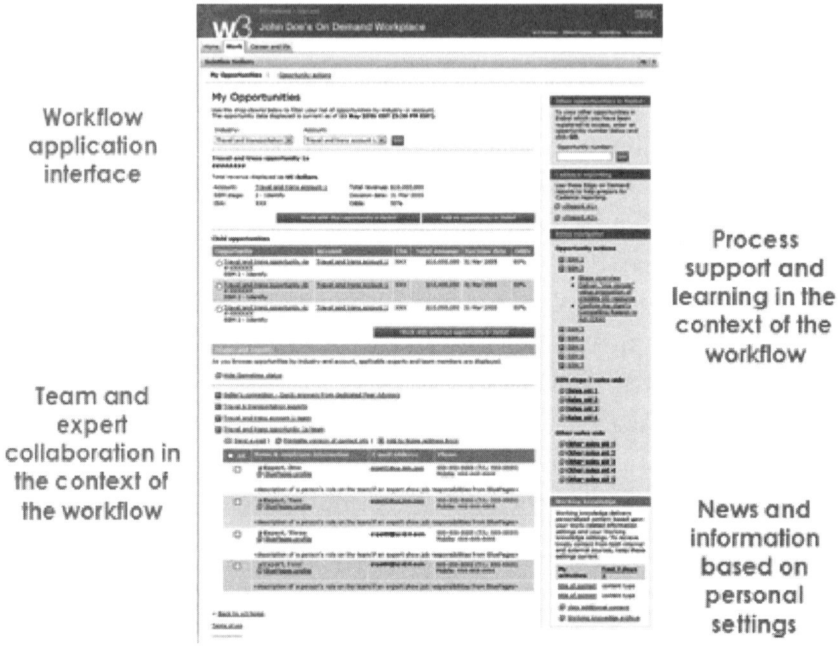

Workflow application interface

Process support and learning in the context of the workflow

Team and expert collaboration in the context of the workflow

News and information based on personal settings

Source: IBM. Used by permission.

The IBM Manager Portal

Managers, too, have an On Demand Workplace devoted to achieving their objectives. As is the case with the sellers, managerial success depends on marshaling resources and executing on numerous expectations. The IBM "Manager Portal" brings tasks and applicable resources together in one place for IBM's thirty thousand managers. The portal aggregates more than two thousand manager resources and serves personalized content to managers in seventy-eight countries in nine different languages. A single update to content updates it globally, wherever that content resides.

Here is what is currently offered to IBM managers:

- *Manager News* brings timely articles, information, alerts, and resources to managers according to their local or geographic profile.

- *Work with Your Employees* is an online tool that enables managers to change their employees' work information, update employee performance reviews, change employee salary and compensation information, promote and transfer employees, and manage other employee functions such as awards or individual development plans.

- *HR Management Reports* provides managers with a quick link to departmental and employee web reports.

- *Leader Spotlight* showcases great IBM managers and leaders. This new feature will highlight global managers who are "walking the walk" and exemplifying IBM's leadership competencies.

- *LEADing@IBM Top Reads and Recent Updates* gives managers a glimpse into the most sought-after information on the IBM's prime leadership development website.

- *Personalized Learning* gives managers direct access to recommended learning activities, based on their profiles.

- *Act Now!* is an up-to-the-minute alert mechanism that informs managers of key business deadlines or when action needs to be taken on specific business commitments during key HR cycles.

- *Manager Resources* is a comprehensive tool that provides managers with access to the following resources:

  - *Manager Tools* offers quick links to the tools that managers use each day in the course of performing their jobs, such as job postings, IBM's travel website, expense reimbursement, and asset management tools.

  - *Checklists* provides managers with checklists and answers to frequent, pressing questions: How to transfer an employee; how to put an employee on leave of absence; how to hire a new employee; etc.

  - *Policies and Practices* provides managers with quick links to important IBM HR policies such as diversity, equal opportunity, IBM workforce flexibility, etc.

- *Build Your Expertise* provides direct access to IBM management development's career and learning programs.

- *Helpful Links* provides managers with helpful quick-links to IBM HR professionals, HR phone lists, and manager forms.

Figure 8.2 is the main page of the manager portal for China.

What can we learn from what IBM has done for their sellers and managers? How does IBM's work exemplify effective performance support?

Figure 8.2 IBM's Manager Portal for China

Source: IBM. Used by permission.

EIGHT PRINCIPLES FOR PERFORMANCE SUPPORT

1. Great Performance Support Is Tied to the Achievement of Important Business Objectives

Perhaps the most important thing that IBM did before it started its Seller's Workplace and Manager Portal projects was to examine business needs and objectives. What are the most critical objectives the business needs to accomplish and who are the people most critical to accomplishing these tasks? That is how the IBM Learning and ODW organizations chose the roles they would enable and received the necessary sponsorship and funding.

IBM also made sure that these support systems focused on the business objectives of the people they are serving. In the case of salespeople, they focus on generating revenue. In the case of managers, the goal is to ensure a motivated and productive workforce. In both cases, the systems gave users extra time to work on the achievement of their objectives. IBM reports that in 2005 the Manager Portal delivered $14M in productivity (time savings) to managers, and 65 percent reported that the portal increased their ability to make effective decisions.

The most prominent portlet in the Seller's Workplace is the My Opportunities portlet, shown in Figure 8.3. It is here that sellers work with the information they need to generate revenue.

Tony O'Driscoll, leader of IBM's Performance Architecture Analysis and Design Group and one of the creators of the Seller's Workplace, emphasized how the business objective was always kept at the forefront: "Most applications today are designed to serve the work process that they automate. Their interfaces do take into account the context within which the seller operates. This design allowed us to mask the complexity of the various applications that sellers use to do their jobs—to sell IBM products and services—by surfacing information, learning, and expertise within the seller's work context. This allows them to save time by not having to navigate multiple applications but instead to focus on the task at hand and have the interactions between the seller and the applications managed by the workplace. The ultimate result is more face time with customers and less time spent navigating the complexity of the enterprise."

2. Great Performance Support Helps Users Define, Track, and Achieve Goals

In the Seller's Workplace, the Sales Navigator portlet presents sales process goals, configures itself to where the seller is on a particular opportunity, and emphasizes

Figure 8.3 The My Opportunities Portlet Within the Seller's Workplace

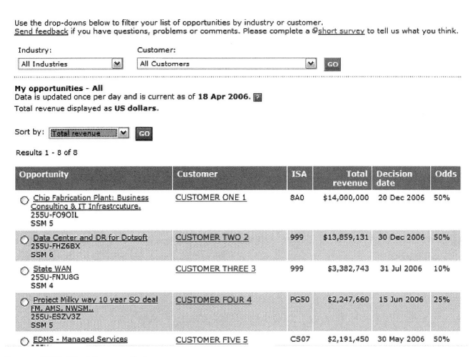

My opportunities

Use the drop-downs below to filter your list of opportunities by industry or customer.
Send feedback if you have questions, problems or comments. Please complete a *short survey* to tell us what you think.

Industry: Customer:

[All Industries ▼]   [All Customers ▼] [GO]

My opportunities - All
Data is updated once per day and is current as of **18 Apr 2006.** ?
Total revenue displayed as **US dollars.**

Sort by: [Total revenue ▼] [GO]

Results 1 - 8 of 8

Opportunity	Customer	ISA	Total revenue	Decision date	Odds
○ Chip Fabrication Plant: Business Consulting & IT Infrastrcuture, 255U-FO9OIL SSM 5	CUSTOMER ONE 1	8A0	$14,000,000	20 Dec 2006	50%
○ Data Center and DR for Dotsoft 255U-FHZ6BX SSM 6	CUSTOMER TWO 2	999	$13,859,131	30 Dec 2006	50%
○ State WAN 255U-FNJU8G SSM 4	CUSTOMER THREE 3	999	$3,382,743	31 Jul 2006	10%
○ Project Milky way 10 year SO deal FM, AMS, NWSM., 255U-ESZV3Z SSM 5	CUSTOMER FOUR 4	PG50	$2,247,660	15 Jun 2006	25%
○ EDMS - Managed Services	CUSTOMER FIVE 5	CS07	$2,191,450	30 May 2006	50%

Source: IBM. Used by permission.

the work that remains to be done. Figure 8.4 shows the Sales Navigator. Note that it is offering support in the "identify" stage of IBM's Signature Selling Method (SSM) in response to an opportunity opened in the My Opportunities portlet. Figure 8.5 demonstrates the way the tool drills down and provides context-sensitive best practices. The Sales Navigator is a Sidekick tool that helps carry out *this* stage of the sales effort by helping individual sellers track progress, effort, and results.

3. Great Performance Support Focuses on What Really Differentiates Great Performance

Do we typically know what efforts make a difference? Do we know what *really* matters to people as they go about their work? Those questions are critical to the creation of effective on demand resources.

Figure 8.4 The Sales Navigator Portlet

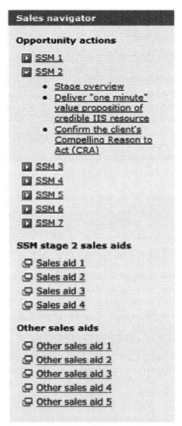

Source: IBM. Used by permission.

Figure 8.5 The Sales Navigator Provides Guidance

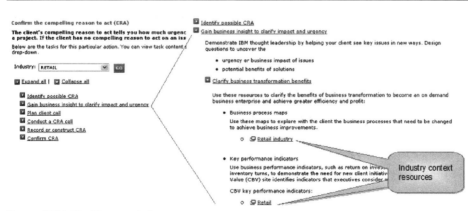

Source: IBM. Used by permission.

IBM is committed to a process that carefully defines what constitutes smartness. They do that by identifying the differentiating practices of exemplary performance, as opposed to typical performance. Then they use that intelligence as the basis for performance support.

What activities and behaviors are most critical to successful sales? What gets in the way? What about managing? What efforts contribute most to effective management? What interferes with those efforts?

IBM's Robert Weintraub said this about where their performance support comes from: "In some cases, we are using ethnographic analysis to understand the workflow of high performers in key roles in the organization. We immerse ourselves in their work lives and analyze what differentiates high performance. We then use the results of that analysis to determine what performance support should be used and, specifically, what function a system or portlet should provide. Furthermore, we create 'wireframes' and prototypes that our target audience can see and use; and we get candid feedback."

The Manager Portal was designed by a manager productivity team—a global, matrixed, core team of thirty IBM-ers from six IBM business units. Michael Fontaine, the director of HR IT strategy and one of the leaders of the effort, said, "We engaged a select group of managers to help identify the tasks required to do their job. This not only became the basic premise of the Manager Portal, but also led to a global survey and focus groups with 10 percent of the IBM manager population. That initial work, and that which has followed, is built on our commitment to develop manager enablement solutions through in-depth user requirements."

4. Great Performance Support *Recognizes and Delivers* the Help That People Need

IBM's On Demand Workplace has been designed to deliver support in the context of the task at hand. Through portlets, the system is "aware of" the work the user is doing and then offers guidance and resources even before the user knows to seek it.

For example, a salesperson might be in the Workplace to check progress on particular opportunities. Each of those opportunities can be advanced in numerous ways. How should the seller proceed most productively? The Sales Navigator offers suggested practices. "Why not learn from others' experiences?" it might suggest. The Working Knowledge portlet might chime in: "Here are some current news articles about key issues and opportunities in your industry that can help you with your client."

The Manager Portal goes even further and demands performance from managers. "Act now!" it states. "There is a deadline approaching, and here is what you need to do." When IBM is clear about the goals of workers and the best ways to achieve those goals, their performance support systems do not wait to be asked for help.

5. Great Performance Support Helps People Collaborate and Look at Their Work from Several Perspectives

While most would agree that collaboration is good, it does not dependably happen all the time, not anywhere. Over 40 percent of IBM's workforce works from their home offices. The context and patterns of work have changed, and IBM has set out to enable collaboration across lines of business, geographies, and a remote and mobile workforce. Connecting with and gathering ideas from others, reaching for new sources, and being systematic about it—all are significant challenges.

IBM's collaboration portlet in the Seller's Workplace is "Teams and Experts," shown in Figure 8.6. When salespeople are working on an opportunity, they might need the help that can only come from collaborating with the right person, at the right time.

The Teams and Experts portlet points to collaborators within the context of the opportunity. It might be someone on the account team or someone representing the opportunity team. It could be an IBM expert in the associated industry, as in the case pictured in 8.6, Travel and Transportation. Through the Teams and Experts portlet, IBM points to people based on their expertise profile. A new ability to find an expert specific to the opportunity they are working on and having the ability for dynamic collaboration enable sellers to instantly build off the expertise of their colleagues. Or there might be a need to send a call for help to a network of IBM salespeople through the "Seller's Connection." These contacts are established and maintained through instant messaging, email, or phone. As the system senses location in the sales process, ready access is tailored and provided—with an instant message link indicating availability.

In a fast-moving, complex, and sophisticated work environment, an expertise profiling approach facilitates critical connections. This proactive system brings the right people together at the right time, in the right way.

Figure 8.6 The Teams and Experts Portlet in the Seller's Workplace

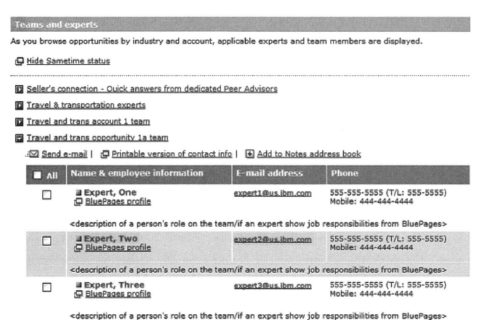

Source: IBM. Used by permission.

6. Great Performance Support Speaks in the Language of the Work and Worker

Like people in any profession, we succumb to the use of jargon—that of instructional technology, instructional design, adult learning, information systems, and so on. Such language separates us from the business and from the users of performance support.

Note the titles of the various aids in the Manager Portal: News, Tools, Checklists, Policies and Practices, Build Your Expertise, Contacts, Work with Your Employees. All are plain-spoken and clear. If you are a manager who needs an answer from the more than two thousand resources out there on the system, what you need is recognizable and only a few clicks away.

When what users need is learning, IBM often gives them three choices: "Show me," "Guide me," or "Teach me." This is plain language for features that serve up learning in leading-edge ways. Learning and support are embedded and delivered in the context of the work being performed. Imagine that you are a seller who is preparing for a meeting with a chief financial officer. While you are experienced in the industry, this is the first time you have been able to schedule a conversation at this level in a large, global organization. You feel pretty good about what you are going to say and do, but would like to be even more fluent on a few related topics, just in case. With the Sales Navigator, when salespersons are being guided through pertinent phases of the sales process, they are continually and consistently offered opportunities to enhance their performance through the familiar "Show me," "Guide me," "Teach me." Figure 8.7 exemplifies this. An "opportunity plan" is a key aspect of IBM's sales methodology. Note the context. Note the options.

7. Great Performance Support Provides What Is Needed, No More, No Less

When managers need to execute a task immediately, having the tool, checklist, policy, or practice at hand is all they need. When sellers are about to call on clients, some quick advice to help them move their opportunity to the next stage is all they may need. Learning from best practice to help enable the execution of work is the goal of these role-enabled workplaces.

Thus, in the Manager Portal, there is easy access to recommended learning modules and articles. In Seller's Workplace, the Working Knowledge portlet is pervasive and offers reading material, assets that are pertinent to the seller's tasks

Figure 8.7 The Sales Navigator Portlet Allows the Seller to Be Shown, Guided, or Taught

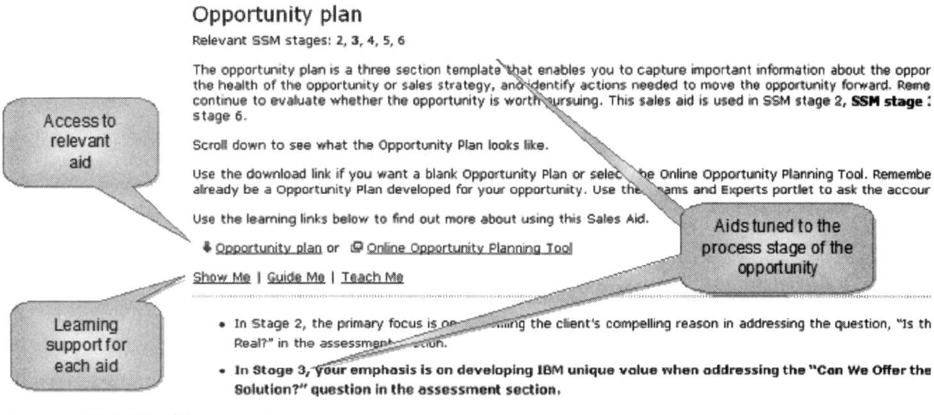

Source: IBM. Used by permission.

and to their growth and maturation. The sellers and managers are acting and developing simultaneously, in the context of work.

8. Great Performance Support Helps People Act Smarter Than They Are

Imagine a veteran seller who is expected to sell new products to new audiences and in new ways. Imagine a new manager. She might be expected to manage a group that spans the globe. Not only must these professionals do their current jobs well, but they are required to be ready for challenges that happen tomorrow or next week, challenges that are brand spanking new.

In the "good old days," the sellers and leaders would sign up and attend classes. While they still do some of that, now much more support is provided to them in the workplace. This support is available on demand, in the context of work. You have seen examples throughout this chapter for both sellers and managers. They have tools that encourage real-time collaboration. They have access to information and guidance, human and technological, when they confront their workplace challenges. And perhaps most interesting of all, their growth and directions are set through analyses that carefully define what excellence looks like. Such study then serves as the backbone for performance support.

Recently, IBM asked salespeople in the United States and Europe about their experiences with Seller's Workplace. Here are a few of their comments:

- "It provides information regarding my accounts, markets, trends, competition. With Seller's Workplace, I have that all at my fingertips."

- "By using the Seller's Workplace, you can quickly identify the opportunities that are at the different sales stages that need your attention."

- "It gives me navigational direction as a leader on where to focus my time."

In their words, it significantly enables better performance.

Nancy Lewis, IBM's vice president of On Demand and Sales Learning, emphasizes the importance of IBM's foray into work-embedded learning: "We have to take it upon ourselves to rethink training and learning. There will never be enough time to learn everything we need to learn. There is such a rapid churn of skills and knowledge required to maintain job performance that learning can no longer be provided as a set of events. And that involves new ways of thinking about an approach to learning. At IBM, we think there's a pressing need for a learning model to incorporate, fundamentally, the on-the-job aspect of how people learn."

YOU DON'T HAVE TO BE IBM

We are thrilled to have IBM as our anchor example in Chapter 8. As you can see, IBM elevates performance support through their commitment to on demand learning and resources. They recognize the power of infusing information, guidance, lessons, people, and practices into the workflow, where tasks are done. Their efforts show that the subtitle of this book can indeed come to fruition. IBM is in transition from learning in the classroom to learning on demand everywhere.

But you don't have to be IBM to create programs that are congruent with these principles. A non-profit can collect relevant resources for home buyers in one place, in a language other than English, and through an elegant interface to help them find just what they need, no more, no less. A senior citizen can go online and answer questions posed by a website that then directs him to an appropriate prescription drug plan. College students can join together online at MySpace or Facebook to talk about graduate school in psychology or what to do to prepare for a blind date. Those same college students enjoy support in the workflow as they write their papers and are immediately informed of spelling and grammar mistakes. A new mom eager to capture those first steps taken by her daughter can get the very best price for a coveted digital video camera by turning to online buying support. And small and medium-sized business can encourage project managers to use HELP systems available online at reasonable prices.

What IBM has done is to innovatively bring these principles together in their efforts on behalf of sellers and leaders. That's why we invited them to help us breathe life into these principles.

REVIEW OF CHAPTER 8

In this chapter, we presented eight principles for effective performance support:

1. Great performance support is tied to the achievement of important business objectives.

2. Great performance support helps users define, track, and achieve goals.

3. Great performance support focuses on what *really* differentiates great performance.

4. Great performance support *recognizes and delivers* the help that people need.

5. Great performance support helps people collaborate and look at their work from several perspectives.

6. Great performance support speaks in the language of the work and worker.

7. Great performance support provides what is needed, no more, no less.

8. Great performance support helps people act smarter than they are.

PREVIEW OF CHAPTER 9

The next chapter is about moving from good intentions to tangible programs that make a difference in the lives of people.

Chapter 9 recognizes that performance support demands much of individuals and organizations. The form is new. The technologies are emergent. The expectations are substantial. The collaborations are vexing. Performance support, to be born and used well, will not happen without serious planning and commitment.

Chapter 9 is about implementation. Who creates such programs? Does performance support stand alone, or should it be a component in a blend? What kinds of people serve on these teams? What do they do? What is the role of the sponsor? What can people and units do to increase the likelihood of success.

RESOURCES

Dickleman, G. (2001). Award-winning performance and consulting: An interview with Burt Huber. *Performance Improvement,* 40(7), p. 28–33.

Gery, G.J. (1991). *Electronic performance support systems.* Tolland, MA: Gery Performance Press. (Previously published by Ziff Institute and Weingarten Publications, 1991.)

Marion, C. (2002). Attributes of performance-centere systems: What can we learn from five years of EPSS/PCD competition award winners? *Technical Communication,* 49(4), 428–443.

9

Strategies for Implementation

Coordinating classes presents one kind of challenge. There is much to be done, of course, but the task is typically within the control of learning and HR people. With performance support, the order of magnitude of the challenge is different. The form is new and demands fresh and pervasive choices by employees, managers, and executives. Success depends on influencing what is resident on the desktop or, in some cases, the precious real estate on mobile devices. Technology is at the heart of the matter. Costs can be great and extend beyond initial development. And efforts associated with performance support span the organization.

In this chapter, we acknowledge that the shift to performance support is no small matter. We share what we know of emerging ideas about implementation. We present eight implementation strategies here, ranging from sponsorship to multidisciplinary teams, measurement, communications, and change management.

Here we attempt to cope with what Gloria Gery called "the law of diminishing astonishment," as people who originally thought performance support was a nifty idea lose their energy and taste for it.

165

Blending is highlighted in this chapter. In 2005 McManus and Rossett interviewed six professionals engaged in implementing performance support. Every one of them noted that performance support tools were but one element in larger blended initiatives, often including classes and coaching.

PLACE PERFORMANCE SUPPORT IN A BLEND

Why are we featuring the juncture between blending and performance support? To answer that question, we visit the University of Tennessee football team.

Ordinarily, we wouldn't write about TN football or CA football either. What drew attention was the Tennessee team's reliance on a bright orange card, a THINK card, distributed to players before they even get their hands on a game playbook. Glier (2005) wrote in *USA Today:* "It is an orange card small enough to fit into their wallets. On the front it says, 'THINK,' followed by a series of questions designed to help the player assess his behavior and make the appropriate decision. On the back of the card are the home and cell phone numbers of the Tennessee coaching staff so players can call for help."

That orange card is Planner performance support for the TN football player. It is a small, colorful job aid dedicated to helping each player reflect on and then improve choices. It is there to encourage good behavior and to facilitate contact with coaches.

The only problem was that it didn't work. While famous for great football, the Tennessee players also received public note for some awful off-the-field activities. According to *USA Today,* there were at least twenty incidents, including shoplifting, assault, gun charges, and failing a drug test.

That THINK card was good, but it was not sufficient. Glier reported, "The THINK card is part of a safety net of counselors, tutors, and role models the university has been constructing since 1995 after eight football players had run-ins with the law in a one-year span."

In a 2006 white paper for the American Management Association (www.amanet.org/blended/), Rossett and Frazee defined blending this way:

> Blended learning (BL) integrates seemingly opposite approaches, such as formal *and* informal learning, face-to-face *and* online experiences, directed paths *and* reliance on self-direction, and digital references *and* collegial connections, in order to achieve individual *and* organizational goals.

Blending typically involves an integrated combination of approaches, such as coaching by a supervisor, participation in an online class, attendance at a workshop, guidance from a performance support tool, breakfast meetings with colleagues, competency statements, reference to documentation, e-coaching by an expert, and participation in an online community. With a blended approach, the organization provides several coordinated ways of reaching strategic goals. Think back on the football players. Nice as that orange card was, it could only be one element in a system.

Let's move from Saturday to Sunday, and off the football field and into a house festooned with flags proclaiming it a real estate "Open House." Like a bee to honey, one of the authors was drawn inside. Within was a youngish woman, the real estate agent. Before enjoying a house tour, the agent was determined to engage in dialogue. She wanted to "qualify" her customer. Her questions were prompted by the software she was running on the computer that sat in front of her.

This is what happened:

> I swung over so I could see the screen and watched as it took her and me through questions that determined my eligibility for such an expensive dwelling, my needs for space, trees, bathrooms, garages. . ., my preferences as opposed to needs, and my house and credit history. Different responses led to different questions and a set of recommendations, including references to other listings that appeared more appropriate to me than the house in which we were sitting. With the click of a single button, she was provided with rationale for those recommendations, based on the information I provided in response to her questions and the company's housing stock.
>
> It was impressive. This relatively inexperienced salesperson was rendered more effective by her Sidekick performance support tool. Because I was interested, she also showed me short classes she could take online and coaches she could schedule to meet with, if she had questions.

The agent was out there on her own, but not really on her own, not the way it once was. The blend, featuring the performance support program, bolstered her sales skills and knowledge. No question about her willingness to use the program. Why? It flat out elevated her performance. Anybody could see that. No doubt she could too.

There are good reasons to house performance support within a blend. Studies report increased productivity for those using a blended approach, as opposed to e-learning alone (Thomson/NETg, 2003). Other studies have reported enhanced employee retention (Bersin, 2004; Nelson, 2005). Zenger and Uehlein (2001) reported that blended learning has been shown to achieve the same results as instructor-led training in 40 to 60 percent less time. While more investigation is necessary, these studies begin to establish a case for blending.

TARGET PRIORITY TOPICS

Stuart Grossman, now at Amgen in Thousand Oaks, California, has developed a handful of performance support tools for corporate and government clients. When asked about implementation, he remarked on the importance of topic selection. He said this in an email: "The project must be of high value to the people who are expected to use it and the people who own it or it will die on the vine because it is not used or updated regularly."

Grossman knows that performance support does not work particularly well with what one of the authors calls "Eat your vegetable projects." These efforts, spearheaded by leadership and lacking grass root support, are intended to encourage employees to do what they might not ordinarily do of their own volition.

Two such experiences come to mind. They involved situations in which leadership wanted employees to do something that they weren't all that inclined to do. Employees were not forcefully against it. It wasn't repulsive to them. It just wasn't top of mind. In one case, the audience was global salespeople, and the favored goal was consultative selling. Their Planner performance support tool was developed to aid them in preparation for interviewing potential customers. The other project targeted training professionals who were being nudged, through the availability of a performance tool, to think more broadly about interventions other than classroom training.

Performance support, in isolation from other approaches, will not compel people to do something that they are not inclined to do. Employees will not sell consultatively, deploy technology, or do anything else because software has appeared on their desktops, cell phones, or personal digital assistants. It is more likely that they will ignore that program and proceed with their habits and pre-occupations.

It is better to use the power of performance support to help people accomplish the things they are already inclined or required to do, and to help them to do those things better. Medicine provides a good example. As a doctor approaches a hospital bed, radio frequency identification (RFID) notifies her personal digital assistant about this patient's condition, history, medication, and recent test results. Of most interest in this example, the physician is also alerted to a new publication relevant to this patient's disease state. Standing beside the bed, the doctor is able to search the text.

ASSURE EXECUTIVE SPONSORSHIP

Successful implementation of performance support, not surprisingly, requires consistent and active sponsorship. The U.S. Coast Guard's leadership development program provides an example. In the past, ship executives helped junior officers select classes in somewhat idiosyncratic fashion. The Coast Guard (CG) endeavored to support their senior leaders in getting the right people to the right development at the right time. Figure 9.1 is a screen from the Unit Development Leadership tool. The online program enables diagnosis of individual needs and interests and then links resources to these personalized results.

Because so much was new about the Unit Development Leadership Program (ULDP), it required sponsorship. Fortunately, the CG got it. For the ULDP prototype rollout, a message was sent to all personnel from the Commandant. As the top stakeholder and ranking officer, he advanced the program by outlining how the ULDP matched his strategic goals for the CG.

Gary Dickelman (epsscentral.info), when asked about implementation of performance support, spoke first about sponsorship. He reports that he no longer focuses on mid-level managers. He seeks referrals to "C" level leaders. Once in touch with executives, he makes his case with examples that point to increases in revenue and decreases in costs. It's all about measures, he said, "Start there."

Figure 9.1 U.S. Coast Guard Unit Leadership Development Program Welcome Screen

Source: © 2005 U.S. Coast Guard. Used by permission.

When he walks through the door, Dickelman reports that he is prepared to share business cases. He is ready to talk about tangible improvements, based, for example, on a project for the Internal Revenue Service. He directed their attention to eight tasks, although there were hundreds more that could have been attended to. Through performance support for the selected eight tasks, the IRS reduced training and increased accuracy and completed work. He is able to point to $4M in savings. That story rivets sponsors.

Is your sponsor really a sponsor? Exhibit 9.1 raises questions about the role of executive sponsors in implementing performance support.

ESTABLISH A CROSS-FUNCTIONAL TEAM

In most organizations, the chief information officer "owns" information, Information technology controls instrumentation and software, and the definition of roles for managers and supervisors "belongs" to HR and training. As McManus and Rossett (2006) wrote, "Aligning these different entities requires sponsorship, finesse, articulated and shared goals, collaboration, and some good luck." One of McManus and Rossett's respondents, representing a global restaurant company, put it this way, "Get a multi-functional team." When his organization moved

---

Exhibit 9.1 Reflect on Executive and Performance Support

- Does the executive know what performance support is and what benefits the approach brings?

- Does the executive know the difference between performance support and training, why those differences are interesting, and how the two forms complement each other?

- Does the executive know how performance support programs typically fail?

- Where obstacles are anticipated, what mitigation is the sponsor helping to put in place?

- Has the executive worked to ready the IT organization and line leaders for performance support?

- Has the executive communicated the link between the support and strategic goals?

- Can the sponsor describe measures that will determine whether the program is working and how to use the data to continuously improve it?

- Is the executive sponsor ready to invest in maintenance and update?

toward online performance support, their team included the corporate office, field personnel, restaurant managers, and others with a stake in the initiative.

Who should be at the table to assure creation of the right system and a hospitable environment once it is released to the people who need it? Ask:

Who Represents the Content and the Message? Who knows what must be said? Who knows what knowledge underpins performance? Who knows what constitutes quality and where the processes break down? Who knows why things go well and why they go awry? That person or persons must be in a position to say "that is what we want to say about the new product" or "that is the rule we want to establish about qualifying for loans of that size."

Who Assures Timeliness and Maintenance? Who has a long view? Who can command attention once the program is no longer new or sexy? This person must be able to assure continued resources when others have moved on to the next new thing.

Who Represents the People Who Will Be Using the Program? Who knows their priorities, needs, concerns, and workplace constraints? That person or persons must be familiar with what goes on at work today and be knowledgeable about the near future too.

Who Represents Line Managers and Supervisors? Who can attract their attention and demonstrate value to them? Who can make certain that the performance support reflects their priorities and relevancies?

Who Represents the IT Organization? Who makes decisions about hardware and software for employees? Who controls what is installed on individual computers and mobile devices and how such programs are distributed and maintained? Who knows the software architecture and can assure that the tool is congruent with current and future efforts? Who will participate in selecting tools and in implementing them in the organization?

Who Holds the Purse Strings? Who approves the money for planning and development? Who assures that maintenance will be supported? Who will decide what is done inside and when to turn to vendors?

Who Owns Orientation and Other Key Classes? Who owns these events? Who can alter them? Will performance support tools be introduced and honored during these programs? Will individuals who look to performance support resources be respected for their curiosity and attention?

Who Represents Performance and Outcomes, Learning and Development? Who convenes this team? Who brings the group together throughout the process? Who assures a focus on outcomes and results? Who controls the tendency to pile on the content and maintains attention to what people need to achieve strategic goals? That person or persons must assemble the group, balance priorities, ask questions, and gather data about use, satisfaction, and value.

Cichelli and Marion (2004) wrote this about teaming on a successful performance support program built for the National Park Service:

> From a development standpoint, the system illustrates the value of coordinating the efforts of ISDs (instructional designers), who laid out the process in the proper detail and wrote explanations that performers would find clear and helpful, with those of ITs, who developed the sophisticated data modeling the system was built upon and used the appropriate technology (Microsoft.NET) to interact with the Oracle databases. By themselves, the ISDs would have been able to clarify and guide users through the processes, and to provide them with supporting materials, but the automation they would have been able to provide would have been much more limited and less sophisticated. By themselves, the ITs would have been able to design two easy-to-use applications, but they would not have addressed supporting performers through the entire work process, and both the work process and the two applications would have required substantial training. In this project, the contributions of both sets of professionals were enhanced through teamwork and a common vision that ultimately benefited performers.

PILOT AND CONTINUOUSLY IMPROVE

Because performance support is a new form, there will be glitches. Something new, complicated, and technology-based has a tendency to stumble. The goal, then, is to use a pilot to anticipate problems—in order to improve the program, fertilize the organization to appreciate it, and build support within the organization for the hard work to come.

Unfortunately, evaluation does not happen in most organizations. The environment in most organizations is not data rich. And when it is, that data is more likely to go in a file cabinet than to influence decisions. An Accenture survey of executives (Cheese, 2004) reported that only 18 percent received weekly or monthly reports about the effectiveness of their learning programs. That number exactly matches the one Rossett and Tobias (1999) found five years earlier when they asked workforce learning and performance professionals about their evaluation efforts.

When moving forward with contemporary approaches to technology, learning, and performance, such as those reflected in performance support, it is critical to include vivid and actionable measurement. Gary Dickelman said this about evaluation: "Nobody does it much. They don't know what to measure. They need to make these measurements so they can eventually make the case to keep going forward. Otherwise, they lose support for the efforts because they don't have a good handle on what difference performance support is making on key business results."

Rossett and McDonald (2006), in an article focusing on the changes in continuing medical education (CME), wrote: "Technology can narrow and sometimes remove the gap between learning and work. Thus the increase in technology-based CME offers opportunities for more expansive and authentic evaluations that are situated within learning, information, and practice. Questions about impact would be asked in juxtaposition with the work, when the physician is making diagnoses, ordering tests, communicating with colleagues and patients, undertaking research, and selecting treatments."

As reported by McManus and Rossett (2006), the Coast Guard's leadership program was released as a "pilot," with expectations set accordingly. Although the Commandant wanted to make participation mandatory, the design team lobbied successfully for a six-month trial period. "We wanted to let people play with it," notes the Coast Guard manager, "so we told personnel 'This is version 1.0; there are going to be issues, please help us make it better.'"

MEASURE AND CONTINUOUSLY COMMUNICATE

Data gathered during pilot testing can be used in two ways. The first way is described above. By providing insight into use and effect, beta testing allows professionals to tweak or more substantially amend the program and implementation.

The second way to use pilot data involves communication about results and improvements in order to garner support for the effort. Dickelman (2005) highlighted this benefit of proofs of concept. He remarked that these short, crisp prototype efforts and related measurements eventually make the case to advance the project. He pointed to a current project for the automotive industry. Eventually it will be a $4.5M project. Today it is a $250,000 pilot. His advice: "Slice off a representative piece. See that it works. Build support within the organization."

That support will engage people and assure support and resources for the emergent effort and for maintenance. Harvard's John Kotter (1998) emphasized the importance of short-term wins when bringing change to an organization. Colleagues are rarely patient. Keep them posted on progress. They want to know whether the organization and individuals are profiting from performance support. Are employees using the program? Do they return repeatedly? Do they recommend it to their colleagues and associates? How about results? Are salespeople selling solutions more effectively, writing proposals more rapidly, engaging with clients with more fluency and frequency? Are the leaders on ships convinced that they have a better fix on their young officers' needs? Are they able to point them to targeted resources? Are junior officers reporting benefits from the new system?

Kesmodel (2005) wrote about this in *The Wall Street Journal*:

> Technology companies like Google Inc. and Microsoft Corp. are changing the way they develop products by using the masses to identify problems in their unfinished programs, known as beta versions. For years, the term "beta" referred to a relatively short period of testing by a select group of outsiders. These days, beta editions are not only released to the public, but also stay in that mode for months, or even years. Google News, Google's news aggregator, has been in beta for three years. Microsoft's anti-spyware application has been in beta for nearly a year.
>
> Betas also have become a marketing device in a fiercely competitive industry, allowing software and Internet firms to release new products or services sooner and cultivate early buzz. Betas, which once had been quietly distributed, are trumpeted in press releases and at news conferences.

"I deplore it as a consumer; I admire it as a marketing profes-sional," said Peter Sealey, a marketing professor at the University of California at Berkeley and former chief marketing officer at Coca-Cola Co. "I can't come up with anything else in the entire marketing world where marketers knowingly introduce a flawed or inadequate product [and] it helps grow your user base."

If performance support is to contribute to individual and organizational per-formance, just about everybody needs to be talked to about the program and kept up-to-date on use, satisfaction, and results.

ADVANCE THIS NEW WAY OF DOING BUSINESS

The idea of performance-centered design (PCD), with performance support as a stellar instance, is new to many people and organizations. It represents a sea change for training and development.

According to Craig Marion (1997), PCD "is designed around performance, is intuitive to its users, and enables them to perform their normal work with obvi-ous gains in speed and efficiency without ever attending training classes or look-ing things up in books. It reflects their own conceptualization of their work and incorporates their language, idioms, metaphors, and understanding of how to perform tasks."

Marion and colleague Janet Cichelli (Cichelli & Marion, 2004) offered a fine example of a performance-centered approach, their Business Plan Developer for the U.S. National Park Service. National Park Service personnel, novices at busi-ness planning, are stepped through organizational activities and team building at the get-go. Then they are introduced to two applications, one for gathering data and the other for writing the plan. Use of the two applications is tied to the key deliverable, production of the business plan.

Frank Anderson and Chris Hardy (2005) described this new way of doing business in Figure 9.2, adapted by us for this book. Performance support is not training, although it is a good partner to training. What you see in Figure 9.2 depicts the possibilities. More democratic in its essence, performance support elevates the role of the individual and advances knowledge sharing and continu-ous access.

Figure 9.2 Performance Support in Context

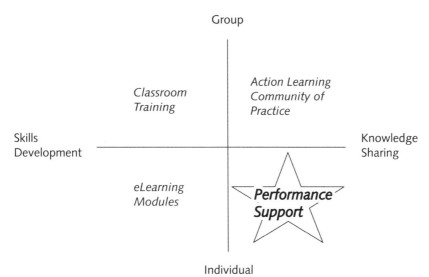

Source: Adapted from Anderson and Hardy, 2005.

In the past, the real estate agent or customer service representative tried to remember what was learned in class two months or even two years ago. Now, with a shift to just-in-time resources, the organizations' collective smarts are available where the work gets done, when it gets done. What real estate agent wouldn't want help in planning an approach to a customer, smartening up about patio homes or a new loan product, or using the tool as a Sidekick to enhance interactions with customers? What customer service rep wouldn't appreciate access to tips on how to handle a customer with a particular complaint?

But not everyone is keen on this new way of doing business. McManus and Rossett's 2006 study found managers who were described as "old school," not fully at ease with performance support or even the use of computers. What's to be done?

The answer, we think, is frank conversation leavened with examples. It is important to talk about and instantiate the new approach, to engage colleagues in reflections on what is admittedly a new strategy, and to compare the old way with the new. Success is most seductive. Measure results. Those numbers will foster and maintain enthusiasm.

People throughout the organization will wonder, "Where did the training go? What about our classes?" Admit to new experiences, assets, roles, and activities. Prepare to counter objections by pointing to benefits and results. Recognize units and individuals engaged in successful implementations for just-in-time approaches. Exhibit 9.2 spotlights learning and performance professionals. Are they advancing the conversation? Are they fertilizing the environment for performance support?

IMPLEMENT AS CHANGE MANAGEMENT

Alexander Hamilton articulated the problem for those interested in implementing any significant change, including, of course, performance support: "Experience teaches, that men are often so much governed by what they are accustomed to see and practice, that the simplest and most obvious improvements, in the [most] ordinary occupations, are adopted with hesitation, reluctance, and by slow gradations. The spontaneous transition to new pursuits, in a community long habituated to different ones, may be expected to be attended with proportionably greater difficulty."

In *The Prince,* Niccolo Machiavelli made the same point: "There is nothing more difficult to take in hand, more perilous to conduct, or more uncertain in its success, than to take the lead in the introduction of a new order of things. Because the innovator has for enemies all those who have done well under the old conditions and lukewarm defenders in those who may do well under the new."

Gary Dickelman wrote in his July 25, 2005, entry at the epsscentral blog:

> "I am reminded of Geoffrey Moore's book, *Crossing the Chasm*—the classic 'high-tech-product marketing 101' text that talks about innovation in terms of early adopters, early majority, late majority, and so forth. The concern of the IT or business executive who has internalized Moore's thesis is that performance support solutions and the technologies that enable them are the stuff of 'early adopters' and thus represent much risk on many levels. They think, for example, that there is not a large installed base, that the underlying technologies are untested on an enterprise scale, and that it is only a few lovers of high-tech toys in their organizations who are their champions. I submit that this point of view with respect to most classes of performance support development tools today is no longer valid."

Exhibit 9.2 The Role of the Learning Professional in Advancing Performance Support

Is the Learning Professional Leading the Way?

- Does the learning professional know what performance support is and the benefits it brings?

- Can the learning professional compare performance support and the ways the organization has delivered on its promises about learning and performance? Can this professional mount a conversation about the shift from a "culture of training" to this new model?

- Is the learning professional aware of how roles change with performance support?

- Does the learning professional know how programs typically fail? Where obstacles are anticipated? What mitigation is being put in place?

- Has the learning professional worked with line managers to define and advance their roles as coaches and guides?

- Has the learning professional developed or acquired assets that will compel employee attention and loyalty?

- Has the learning professional experienced performance support?

- Has the learning professional worked to strengthen the technology infrastructure for delivering the support?

- Has the learning professional altered the orientation to point to examples of just-in-time assets and altered the messages to reflect respect for looking to references when needs arise?

- Has the learning professional developed, piloted, and improved guidance systems that help employees find what they need when they need it?

- Is the learning professional engaged in selecting "sweet spots" for performance support topics and initiatives most likely to benefit from guidance in the workplace?

- Has the learning professional gathered data on the effectiveness of the program? Is that data improving the program and the implementation? Is that data appearing in front of people who ought to see it?

(See Chapter 7 for a list of these tools.)

What to do about this ancient and modern resistance? Table 9.1 draws on the change management literature, especially the work of Kotter (1988) and Rogers and Shoemaker (1971).

REVIEW OF CHAPTER 9

In this chapter, we introduced eight strategies for implementing performance support:

1. *Place performance support inside a blend.* When McManus and Rossett (2006) studied implementation for performance support, their subjects unanimously favored PST as one part of a blend. Blending typically involves an integrated combination of approaches, such as coaching by a supervisor, participation in an online class, attendance at a workshop, guidance from a performance support tool, breakfast meetings with colleagues, competency statements, reference to documentation, e-coaching by an expert, and participation in an online community. With a blended approach, the organization provides several coordinated ways of reaching strategic goals.

2. *Target priority topics.* Rather than exhortations, use the power of performance support to help people do the things that they already want to do or are required to do, and to help them to do those things better even than before.

3. *Assure executive sponsorship.* Here are just a few of the questions to consider when enlisting executives as active and consistent sponsors for performance support:

   - Does the executive know what performance support is and what benefits the approach brings?

   - Does the executive know the difference between performance support and training, and how they might complement each other?

Table 9.1 Treating Performance Support as a Change Management Challenge

Change Strategies	Applications to the Implementation of Performance Support
State the *advantages*	Why was the investment made? What difference is the performance support intended to make? How does this initiative match the organizational strategy? How have others benefitted from performance support for similar challenges?
Establish *compatibility*	How does the performance support advance shared goals and strategic directions? How does it match what people are already required to do? How does it match with top priorities and key obligations? How does it help people save time? How is it integrated into existing programs, such as orientation and compliance classes?
Keep it *simple*	If performance support is required to use the performance support, abandon all hope. Is the program easy to use? Does it match the challenges individuals confront at work? Is the language natural? Is jargon outlawed? Are guidance systems obvious and available? Are effort and progress tracked?
Set up *trials*	Has the program been tested? Has it been tested in the field by the intended users? Has it been improved as a result of the testing?
Allow them to *witness the impact*	Do people know what difference the program is making? Do they know how people are using it and how it is benefitting the users? How is data being gathered and transmitted to improve the program and inform colleagues? Deutschman (2005) noted that narratives change behavior, that stories more than facts move people. It is critical to encourage users to tell the stories of how the performance support has influenced target goals.

- Does the executive know how performance support programs typically fail? Where obstacles are anticipated, what mitigation is the sponsor putting in place?

- Has the executive worked to ready the IT organization and line leaders for performance support?

4. *Establish a cross-functional team.* Rossett and Tobias' 1999 study identified boundaries and white space in organizations, a situation that imposes barriers to the implementation of performance support. The best solution to this problem is to acknowledge it and gather a team that can transcend distinctions.

5. *Pilot and continuously improve.* Something new, complicated, and technology-based has many ways to stumble. The goal, then, is to use a pilot to anticipate issues, in order to improve the program as you go forward.

6. *Measure and continuously communicate.* John Kotter (1998) emphasized the importance of short-term wins when bringing change to an organization. Colleagues are rarely patient. They want to know whether the organization and individuals are profiting from performance support. Are employees using the program? Do they return repeatedly? Do they recommend it to their colleagues and associates? How about results? Gather data and communicate about benefits and modifications.

7. *Advance this new way of doing business.* In the old days, the real estate agent tried to remember what was said in class two months or two years ago. Now, with a shift to just-in-time resources, the organization's collective smarts are available where the work is done. What real estate agent would not want help in planning an approach to a customer, smartening up about patio homes or a new loan product, or using the tool as a Sidekick to enhance interactions with customers?

8. *Implement as change management.* State the advantages
   - Establish compatibility
   - Keep it simple
   - Set up trials
   - Allow them to witness the impact

PREVIEW OF CHAPTER 10

Chapter 10 extends into the future. In what directions are workforce learning and support going? What role will Planners and Sidekicks play?

RESOURCES

Anderson, F.J., Jr., & Hardy, C.R. (2005, May). Agile learning environments: Enhancing performance. *Chief Learning Officer,* pp. 26–32.

Bersin, J. (2004). *Blended learning: Finding what works.* Retrieved February 26, 2004, from www.clomedia.com/content/templates/clo_feature.asp?articleid=357&zoneid=30

Cheese, P. (2004). *The Accenture high performance work study.* Retrieved November 29, 2005, from www.accenture.com/NR/rdonlyres/378B3BDA-9061–4F13-B7F8-B3B026B69705/0/hp_study_2004_exec1.pdf

Cichelli, J., & Marion, C. (2004). Business plan developer. *Performance centered design awards 2004.* Retrieved December 20, 2005, from http://files.epsscentral.info/samples/2004_pcd_awards/BPD/SI-INTL%20inprod.htm

Deutschman, A. (2005, May). Five myths about changing behavior. *Fast Company,* p. 94.

Dickelman, G. (2005, December 12). Personal communication.

Glier, R. (2005, July 27). Is Tennessee football out of bounds? *USA Today.*

Hamilton, A. (1966). The report on the subject of manufactures. In H.C. Syrett (Ed.), *The papers of Alexander Hamilton,* Volume X. New York: Columbia University Press.

Hatcher, T. (1999). How multiple interventions influenced employee turnover: A case study. *Human Resource Development Quarterly, 10(4),* 365–382.

Kesmodel, D. (2005, November 28). For some technology companies, "beta" becomes a long-term label. *The Wall Street Journal Online.*

Kotter, J. (1998). *Winning at change.* Retrieved December 2, 2005, from www.pfdf.org/leaderbooks/L2L/fall98/kotter.html

Leonard, P. (2005). *Blended learning provides efficient, effective, measurable learning.* Retrieved August 1, 2005, from wwwmamanet.org/blended/PatLeonardArticle.htm

Marion, C. (1997). *What is performance-centered design?* Retrieved December 12, 2005, from www.chesco.com/~cmarion/PCD/WhatIsPCD.html

McManus, P., & Rossett. A. (2006, February). Performance support: Value delivered when and where it is needed. *Performance Improvement.*

Nelson, A. (2005). Deploying media-rich learning systems. *Chief Learning Officer, 4(5),* 45–47.

Rogers, E.M., & Shoemaker, F.F. (1971). *Communication of innovations: A cross-cultural approach* (2nd ed.). New York: The Free Press.

Rossett, A., & Frazee, R. (2006). *Blended learning opportunities: A white paper.* New York: American Management Association.

Rossett, A., & McDonald, J. (2006, February). Evaluating technology enhanced continuing medical education. *Medical Education Online.*

Rossett, A. & Mohr, E. (2004, February). Performance support tools: Where learning work and results converge. *Training and Development, 58*(2), 35–39.

Rossett, A., & Tobias, C. (1999). An empirical study of the journey from training to performance. *Performance Improvement Quarterly, 12*(3), 31–43.

Thomson/NETg. (2003). *Thomson job impact study.* Retrieved February 17, 2003, from www.netg.com/Upload/uk_ThomsonJobImpactStudy.pdf

Zenger, J., & Uehlein, C. (2001). Why blended will win. *T + D, 55*(8), 54–60.

CHAPTER

10

Into the Future

W e commence each year by consuming a feast of "Best of" lists. What technologies are in our immediate future? What gadgets? What do experts see happening to e-learning? To training and development? The 2006 lists include words like video podcasting, mobile learning, mashups, wikis, personal media aggregators, video, and $100 laptops. All present opportunities for moving knowledge from the classroom to knowledge everywhere.

The last two items on the list grab attention: video? $100 laptops?

Video intrigues because it is soooooo last century, and yet it is also so much more. What is different about video today, of course, is how much is possible for so little cost. The National Research Council of Canada's Stephen Downes was buoyant in *Elearn Magazine's* predictions for 2006:

> This is one of the easiest years to make predictions in some time: 2006 will be the year of video. From video-on-demand services such as sports, to distributed video (Reuters allows websites to run video for free), to vodcasting and other forms of consumer video, we will be awash in video this year. Expect also to see a continuation of the copyright debate, the continuing expansion of distributed web services (the "Web 2.0" phenomenon), and (as a result) an increasing emphasis on free and open content, at the expense of commercial

content. In e-learning proper, the migration away from commercial LMSs to Moodle, Sakai, and Bodington will continue, as will the less visible migration from LMSs altogether. In other words, the universe is unfolding as it should.

Imagine if computing power cost what a cell phone now costs. Nicholas Negroponte's Media Lab at MIT is collaborating with Taiwan-based Quanta Computers to make $100 laptops happen. Think of the access that people in developing countries will have to information, to record keeping, to the rule of law, where contracts can be recorded and accessed, no matter the country. Consider the ability to connect with distant family, potential business allies, or sage advisors, as needed.

In this chapter we wander into the future. Are we certain? Not at all. Are we optimistic? We are most definitely that. Here we attempt to tease out what the riches of technology and imagination mean to people blessed with a performance centric perspective. We begin with key changes in roles and responsibilities, and close the book by admitting to a few hesitations about performance support.

A NEW YOU

Yes, us. It is time to change what learning and performance professionals think about and do. It is time for us to study, learn, and focus in new areas. It boils down to the creation of supportive and information-rich environments and more technology, orchestration, measurement, and responsibility for results. Exhibit 10.1 highlights what professionals will do more of.

Some conventional activities will diminish in importance. First, and not surprisingly, delivery of training in rooms to groups will reduce in importance and frequency. Annual studies by ASTD and *Training* magazine confirm the slow, steady trend away from classroom delivery.

Once upon a time, people in our profession were in large part measured by their moments in rooms with students. While that will remain a portion of the work for some, no longer will it be at the center of the skill set. The profile of the classroom instructor will diminish, but of course not the importance of spreading expertise where it is needed. No longer will success in our profession be measured by the ability to stand and deliver training events.

Exhibit 10.1 More Focus on These Things in the Future

More . . .

- Performance support, where information and advice are delivered where and when needed

- Concern about results

- Measurement of results

- Use of results to plan and improve programs

- Interest in individual satisfaction and engagement

- Blending of education and support, formal and informal approaches, technology, and face-to-face options

- Creation of assets that can be accessed as needed

- Partnership with the line, where their needs and opportunities are anticipated

- Services and assets delivered where they are needed

- Orchestrations of programs that reach into the workplace and nudge employees, managers, supervisors, and even executives into roles associated with continuous growth and development in the context of work

---

Another task with lesser prominence will be design and development of training courses with collateral instructor and student guides. The professional will now be expected to create more kinds of materials, instructional *and* informational, many of which have been described in this book. Professionals will also work with vendors in the production of high-value assets, including performance support. Some will themselves acquire specializations in the creation of performance support Planners and Sidekicks. And some will become project managers, charged with coordinating the efforts of many to surround employees with resources and tools required to elevate performance.

When we look to our success, we envision a shift away from counting noses in classrooms, butts in seats, and hits on websites to the search for more subtle influences on strategic outcomes and daily habits. Are salespeople more fluent as they close sales? Do they close more sales? Do customers return to them for advice, even if it does not lead to an immediate sale? Do salespeople participate in online communities? Do they contribute to knowledge bases? Do they learn and seek informaton continuously? Do they acknowledge the need to learn about products, services, and vertical markets throughout their days and across their work lives?

It is common practice to give short shrift to Kirkpatrick's Level 1 evaluations, the level that represents an individual's satisfaction with the experience or program. Such individual satisfaction has often been cast as less worthy than higher Kirkpatrick levels, where outcomes are examined. While results are, of course, the reason for the effort, satisfaction and appreciation grow in importance in a performance-centric world. What salesperson or customer service rep or firefighter will look to performance support resources if he or she does not appreciate them? As organizations move away from classrooms and into blends delivered at work, employee approval elevates in importance. That positive reaction is critical, although not sufficient.

And there is one other matter. Recent practice esteems constructivist approaches. There isn't a graduate or certificate program that does not favor scenarios, cases, and problem-based learning. While it is hard to argue against these vivid, authentic, and engaging approaches, Paul Kirschner and colleagues (2006) raise questions about the wisdom of using minimally guided instruction, such as inquiry, problem-based, or project-based learning for novices or when new topics are introduced. They make this statement, "Controlled experiments almost uniformly indicate that when dealing with novel information, learners should be shown what to do and how to do it" (p. 8).

This does not mean the end of cases, webquests, scenarios, or realistic opportunities to practice. What it does encourage is more attention to preparation and orientation, to providing directions and worked examples, especially at the get-go. Rossett & Frazee (2006), while describing three forms for blended learning, encourage an anchor blend, where individuals new to the subject, role, or way of learning, are introduced in the classroom and then set free to use online resources, such as performance support.

A NEW THEM

The workforce is changing, as are the students who swiftly become the workforce. Ascione (2006) said this about students: "Today's students are 'digital natives' who someday will end up in digital schools. The question is what those digital schools will look like, what the rate of adoption will be, and what policy decisions will surround that process." Ascione's assumption, and one that holds true for many workplaces and homes in the developed world, is that technology and information, lessons, instructors, and events, not to mention music and entertainment, will be ubiquitous.

Work, learning, and reference are growing more identified and continuous (Tapscott, 1996). Responsibility thus shifts to the individual, student, or worker, who is expected to figure out what is needed, to take advantage of surrounding resources, and to go get them. There's the rub. Many are not ready for this independence.

And many prefer what they know—classroom experiences led by instructors—and are not particularly adept at getting their needs met independently, including through performance support. A proprietary study for a U.S. government agency found that, while executives and managers were keen on the shift to self-reliant technology-based learning, employees were less so.

In the best of all possible futures, jobs are redefined, performance management matches the new realities, and supervisors and managers are keen to nudge and coach their employees toward new roles, independent growth, and expectations for self-reliance.

But what happens when the world is imperfect? Rossett and Frazee (2006), Rossett and Schafer (2003), and Dunlap and Grabinger (2003) have tackled that question. Stretching the literature on self-reliant learning to the challenges presented to individuals by performance support, they tout approaches that encourage individuals to persist, refer, and benefit from an information-rich environment. Will employees look things up? Will they call upon these support resources, human and technological, when confronted with a problem or an irritated customer? Will they contribute to these resources? Will they keep coming back for more ideas and development?

There are reasons to assume that the transition will be halting. Exhibit 10.2 presents strategies to advance individual success in a performance-centric world.

ALMOST UNREMARKABLE

What if this new way were no longer worthy of remark? What if performance support was so integrated into work and life that it was scarcely noticed?

Exhibit 10.2 Helping People Embrace Performance at Work

- Provide obviously useful content.
- Be explicit about how the resources advance personal goals; provide examples and testimonials.
- Be explicit about how the resources advance organizational goals; provide proof and testimonials.
- Configure support so that it responds to typical and important dilemmas or challenges; personalize it as appropriate.
- Remind users of all they already know and how their knowledge helps them use the support.
- Provide examples of how the performance support resources have contributed already.
- Provide choices in amount of support: from hand-holding by a tool that does most of the work to a trusted, occasional advisor, to a provider of rare tips and hints.
- Ask for reflections on the value of the support; ask for suggestions about how it could be more useful.
- Report on adjustments and updates to the tool, especially on changes derived from user input.
- Provide rationale for why information and guidance were directed to that user.
- Ask supervisors to encourage employees toward performance support by remarking on the support they themselves use and on ways that employees can do the same.
- Honor efforts by employees to organize and maximize their resources.
- Build introduction to and examples about using performance support into orientation, training, and coaching.

Sherpa Performance Guides provides an example. The small San Diego-based company delivers a program designed to enhance effectiveness by increasing the capacity and support users enjoy from their personal information managers (PIM). Outlook, GroupWise, and Entourage are PIMs.

Sherpa Performance Guides embed a checklist inside the appointments located in the PIM itself. Embedded inside the calendar object is a hyperlink to performance support.

Once at the Sherpa Guidebook, individuals who have studied up on Sherpa.com access the latest Sherpa Beta Session Checklist content. They are reminded about key skills taught in classes focused on time management and productivity. They learn about externalizing (clearing the mind of tasks and other commitments), load balancing (adjusting project, task, and other priorities based on resource allocation), and making intentions (matching tasks with available resources).

Another example of the omnipresence of performance support was provided by the sister of one of the authors. Scheduled for a dim sum lunch with pals, she worried because she didn't know anything about dim sum and wasn't sure her pals did either. She turned to performance support in the form of *Dim Sum: A Pocket Guide* (Li, 2004). Queried about how the meal turned out, she reported, "Yup—used the book. Had an awesome lunch. Girls were grateful for my experience in 'dim summing,' and the cheater's handbook helped me look like I knew what I was doing." Her resourcefulness wasn't the least bit remarkable for her, and it enabled her and her friends to extract special joy from their lunch.

IS NOTHING SACRED?

Much that was taken for granted is now open to reconsideration because of the convergence of information and effort. Consider the topic of students, schools, and testing. Obviously, cheating is bad. That hasn't changed. But what about a young girl who turns to the Internet to help her take a test in her middle school classroom?

Gamerman (2006) described a thirteen-year-old in the middle of a vocabulary test. When stumped on the definition of "desolated," she turned to an online dictionary and soon won an A on the test. Was that cheating? Or was it the appropriate use of Sidekick performance support.

In this teen's world and in a growing number of institutions, the child is encouraged to look beyond memory to Sidekick support resources. How could this be? This is the way Ellen Gamerman (2006) put it in *The Wall Street Journal*: "In a wireless age where kids can access the Internet's vast store of information from their cell phones and PDAs, schools have been wrestling with how to stem the tide of high-tech cheating. Now, some educators say they have the answer: Change the rules and make it legal. In doing so, they're permitting all kinds of behavior that had been considered off-limits just a few years ago" (p. 1).

It boils down to questions about what we want children to learn in schools. Gamerman continues, "The real-world strengths of intelligent surfing and analysis, some educators argue, are now just as important as rote memorization."

This shift in expectations goes beyond the schools and into the world of workforce learning and performance. It affects sales, customer service, repair, and even leadership, as you saw in Chapter 8. The middle-schooler who is encouraged to look things up and beam messages back and forth with a classmate might just be more likely to grow into a seller or leader who refers to resources in the workflow and more naturally collaborates with colleagues.

Gamerman's (2006) article made another key point. The middle-schooler didn't get her A, the teacher explained, because she used the Internet to define "desolated." Her grade was earned because she generated a good sentence that used the word. The Internet helped, but it did not assure her grade. A clever blend of instruction and performance support made it happen.

CONVERGENCE!

Sherpa Performance Guides is devoted to helping people acquire new personal productivity habits. In the past, growth and change would have depended on classes.

While classes are still important to the Sherpa approach, the company now attempts to influence gnarly challenges when people are experiencing them, through that pervasive workplace tool, the PIM. They call it their "workflow" program.

Here are the principles that drive Sherpa's Workflow Program:

1. *Visual volume reduction:* Reducing unnecessary informational stimuli increases focus, heightens attention to priorities, and leads to better decision making.

2. *Intentionality:* Being systematic about deciding what to do and specifying exactly when and where to do it increases the likelihood of task completion.

3. *Tyranny of the inbox elimination:* Maintaining focus on intentions—without having attention diverted by information inflows or pressing but lower priority items.

How does Sherpa propose to accomplish and sustain such ambitious goals? They use blended learning and situate much of their effort where work and distractions happen. They insinuate support into daily challenges. Their program involves custom configuration of the PIM; face-to-face training; and live, weekly e-coaching sessions with a Sherpa guide.

The approaches confront reality. The training and coaching sessions are powerful, of course, but they end. What lingers is the PIM. Within it is the performance support, at work, converged with mundane and vivid pressures.

PERFORMANCE SUPPORT IS NOT MAGIC

Intel's Frank Nguyen (2006) said, "My perception is that many human performance technologists and trainers still perceive performance support tools as an enigma: They understand what they are, what they can offer, but most do not know where to begin designing or building one. In addition, the vast majority of performance support systems that have been developed over the years are targeted at a very specific performance problem (supporting help desk agents with common issues, field sales employees with product information, employees with performance on a software task). Oftentimes, the performance support system cannot be duplicated or extended to another performance problem without significant modification or enhancement, which can be expensive and time-consuming."

Seconding Gary Dickelman's view expressed in Chapter 7, Nguyen grew more optimistic:

> Fortunately, this appears to be changing. New technologies have been introduced and are being introduced to the market that will make it easier for human performance technologists to select from a variety of performance support interventions to mitigate a performance problem. For example, Laffey (1995) suggested that performance support systems could be "dynamic." In other words, rather

than be prescribed static systems, they could learn about the user and adapt content accordingly. While this was difficult if not arguably impossible to do in 1991, the advent of technologies available today, such as XML, RSS, and others, make it possible to profile a learner, intelligently deliver content based on their personal attributes, and even deliver content they subscribe to.

Figure 10.1, provided by Intel's Nguyen, illustrates the use of workflow diagrams derived from the business process modeling world. Rather than provide employees with FAQs or a search engine, visual representations of the work first explain and then support it, delivering instant access to appropriate support content.

Figure 10.2 illustrates a similar notion, but this time applied to equipment repair. Instead of flipping through volumes of paper-based manuals to find parts or repair procedures, technicians can instead navigate through a three-dimensional CAD diagram derived from the engineering field to locate the appropriate support information.

Figure 10.1 Performance Support Emerging from Business Process Modeling

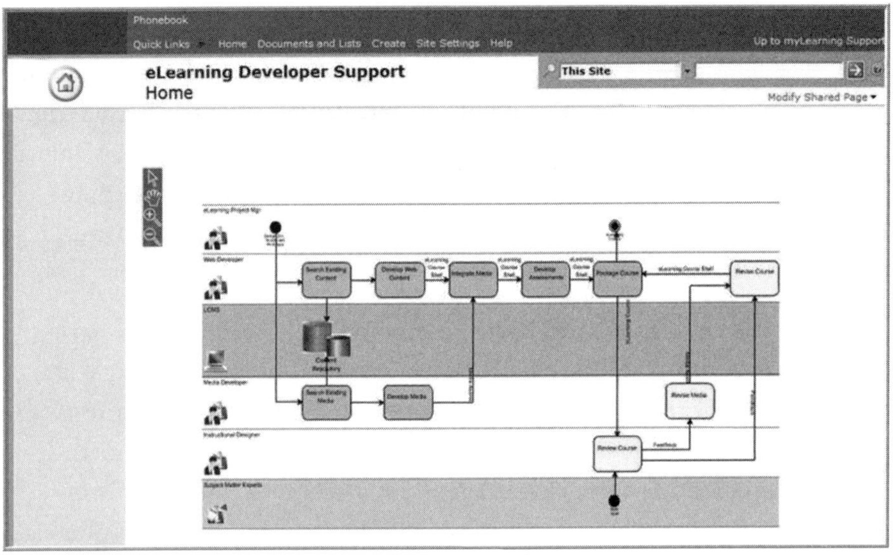

Source: Intel. Used by permission.

Figure 10.2 Performance Support Content Linked to Visuals from Equipment Diagrams

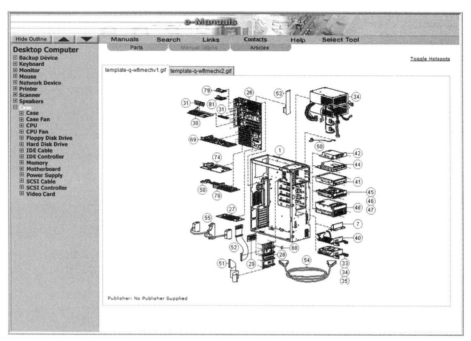

Source: Intel. Used by permission.

SMALL, MOBILE, AND PERSONALIZED

Reynolds (2006), in a blog about technology and learning, opined that education "still hasn't come to grips with what handheld devices really mean in terms of learning, but 2006 is the year when educators and content providers will start to get serious about the possibilities. Pushing learning content to hand-helds will be a big priority for the year, as will using these devices as extensions of larger learning frameworks like LMS (learning management system) platforms."

Learning via mobile devices may be late to the game, but small and mobile resources, with information and guidance delivered when and where needed, are happening today, and will be very much a part of the next decade.

Think back on the first time a rental car return agent checked in a car and handed over a receipt without moving his feet or asking you to move yours. That technology was a harbinger of wonders to come. Have you watched as the size of that support device has shrunk and speed and capacity have grown?

Another example was provided by torrential downpours. A few years ago, one of the authors returned from a rained-out vacation in Palm Springs to find that her roof had caved in to her bedroom. That unhappy moment was soon followed by a visit from the insurance adjuster, who said, "Too bad it was water damage. If that tree out there had fallen on the roof and knocked it into your bedroom, then we could pay for it all. Now we can't. Really too bad about that."

Definitely too bad. Still the company was able to pay for some portion of it, based on arcane regulations and policies. The adjustor did some measuring, asked some questions, and came up with a number. Peppered with questions, and some emotion too, he pointed to his computer. There were questions there, almost identical to the ones we were asking, with answers based on the insurance contract we had signed. The computer presented responses in friendly and soothing language—with hyperlinks to the contract.

That agent did a better than decent job with a cranky customer and difficult situation, in part because he had access to mobile support populated with assets that targeted likely customer concerns and questions. Even though the outcome was grim, it was hard to argue with it or the expertise delivered by the agent supported by his trusty tools. The agent had access to what he needed in the destroyed bedroom, in right-sized bites, and targeted to the issues that arose.

That was good for today. Consider tomorrow in a world smartened up and personalized by RFID (radio frequency identification tags). While shoppers move through the aisles at the supermarket, they can ponder their selections supported by recommendations keyed to budget, dietetic restrictions, haute cuisine combinations, or nutritional recommendations. Doctors too can enjoy small, customized messages that help them do their jobs better. For example, they can examine drug interactions and up-to-the-minute research based on RFIDs tagged to patient charts.

Williams (2006) discussed how body area networks (BANs) will free us from cumbersome cuffs or monitors to answer questions about our blood sugar or hydration needs. He explains:

> Body area networks rely on sensors embedded into "smart" fabrics and materials (researchers at MIT, for example, have built electronic circuits entirely from textiles). These sensors will eventually appear in a range of consumer products—from shoes to keyboard to jewelry and even makeup. They will monitor changes in our temperature and

other vital signs, as well as in our emotions and physical activity. They will transmit the results to interfaces that are already integral parts of our lives, such as cell phones, video screens, and appliances. Consumers, if they wish, will be able to set those sensors so that they transmit data to family, health practitioners, and trainers. However, the overarching goal is not to alert others in case of medical emergency but rather to monitor and respond to our own constantly shifting interior landscapes. This wellness-management model promises to reduce health care costs. (p. 37)

TAMING A DATA-RICH WORLD

Is there such as thing as too much of a good thing? Could organizations provide their people with too many resources and too little guidance?

In Chapter 7, we pointed to approaches used to sort and sift information. In Chapter 8, IBM described performance support put in place to make their plentiful resources even more valuable for sellers and managers.

Joe Williams, principal of Exegi Inc., knows that there is such a thing as too much of a good thing. He was brought in to help a large retail food company cope with this challenge. In his sidebar, he highlights two realities for the future. The first is organizations and employees flooded with valuable information. The second is the need to find a way to identify the right resource for this need at this time.

Is There Such a Thing as Too Much Information?

JOE WILLIAMS

The Need

A very large grocery company in the United States has an IT group of over a thousand employees. These technical professionals swim daily in a sea of information and continuous learning. However, getting access to these resources was often difficult and confusing. The result? They perceived lost opportunities to leverage valuable information, increased costs of redundant training events, and less effective workers.

(Continued)

The Solution

We envisioned a single point of contact for employees to access training, information, and tools to help them do their jobs more effectively. To achieve this goal, we designed a reference-based learning portal that provides a blend of training and support for job performance. From this portal, users can gain access to resources and stay informed about what's happening in the IT community.

The heart of the system is in the five menu items along the top of the home page. From that top navigation bar, users can discover the range of support options, from training to job aids, available to help them do their work more effectively.

- *Get Training* links users to hundreds of courses that address both technical and "soft" skills as well as the schedule of planned classroom training. Users can even request a course that meets their unique needs.

- *Get Information* provides access to online books, articles, and white papers, as well as links to other sites with useful information.

- *Work with Others* is a forum for internal study groups, allowing online discussions as well as scheduling in-person study groups.

- *Ask the Expert* captures the knowledge of the company's experts. Users can learn who has expertise in a particular area and contact him or her. Presentations on particular subjects are archived here, and live chats can be scheduled to provide knowledge transfer from experts to novices.

- *On the Job* provides useful tools to enhance performance. Here users find job aids and best practices, such as reference architectures for application design.

The Effects

Since coming online in late 2004, popularity has grown steadily, based on the number of hits on the site and on usage statistics for online courses. User surveys indicate that people are still relying largely on traditional training resources, but are increasingly accessing the site for job aids and current information and news affecting the IT community. We're achieving the desired goal of providing a forum for IT workers to share their knowledge and learn from others.

WHAT IS IT?

Is it a job aid, a computer, a cell phone, e-learning, or performance support? The distinctions were once clear. They are not clear today.

Come to the doctor's office. It was surprising to see a well-thumbed *WebMD* magazine in the waiting room. But *WebMD* is an online health website?!? Or is it a glossy magazine? The confusion is confirmed by the popular Babycenter.com, which is taking its dot comness to print in stores and offices near you. Turns out, according to Lee (2006), publishers believe that print readers spend more on the products they see in ads than do online readers. Enter magazines crafted for women with various relationships to babies. Babycenter.com has one for expectant moms, another for the parents of the newborn, and yet another for the toddler's mother. Not surprisingly, both the content and the ads alter to match the mom.

Newspapers, on the other hand, are pushing their content online. No problem following San Diego's pension scandals or the Padres while on the road in Singapore. The newspaper is online.

The content is swinging both ways, with more to come. What is a podcast delivered on a cell phone or to an MP3 player or streamed on a laptop? Is it e-learning? Is it knowledge management? Is it performance support? If the content supports a tour of the new Tate Gallery and helps us to understand and appreciate contemporary art, is it performance support or e-learning?

The trend intrigues. Some users will locate a recipe or advice or guidelines that they want and print them for reference when needed. Others will load an e-coach's podcasted advice on a cell phone and take it along on the sales call. And some will take advantage of mobile book-like devices.

The battery capacity of a new device by Sony is astonishing, with claims that you can read the equivalent of fifteen books without a power charge. That could be a lot of guidance and documentation available pretty much wherever you want it. Is it performance support? Is it instruction?

This raises questions about those old, favored distinctions. Intel's Frank Nguyen (2006) believes that the walls between interventions are blurring:

> Training and performance support will become complementary rather than opposing interventions. In particular, the lines between e-learning and performance support will blur. Related to the technology evolution mentioned earlier, certain LMS and LCMS vendors are introducing capabilities to maintain deep links into learning objects stored inside traditional training content repositories. While some-what trivial at first glance, this capability can be a very powerful tool for a human performance technologist or trainer. For instance, in a business process performance support system, one might traditionally link to a help file or web page on the intranet to deliver support content for a task or procedure in the workflow. In the future, one can link directly to a relevant learning object inside the LCMS originally developed for e-learning delivery. The same approach can be applied to content-sensitive help for software procedures, frequently asked question pages, and any other problem-specific support system. By doing so, this reduces the redundancy in content development time and cost and improves data quality, as content no longer needs to be developed and maintained in two different systems for training and reference purposes.

A GRAIN OF SALT

Should we pause before we wholeheartedly embrace this form? While we encourage the shift to performance support, the time has come to admit some concerns. Three concerns to conclude what has been, admittedly, a performance support love fest.

Beyond Knowledge Transmission

Dave Jonassen (2005), in a piece posted on the *Instructional Technology Forum,* noted that the purpose of education is the solution of problems. He contrasted problem solving with knowledge transmission, pointing out that most education models tout content acquisition over and above engagement with authentic challenges. Jonassen wrote, "The knowledge transmission paradigm of education assumes an absolutist epistemology, where content is believed to represent the truth."

Much of performance support is, of course, a collection of content, intended to inform and guide as needed. But does the user know how to use it? Does he know when to use it? Is content connected to the problem or concern? Does she use it wisely and well? Can she find what she needs? Can he adjust for this situation and client? Does she possess the necessary scaffolding, experiences, and ethical tenets to sift and sort and perform? Does he know the limits of his ability to use the support? Does she appropriately question the quality of the advice?

Let's apply this concern to what would have to be one of the most difficult moments—the grim circumstance of what to do when a friend is threatening suicide. Concerned, you go to a website that promises to help. Even though you scrupulously follow the advice, it doesn't go well at all. Your friend almost succeeds. It was a close call.

It would have been far better to press your friend to seek professional help, and even to accompany him for that counsel. The online support gives the illusion you know what you're doing when you don't know much at all. Instead, it should help recognize a situation that is not for novices. It should alert you that you have reached the limits of your knowledge.

No sin if you feel all pumped up about removing the odor of fish from a house or preparing the wall for painting. How much harm can you do? But when a life is at stake, performance support could be boosting confidence when it ought not.

Much knowledge work can be aided, of course. For the above painful example, performance support does have something to offer the individual who seeks to assist a distressed friend: How to find a local Spanish-speaking psychologist. How to find one who specializes in suicide or depression. How to find one on the south side of town or one who works nights. But when it comes to connecting complex principles to unclear conditions, well, it makes sense to find someone who has experience with solving these kinds of problems over time and with many people and circumstances. Yes, education. Good and plentiful education. Performance support is no substitute for education in such a case.

That's the first concern about performance support. The second reminds us that not everybody will be able to use support without a hitch. The technology can be an impediment, both in its use and in access to it.

The Less-Savvy User

An article about online dementia care reminded of the many with learning and performance needs. Not all will thrive when expected to take on their own support. McDonald, Stodel, and Casimiro (2005) described an online facilitator who said, "The learners need a basic computer course in order to navigate the course more efficiently and effectively—how to operate the computer, how to access different programs, how to use a mouse, how to write an email, how to post an answer on the forum, how to move to and from one part of the course content to another without getting lost, how to navigate the system, [and] how to import text for another program."

Left to their own devices, many won't or can't or shouldn't act on their own—even with a little help from the Internet. Many need parents, teachers, older siblings. *The Wall Street Journal Online* (December 30, 2005) revealed one of the problems associated with a pull-driven world. What were the top search terms at Yahoo in 2005? Britney Spears, 50 Cent, Cartoon Network, and Mariah Carey. Paris Hilton and Eminem were not far behind. If you think this is a Yahoo problem, let's look at AOL. Their top items were lottery, horoscope, and tattoos. No kidding.

Look what moves people to take advantage of the rich resources of the web. It makes you wonder whether school children will search long and well. Will employees leverage their resources? Will individuals use home and mobile assets to create better lives and communities?

As we place more learning and support resources in the hands of individuals, we must remain cognizant that there are those who will require support and guidance to benefit.

Over-Reaching

The third concern is not as serious as the first two. But it matters. It is the problem of performance support usurping the textured and human judgments that make us who we are. It is support that sticks its nose just about everywhere. Is there such a thing as a performance support system that is too smart for our own good?

We now have tools that pick music, dates, and retirement locations for us. Rather than sampling music, chatting with friends, borrowing DVDs, and wheedling away hours in unfamiliar locations, performance support saves time. But is it stealing opportunities for experiences? Is the iPod pointing you to tunes like those you already favor? Will it surprise you? Will it expand your musical tastes? Does support reduce the likelihood of innovation?

Let's consider dating and retirement. Instead of playing the field and spending time with many people and in many places, less is invested in the process. Online tools query the user, and then programmed logic points to likely people and locations. Charlotte or San Diego? Charlotte or Mary Lou? The tool points the way. But is something lost in the process?

STILL, A VERY GOOD THING

Rossett and Mohr (2004) told a popular story about Dr. Albert Einstein. When a reporter asked whether he could have the great man's phone number, Einstein replied, "Certainly." Then he picked up the phone directory, looked up his number, wrote it on a slip of paper, and handed it to the reporter. Dumbfounded, the reporter said, "You're considered to be the smartest man in the world and you can't remember your own phone number?" Einstein's reply: "Why should I memorize something when I know where to find it?"

That is exactly the point.

But there is even more to say about it today and in the future. Your address book is a fine example of Sidekick support. We all profit from expanded immediacy, tailoring, mobility, and personalization, from address books that go where we go and allow us to electronically search for the person we met in Dallas or Dublin two Decembers ago.

This chapter and the book are chock full of examples of support that goes along for the ride, delivering advice and guidance when needed, or just before or after. It saves time. It saves money. Used appropriately, performance support even saves lives.

Remember the Coast Guard and support for boarding officers? Remember pre-flight check lists. Consider the IBM and Intel examples that touch support for everything from manufacturing to selling to leadership. Think back on the auto repair support beamed to the eyelids of mechanics. Appreciate portals that help you find just what you need when you know it is out there somewhere, if only you could find it, whether the topic is earthquake mitigation, retirement, leadership, or hip hop.

This started out to be a revision of *A Handbook of Job Aids.* That did not turn out to be the case. It's a whole new story and a whole new world. We hope you are as delighted about it as we are.

RESOURCES

Anderson, F.J., Jr., & Hardy, C.R. (2005, May). Agile learning environments: Enhancing performance. *Chief Learning Officer,* pp. 26–32.

Ascione, L. (2006, January 12). *Major study to probe ubiquitous computing.* Retrieved January 12, 2006, from www.eschoolnews.com/news/showStoryts.cfm?ArticleID=6060

Bersin, J. (2004, February 26). Blended learning: Finding what works. *Chief Learning Officer.*

Davenport, R. (2006, January). The future of the profession. *Training and Development, 60*(1), 41–46.

Dickelman, G. (2005, December 12). Personal communication.

Dolezalek, H. (2006, January). Who has time to design? *Training, 43*(1), 24–28.

Downes, S. (2006, January). Predictions for 2006. *elearn Magazine.*

Dunlap, J.C., & Grabinger, S.(2003). Preparing students for lifelong learning: A review of instructional features and teaching methodologies. *Performance Improvement Quarterly, 16*(2), 6–25.

Gamerman, E. (2006, January 21). Legalized cheating. *The Wall Street Journal Online,* p. 1.

Johnson, B.C., Manyika, J.M., & Yee, L.A. (2005). The next revolution in interactions. *The McKinsey Quarterly, 1.*

Jonassen, D.H. (2005). Let us learn to solve problems. *Instructional technology forum.* Retrieved February 9, 2006, from http://it.coe.uga.edu/itforum/paper83/paper83.html

Kirschner, P.A., Sweller, J., & Clark, R.E. (2006, January). Why minimal guidance during instruction does not work. *Educational Psychologist, 4*(1).

Laffey, J. (1995). Dynamism in electronic performance support systems. *Performance Improvement Quarterly, 8*(1), 31–46.

Lawler, E.E., III, & Mohrman, S.A. (2003). *Creating a strategic human resources organization.* Stanford, CA: Stanford Business Books.

Lee, L. (2006, January 9.) Call it Guttenberg's revenge. *BusinessWeek,* pp. 29–30.

Li, K.S. (2004). *Dim sum: A pocket guide.* San Francisco: Chronicle Books.

Lucas, C. (2005, December). Grade-a-matic. *Edutopia: The new world of learning.* Retrieved January 18, 2006, from www.edutopia.org/magazine/ed1article.php?id= art_1411&issue=dec_05

Marion, C. (1997). *What is performance-centered design?* Retrieved December 12, 2005, from www.chesco.com/~cmarion/PCD/WhatIsPCD.html

MacDonald, C.J., Stodel, E.J., & Casimiro, C. (2005, December). Online training for healthcare workers. *eLearn magazine.* Retrieved December 14, 2005, from http://elearnmag.org/subpage.cfm?section=case_studies&article=33–1

McStravick, P. (2006, January). Looking forward: The learning and development industry in 2006. *Chief Learning Officer, 5*(1), 52–56.

Meyer, K. (2005, December 30). Tabs on tech. *The Wall Street Journal Online.*

Nguyen, F. (2006, January 26). Personal communication.

Reynolds, R. (2006, January 2). Technology trends for 2006. *Xplanezine Futuremeter.* Retrieved February 9, 2006, from www.xplanazine.com/archives/2006/01/technology_tren.php

Rossett, A., & Frazee, R. (2006). *Blended learning opportunities: A white paper.* New York: American Management Association.

Rossett, A., & McDonald, J. (in press). Evaluating technology enhanced continuing medical education. *Medical Education Online.*

Rossett, A., & Mohr, E. (2004, February). Performance support tools: Where learning work and results converge. *Training and Development, 58*(2), 35–39.

Rossett, A., & Schafer, L. (2003, June). What to do about e-dropouts: What if it's not the e-learning but the e-learner? *Training and Development, 57*(6), 40–46.

Tapscott, D. (1996). *The digital economy: Promise and peril in the age of networked intelligence.* New York: McGraw-Hill.

Weinstein, M. (2006, January). What does the future hold? *Training, 43*(1), 18–23.

Williams, D. (2006, February). The HBR list: Breakthrough ideas for 2006, Can I hear me now? *Harvard Business Review, 84*(2), 37–38.

Index

Fogg, B.J., 4

Fontaine, M., 158

Football wristbands: background of, 108–109; as sidekick support for football plays, 109*fig*–110

Formats. *See* Performance support formats

Frazee, R.V., 122, 189

G

Gamerman, E., 32, 191, 192

Gautier-Downes, J.D., 4, 35, 56, 123

Gery, G., 37, 150, 165

Gifford, C., 86

Gilbert, T., 24

Glier, R., 166

Goggins, R., 81, 82, 85

Goggle, Inc., 44

Goodrum, D.A., 48

Google Earth, 77

Google Inc., 176

Google News, 176

Gordon, J., 41

Grabinger, S., 189

Graphical format: college savings shortfall displayed in, 131, 132*fig*; described, 125–127; Snow's Map of Cholera Deaths, 125–126, 127*fig*

Grossman, S., 168

GTE, 31

H

Hamilton, A., 180

A Handbook of Job Aids (Rossett & Gautier-Downes), 22, 29, 49, 204

Hanna, S.E., 48

Hansen, E., 110

Hardin, D., 8

Hardy, C., 177, 178

Harless, J.H., 4, 31, 32, 123

Haynes, R.B., 48

Heller, J., 6

HIPAA, 21

Hoffmeyer, M., 108

Hubbard, L., 48

Human Performance Technology (or Human Performance Improvement), 24

Hunt, D. L., 48

Hutchins, E., 20

Hyperion Solutions Corporation, 96

I

IBM performance supports: abundance and effectiveness of, 131, 163; Manager Portal, 152–154*fig*, 158, 160; On Demand Learning (ODW), 150–151; Seller's Workplace, 151–152, 152*fig*, 156, 157*fig*, 160*fig*, 161*fig*, 162; Signature Selling Method (SSM), 156

Implementation. *See* Performance support strategies

Indianapolis Star (newspaper), 100

Inform and decide formats: coach format, 125, 126*fig*; decision table format, 129*fig*; graphical format, 125–127*fig*, 132*fig*; list format, 124–125; savings options using, 131, 133*fig*

Information: future needs and management of, 197–199; job aids in securing and organizing, 32–33; traditional job aids supporting, 56. *See also* KM (knowledge management)

Information overload, 33

Information Week's 2005 annual survey, 43

Instructional Technology Forum, 200

Integration. *See* Performance support-work integration

Intel, 193, 203

International Data Corporation, 139

Internet: examples of Planners on, 77–78; Google Earth, 77; navigation format used on the, 130; search format used on the, 130–131. *See also* Websites

Interservice Procedures for Instructional Systems Development, 31

Intrinsic support, 37, 38*t*

iViz Group, 96

IvVo, 56

J

Jack in the Box: Computer-Based Training Main Menu, 90*fig*; electronic library used by, 87–88, 89; New Product Sidekick Performance Support, 68*fig*; Reference Materials, 89*fig*

JM Family Enterprises' Toyota dealership, 43

Job aids: assessing employee skills and abilities to use, 28–29; benefits of, 5–7; early form of, 31–32; employee motivation to use, 29; implications of using, 32; resistance to, 121; supporting procedures and information, 32–33; thought-provoking, 33–36. *See also* Performance support

Johnston, B.R., 48
Jonassen, D., 200–201
Jupiter Research, 63

K

Kasvi, J.J., 48
Kesmodel, D., 176
Key learning indicators (KLI), 92
Kirkpatrick's Level 1 evaluations, 188
Kirschner, P.A., Sweller, J., & Clark, R.E., 188
Klein, J.D., 48
KM (knowledge management), 46. *See also* Information
KMWorld (journal), 46
Knapczyk, D., 48
Knowledge engineering, 43–44
Kotter, J., 176, 180

L

Ladd, C., 48
Laffey, J., 193
"The law of diminishing astonishment," 165
Learning: blended, 166–168; LMS (learning management system), 194, 200; moving STM into LTM for, 20; ODW (On Demand Learning) [IBM] approach to, 150–151
Leclair, R., 48
Lee, L., 199
Leighton, C., 48
Levy, J., 9, 42
Lewis, N., 162
Li, K.S., 191
Library of Congress inline learning center demonstrations: background of, 105–106; Bubble Text Documents Necessary Steps page, 107*fig*; compared to Salesforce.com Interaction Coach, 116; rollout of, 108; Show Me How page of, 106*fig*; using technology to streamline development, 108; Text Within Bubbles Provides Demonstrations page, 107*fig*
Lifting Equation (NIOSH), 81–82
Lifting operations calculator: background of, 81; online calculator does the math for you, 84*fig*; paper-based calculator for analyzing lifting operations, 83*fig*; for simplifying a complex assessment, 81–82, 84; tailored-step format of, 124
List format, 124–125
LMS (learning management system), 194, 200

Locating information formats: navigation format, 130; search format, 130–131
LTM (long-term memory), 19–20

M

McCabe, C., 48
McDonald, C.J., 202
McDonald, J., 175
Machiavelli, N., 180
McKellar, H., 46
McManus, P., 48, 67, 172, 175, 178, 182
Macromedia Captivate, 108, 141
McStravick, P., 137, 139
McTighe, J., 78, 80
Magnolia's story, 55–56, 73*fig*–74*fig*
Manager Portal (IBM), 152–154*fig*, 158, 160
MapQuest, 60
MapQuest Find Me, 60
MapQuest Mobile, 60
Marion, C., 149, 150, 174, 177
Measuring results, 175–177
Memory: investing in external support assets versus, 68–69; long-term and short-term, 19–20; processing information using working, 21
Microsoft Corp., 176
Mike's Express Carwash, 100, 120
Mike's Express Carwash poster: background of, 100–101; blended solution using, 101; decision to not use technology in, 133–134; how it works, 101–103; panel 1 restrictions poster, 102*fig*; panel 2 displaying high-risk items, 103*fig*; panel 3 showing items requiring attendant attention, 104*fig*; as "simple tool," 104
MIT Media Lab, 186
Mobile performance support, 44–47, 194–196
Mohr, E., 6, 42, 122, 203
Moore, C., 91, 94, 95
Moore, G., 180
Morrison, J.E., 48
Motorola, 3
MP3 players, 45
My Opportunities (IBM Seller's Workplace), 151, 156*fig*

N

National Institute for Occupational Safety and Health (NIOSH) Lifting Equation, 81–82
National Park Service, 177
National Research Council of Canada, 185
Navigation format, 130

NCR Global Learning, 94, 95
Negroponte, N., 186
Nelson, A., 168
The New Yorker, 3
Nguyen, F., 47, 48, 49, 193, 200
Nielsen, J., 125, 126, 150
NYSE (New York Stock Exchange), 136

O

O'Driscoll, T., 7–8, 41, 155
ODW (On Demand Learning) [IBM], 150–151
Organizational culture: encouraging job aids, 32; performance support readiness of, 122–123
Organizations: battle for talented and self-reliant employees, 45–47; outsourcing by, 137–139*t*; performance support readiness of, 122–123. *See also* Employees; Workplace
Outsourcing: issues to consider in, 138*t*–139*t*; reasons for, 137–138; selecting vendors for, 139–141
Oxley, S., 21

P

Parsimony, 7–8
PCD (performance-centered design), 111, 150, 177
PDA (personal digital assistant): anticipated increase in use of, 45; benefits of using, 9, 41
Pennsylvania state police, 40
Performance support: appropriate times for using, 19–26; audience of, 120–121, 137; Cavanaugh's 2E31 Spectrum of, 37, 38*t*–39*t*; connections between instruction and, 10–11; debate over real purpose of, 66; definition of, 24; economic worth reason for, 8–9; external and extrinsic, 37, 38*t*; future of, 185–204; inappropriate times for using, 26–29; job aids in context of, 5–7; memory versus inventing in, 68–69; parsing, 64–71; resistance to, 121; "smartness" of, 134–137; value of, 144; what it is not, 4–5; what we know and don't know about using, 47–49. *See also* Job aids; Using performance support
Performance support benefits: mobile support as, 44–47, 194–196; overview of, 7–9, 203–204; performance results as, 42; support where the work is done, 43–44
Performance support effectiveness: creating your own, 163; eight principles for, 155–162; IBM performance support examples of, 131, 150–154*fig*, 163; quality issues of, 149–150

Performance support formats: coach format, 125, 126*fig*; combining different, 131; decision table form, 129*fig*; graphical format, 125–127*fig*, 132*fig*; list format, 124–125; navigation format, 130; quiz format, 127–128*fig*; search format, 130–131; step format, 123–124; tailored-step format, 124
Performance support future: convergence leading to, 192–193; digital savvy workforce and, 188–189, 190*e*; emerging from business process modeling, 193–194*fig*; facilitating performance support for less-savvy user, 202; highlights of, 186–188, 187*e*; learning via mobile devices, 194–196; new technological innovations for, 185–186, 199–200; new uses of performance support, 200–202; over-reaching concerns, 202–203; performance support content linked to visuals, 194, 195*fig*; Sherpa Performance Guides example of, 189, 191, 192; taming data-rich world as part of, 197–199
Performance support history: beginnings of performance support-work integration, 37–41; Cavanaugh's 2E31 Spectrum of Performance Support, 38*t*–39*t*; contemporary state of performance support, 41–47; Gery's work on performance support, 37; technological origins, 36–37
Performance support principles: 1: performance support is tied to achieving business objectives, 155; 2: performance support helps to define, track, and achieve goals, 155–156; 3: focus on what really differentiates great performance, 156, 158; 4: performance support recognizes and delivers needed help, 158–159; 5: performance support helps collaboration, 159–160*fig*; 6: great performance speaks in language of work/worker, 160–161; 7: performance support provides what is needed, 161–162; 8: performance support helps people act smarter than they are, 162
Performance support strategies: advancing this new way of doing business, 177–179*e*; assuring executive sponsorship, 169–172*e*; blending strategy, 166–168; establishing cross-functional team, 172–174; implementing as change management, 180–181*t*; measuring and continuously communicating, 175–177; piloting and continuously improving, 174–175; role of learning professional in, 179*e*; targeting priority topics, 168–169

Performance support tailoring: described, 57; finding a destination example of, 58, 59*t*, 60–61*fig*; flip side of, 63–64; parsing, 64–66; pizza delivery example of, 58*fig*; Sidekick and Planner types of, 66*fig*–71

Performance support-work integration: degree of performance support/work, 56–57; finding a destination example of, 58, 59*t*, 60–61*fig*; flip side of, 61–63; history of, 37–41; parsing, 64–66; pizza delivery example of, 57–58*fig*

Performance-centered design (PCD), 111, 150, 177

Personalization: myth of, 63–64; performance support, 8–9

Pilot programs, 174–175

PIMs (personal information mangers), 189

Pipe, P., 32

Pizza delivery performance support, 57–58*fig*

Planners: described, 40, 64; integrated supports, 64, 65*fig*; tailored and standard, 66*fig*–71; when to use, 99

Planners applications: calculator for lifting operations, 81–85; CLO Dashboard, 91–96; electronic reference library, 87–91; examples of, 41, 77–78; sales rep incentive tool, 85–87*fig*; UbD rubric for teachers, 78–81

Planning: integration used in, 61–63; performance support for, 38–39

Pompei, D., 110

Porter, W., 39

The Prince (Machiavelli), 180

Procedures: job aids for, 32–33; SOPs (standard operating procedures) automated, 64; steps to complete task dictated by, 123; traditional job aids supporting, 56

Q

Quality issues, 149–150

Quinn, B., 110

Quitnet.org, 60

R

Rae, S., 41

Raybould, B., 47

Relevance, 8

Reynolds, R., 194

RFID (radio frequency identification): benefits of using, 9; personalization through, 196; tasks accomplished using, 169

RoboDemo, 108

Rocket Software's ActiveGuide Web Studio, 116

Rogers, E.M., 180

Rosenberg, M.J., 24, 25, 42, 48

Rossett, A., 4, 6, 9, 35, 42, 48, 56, 67, 120, 122, 123, 172, 174, 175, 178, 182, 189, 203

Rosson, M. B., 47

Rubistar, 81

Rubric for teachers: background of, 78; to help students create curriculum, 80*t*; ironic twist of, 79, 81; reflecting on performance of, 79

S

Saign, D., 46

Sales Navigator Portlet (IBM Seller's Workplace), 151, 157*fig*, 161*fig*

Sales rep incentive tool: background of, 85; content and delivery of, 86; transitioning to a new sales incentive plan, 87*fig*

Salesforce.com Interactive Coach: background of, 110–111; Coach endeavors to reduce chance of error, 114*fig*; coach format of, 125; Coach helps users tailor the application, 115*fig*; Coach points to action to take, 113*fig*; Coach providing task guidance and context, 113*fig*; compared to Library of Congress' demonstrations, 116; development of, 116; highlights of embedded support by, 111–115; new mindset for using, 116–117; users select preferred level of support, 112*fig*

Saltzman, P., 48

Salvatore, R., 88, 91

SAP (software system giant), 69, 71

SAT (Scholastic Aptitude Test), 22, 32

Saving options decision table, 131, 133*fig*

Schafer, L., 189

Schaffer, S., 9, 69

Schramm, W., 39

Schwab.com, 60

Schwen, T.M., 48

Sealey, P., 176

Search format, 130–131

Self-service workplace, 42

Seller's Workplace (IBM): main page of, 153*fig*; My Opportunities Portlet within, 151, 156*fig*; overview of, 151–152; Sales Navigator Portlet within, 151, 157*fig*, 161*fig*; salespeople on their experiences with, 162; Teams and Experts Portlet in, 151, 160*fig*

Sexual harassment, 67–68, 69

and technology options for, 131–137; out-sourcing decision, 137–139*t*; selecting vendors, 139–141; software tools for, 141–143*t*. *See also* Performance support

V

Van Dam, N., 42
Vartiainen, M., 48
Vendor selection, 139–141
Villachica, S.W., 122
Visual Mining, 96

W

The Wall Street Journal, 40, 176, 191
The Wall Street Journal Online, 202
Washington State Department of Labor and Industries, 81, 83, 84
Waterman, J.D., 46
Waterman, R.H., Jr., 46
WebMD magazine, 199
Websites: American Management Association blending white paper, 166; clearningmag.com, 41; ehelp.com, 64; Ehow.com, 8; EPSSCentral, 111, 144; FEMA's checklist, 34; on influenza maps, 126; Lifting Equation (NIOSH), 81–82; lifting operations calculator, 85; navigation format used in, 130; performance centered design (PCD), 150; Quitnet.org, 60; Rocket Software's ActiveGuide Web Studio, 116;

Rubistar, 81; Schwab.com, 60; search format used to locate, 130–131; on user interface design guidelines, 125. *See also* Internet
Weger, P., 63
Weight Watchers Online, 134, 136
Weintraub, R., 150, 158
Weis, C., 110
Whitney, K., 105
Wiggins, G., 78, 80
Wildstrom, S., 45
Williams, D., 196
Williams, J., 197, 199
Wilson, B., 48
Witmer, B. G., 48
Woods, T., 28
Working environment, 120–121
Workplace: performance support outside of the, 44–47; performance support in the, 43–44; self-service, 42. *See also* Employees; Organizations
Wurman, R.S., 33

Y

Yahoo!, 130, 202
Yellow Pages performance support, 57–58*fig*

Z

Zenger, J., 168
Zeroed-In Technologies, 91, 92, 93, 94, 96

About the Authors

Allison Rossett, a professor of educational technology at San Diego State University, is fascinated by what, in addition to classes and training, influences performance. This enthusiasm began decades ago with her book, *A Handbook of Job Aids,* and continues here today.

Allison is an irreverent keynote speaker, a bang-up ping pong player, and a consultant on learning and performance strategy, development of workforce learning professionals, and analysis and evaluation. Her many honors include induction into the *Training* magazine HRD Hall of Fame, recognition as ASTD's winner for Contributions to Workplace Learning and Performance in 2002, membership on ASTD's International Board, and best book honors for *Training Needs Assessment, A Handbook of Job Aids, First Things Fast: A Handbook for Performance Analysis,* and *Beyond the Podium: Delivering Training and Performance to a Digital World* (2001). Allison also edited *The ASTD e-Learning Handbook: Best Practices, Strategies and Case Studies for an Emerging Field.*

Allison's career has taken her many places, including Taipei, Singapore, India, Australia, Brazil, and all over North America. She lives happily and works excessively in San Diego, California.

Lisa Schafer is a co-founder of Collet and Schafer, Incorporated. She has conducted performance analyses, delivered training solutions, developed systems, and administered industry benchmarking surveys for Fortune 100 clients. She developed an award-winning financial system for a global pharmaceutical company, which successfully reduced employee workload while improving deliverables.

Lisa started her career in human resources, focusing on organization analysis, staffing, process improvement, and employee recruiting and retention. Her business acumen, combined with her experience in data analysis and presentation, human capital, and the appropriate use of technology, enable her to see to the root of a problem and develop effective solutions.

She graduated with highest distinction from Purdue University with a bachelor's degree in management. She earned a master's degree in educational technology from San Diego State University. She is a member of ASTD, ISPI, and WorldAtWork. Lisa lives in San Diego, California, with her two terrific teenagers, Julie and Gregory.